Fending for Ourselves

Fending for Ourselves

Youth in Zimbabwe 1980-2020

Edited by

Rory Pilossof

WEAVER W PRESS

Published by Weaver Press,
Box A1922, Avondale, Harare. 2021
<www.weaverpresszimbabwe.com>

Typeset by Weaver Press
Cover Design: Danes Design
Printed by: DP printmedia, Bulawayo

The publishers would like to express their gratitude to the
CEADZ Consortium for their support in the publication of this book.

ISBN: 978-1-77922-400-2 (p/b)
ISBN: 978-1-77922-401-9 (ePub)
ISBN: 978-1-77922-402-6 (PDF)

Contents

About the Authors

Michael Bourdillon went to school at St George's College, Harare, and subsequently studied Social Anthropology at the University of Oxford. He taught for 25 years in the Department of Sociology, University of Zimbabwe. He has also taught in the University of Calabar, Nigeria, and has directed the Child and Youth Institute in Dakar at the Council for the Development of Social Science Research in Africa. He has been practically involved in interventions for street children and for working children, and has continued to research and publish widely in the field of childhood studies, especially on children's work and on children in poverty.

Eve Musvosvi Chandaengerwa is a lecturer in Sociology at Midlands State University. After graduating in sociology at the University of Zimbabwe, she was awarded an MSc at UZ and a PhD at the University of Pretoria. Her research interests include youth and child rights, socio-cultural anthropology, and the anthropology of health and illness. She has published widely, and is actively engaged in a range of community-based activities.

Simbarashe Gukurume is a Senior Lecturer at Sol Plaatje University in the Department of Social Sciences. Prior to that he was a lecturer and faculty research chairperson at Great Zimbabwe University. Simbarashe holds a PhD from the University of Cape Town. His Masters in Sociology and Social Anthropology and BSc in Sociology were obtained from the University of Zimbabwe. His research focuses broadly on the sociology of youth, informality and informal economies, livelihoods, displacements, the ethnography of money, politics and social movements and Pentecostalism. Simbarashe has been a recipient of the Harry Frank Guggenhcim Young African Scholars, and the Matasa Fellows Network awards.

Eric Kushinga Makombe is a Senior Lecturer in the Department of History, Heritage and Knowledge Systems at the University of Zimbabwe and a Research Fellow in the History Department at the University of the Free State. He holds a PhD in History from the University of the Witwatersrand. His broad research interests are in urban history, human economy and livelihoods, rural-urban linkages, and rural development.

His articles have appeared in *Global Environment* and *Essays in Economic & Business History.*

Felix Maringe is a Professor of Higher Education and former Head of the Wits School of Education. He researches international education and leadership in circumstances of multiple deprivation in different educational settings. His key contribution in this field is the Poverty, Antecedents, Curriculum and Teaching and Learning (PACT) model developed as both an analytic and evaluative model for interrogating the challenges of leading educational institutions in circumstances of multiple deprivation.

Alfred Masinire is Senior Lecturer and Head of the Curriculum Division in the School of Education at the University of the Witwatersrand. His research focuses on rural education, as well as gender and teacher development in rural schools. At the core of his work, he maintains a strong commitment to rurality and social justice. His most recent publications are *Rurality, Social Justice and Education in Sub-Saharan Africa Volume I: Theory* and (with Amasa P. Ndofirepi) *Practice in Schools and Rurality, Social Justice and Education in Sub-Saharan Africa Volume II: Theory and Practice in Higher Education.*

Rekopantswe Mate is a Senior Lecturer in the Sociology Department, University of Zimbabwe, where she teaches development studies, youth studies and popular culture. She does research on social change and how it affects generational and gender relations. Her publications include journal articles, book chapters and encyclopaedia entries on young people and women in Zimbabwe.

Ivo Mhike is a postdoctoral fellow with the International Studies Group at the University of the Free State. His PhD thesis focused on the state constructs of childhood and deviance in colonial Zimbabwe. His research interests include youth cultures in the colonial and post-colonial state, economic change and the transformation of the family unit. He is working on a monograph entitled *Degeneracy and Empire: Childhood, Youth and Whiteness in Colonial Zimbabwe, 1900-c.1960* for the Palgrave Studies in the History of Childhood. Ivo has also taught at the University of Zimbabwe in the Economic History Department.

Rangirai Gavin Muchetu is a political economist who specialises in rural and agricultural development. He obtained his PhD in Global Society Studies from Doshisha University, Kyoto, and is currently studying farmer cooperatives in Shiga Prefecture, Japan, as a postdoctoral fellow. His thesis focused on issues faced by agrarian societies after Japanese and Zimbabwean radical land reforms. His interest is in the forms and character of the collective-action mechanisms utilised to combat post-reform market contradictions. As the realities of unavoidable land reforms settle in southern Africa, it becomes vital to explore such debates to proffer lasting solutions.

Ngonidzashe Muwonwa is an academic and multi-media producer interested in youth identities and popular culture. His youth-centric research utilises participatory methods which resonate with young people's embedded attitudes, desires and practices which normally challenge and subvert adult-constructed normative ideologies of youth. He strongly believes that young people in Zimbabwe and the rest of Africa are precariously perched at the intersection of tradition and modernity, and therefore a non-prohibitive framework of understanding what it means to be a young adult needs to be incorporated in all youth studies to appreciate youth agency and competencies while reducing their vulnerabilities.

Marjoke Oosterom is a research fellow at the Institute of Development Studies, University of Sussex. She has a background in comparative politics and her research concentrates on the effects of violence, conflict and repression on civic and political participation; civic space; and popular and collective action. Her specific expertise is in youth politics; political socialization; the politics of the informal economy; and youth employment and empowerment in fragile and conflict affected settings. Her research is concentrated on Zimbabwe and Kenya. Marjoke leads the IDS Research Strategy on 'Youth Employment and Politics', which encompasses a diverse portfolio of interdisciplinary research projects. She regularly advises donors, policy actors and international organisations that fund and implement governance and youth-focused interventions in Sub-Saharan Africa.

Ross Parsons did his undergraduate studies at the University of Zimbabwe, and his postgraduate work at a variety of institutions including Boston College, the Tavistock Clinic and Johns Hopkins University. He has been a senior lecturer in Anthropology and Psychology at Africa University and has extensive experience as a psychotherapist, writer and social researcher. His publications include

One Day This Will All Be Over: Growing up with HIV in an Eastern Zimbabwean Town.

Rory Pilossof is a member of the International Studies Group at the University of the Free State. His main research areas are land, labour, and belonging in southern Africa. His publications include *The Unbearable Whiteness of Being: Farmers' Voices from Zimbabwe* and (with Andrew Cohen) *Labour and Economic Change in Southern Africa c.1900-2000: Zimbabwe, Zambia and Malawi.*

Brian Raftopoulos is a Zimbabwean scholar and activist. Formally Associate Professor of Development Studies at the University of Zimbabwe, he moved to Cape Town in 2006 and is currently the Director of Research and Advocacy in the Solidarity Peace Trust/Ukuthula Trust, an NGO dealing with human rights issues in Zimbabwe. He is also a Research Associate at the International Studies Group, University of the Free State. He has published widely on Zimbabwean history, labour history, historiography, politics, and economic issues. He was a Mellon Senior Research Fellow at the Centre for Humanities Research at the University of the Western Cape from 2009-2016. He serves on the Advisory Boards of the *Journal of Southern African Studies* and *Kronos, Southern African Histories.* He was a member of the founding Task Force of the National Constitutional Assembly, 1998-2000, the editor of the NCA journal *Agenda*,1999-200, and the first Chair of the Crisis in Zimbabwe Coalition, 2001-2003.

Tony Reeler is Co-Convener of the Platform for Concerned Citizens. He is a Senior Researcher and former Director at the Research and Advocacy Unit, an independent institution specialising in human rights, transitional justice, and governance. He has taught at the Universities of Malawi and Zimbabwe and was the founding director of the Amani Trust in 1993. He was a member of the Council of the International Rehabilitation Council for Torture Victims, 1993-2003, and a member of its Executive Committee. Has published widely in the fields of mental health, trauma, and human rights, and currently works on issues of governance and elections, providing research reports, analyses, and opinion pieces.

Timothy Scarnecchia is an Associate Professor of African History at Kent State University. He is the author of *The Urban Roots of Democracy and Political Violence in Zimbabwe: Harare and Highfield,*

1940-1964 and *Race and Diplomacy in Zimbabwe: The Cold War and Decolonization, 1960-1984*. He has published articles and book chapters on the history of Harare, as well as nationalist politics in Zimbabwe.

Toendepi Shonhe is a political economist at the Thabo Mbeki School of Public and International Affairs, University of South Africa His research interests include land and agrarian change, sustainable rural livelihoods, climate change adaptation and economic development in Africa. His publications include *Reconfigured Agrarian Relations in Zimbabwe*, *The Clash of Visions: Rethinking the land and agrarian questions in Africa* and *Agrarian Transformation under Neoliberalism in Zimbabwe and South Africa: Compromises, contradictions, constraints and cumulative outcomes*.

Introduction

In 2017, the 21st of February, Robert Mugabe's birthday, was declared the Robert Gabriel Mugabe National Youth Day. At the time, Mugabe was 93 years old, yet the irony of naming a youth day holiday after the aged leader seemed lost on the state. The holiday has continued to be respected, despite Mugabe having been ousted from power later in 2017. On 20th of February 2021, Fadzayi Mahere, a prominent lawyer and Spokesperson for the Movement of Democratic Change Alliance, asked on Twitter:

> Using the hashtag #BeingYoungInZim, describe what being a youth in today's Zimbabwe means & looks like for you? Are you winning? Do you enjoy freedom? Are you working the job you dreamed of when you were young? What's on your mind?[1]

The responses presented a depressing picture of what being young in Zimbabwe was like just over 40 years since independence. Many outlined the political, social and economic challenges they faced:

- #BeingYoungInZim is needing to leave the country to pursue your dreams, because Zimbabwe as it is, is an environment that's hostile to creativity and innovation.[2]
- #BeingYoungInZim the only way to see a better future for yourself is dream about being employed out of the country … a passport is jus [sic] as important as your degree.[3]

---

1 Fadzayi Mahere (2021, February), available at https://twitter.com/advocatemahere/status/1363006891421491204

2 K.N. (2021, February), available at https://twitter.com/kuda_nyangoni/status/1363057232053739520

3 Bishop el chapo Bab Lao (2021, February). available at https://twitter.

- #BeingYoungInZim you are called born free but you are not free, freedom is a myth.[4]

- #BeingYoungInZim we see our lives passing by, taking longer to realise our dreams, supporting each other as those who lead the way do not seem unfazed about our tomorrow. So we wake up every single day, do what we are supposed to do with the hope that it will eventually be okay.[5]

- #BeingYoungInZim is just so painful to even imagine.

   No hope

   No future

   No payslip

   No assets

   When you raise your voice to point that out then you are called unpatriotic, criminal and terrorist. What is more terrifying than being a target of this regime?[6]

Others pointed to some positives, such as the ability to make a living farming or mining, but overwhelmingly the responses were negative, and noted the hardships many young people faced trying to survive in Zimbabwe. Many also lamented the false dawns of independence and the 2017 coup/not-coup.

This small and unscientific sample points to many of the challenges young people have faced and continue to face in contemporary Zimbabwe. This collection builds on these insights and explores the youth experience in Zimbabwe during the first 40 years of independence, from 1980 to 2000. The arrival of independence in 1980 ushered in a moment of hope and optimism in Zimbabwe. With peace and majority rule seemingly secured, it appeared that the country was ready to embark on a path of development and growth that would benefit all its citizens. The youth were seen as vital to this new growth, and would be the ones to most benefit from the expansion of educational and

com/Bishopellchapo/status/1363041416373538816

4 Wezhira Wezhinji (2021, February), available at https://twitter.com/philllip_c/status/1363039512394399744

5 Loreen (2021, February), available at https://twitter.com/itsloreen_/status/1363080283550076929

6 Constentine (2021, February), available at https://twitter.com/costa_cnm/status/1363427229376663552

employment opportunities. The future lay with the youth, and the 'born frees' (those born after independence), who would inherit the new, liberated Zimbabwe and prosper.

These hopes and dreams, however, never came to fruition. The anticipation that swept the nation in the 1980s dissipated as violence, corruption, and increasingly authoritarian rule saw Zimbabwe mired in social, economic, and political crises that worsened after the mid-1990s. The 'born frees', who became youths at roughly this time, came of age as Zimbabwe lurched from one crisis to another, crises that linger on today, or have been exacerbated since the change of leadership in the ruling Zimbabwe African National Union - Patriotic Front (ZANU-PF). The removal of Robert Mugabe from power in 2017 bought renewed hope that solutions to Zimbabwe's problems would be found, and that the youth could look forward, once again, to a better future. However, this optimism was short-lived. The economic problems the country faced remain in place, and the state has shown itself to be more than willing to repress political and economic freedoms.

This collection covers a range of topics, including education, work, urban life, involvement in the informal economy, gender relations, and political activity. Importantly, the book explores successive generations of youth, to show how ideas, experiences, and reactions to the social, political, and economic context have shifted over time. Each contribution looks at the evolution of a particular issue during the full 40 years of independence, in order to show change over time and how diverse the range of experiences can be across time and place. While, clearly, many of the issues affecting youth over the past 40 years have been 'bad' (physical and mental trauma, declining employment and educational opportunities, poverty, ill-health) this collection also stresses the agency and resilience of Zimbabwe's young population, and how they have found ways to navigate the political, social, and economic terrains they occupy.

These youth perspectives of Zimbabwe, and its recent past, are vitally important. Zimbabwe is a young country. At present, approximately 68% of its (estimated) 13 million total population are under the age of 35. Over 40% are under the age of 15. Such a large part of the population deserves more sustained research. To date there is no collection on youth in Zimbabwe, and this book is an important contribution to filling this gap in the scholarship. This collection gathers together a diverse range of authors from different backgrounds, institutions, and localities, all offering new dimensions of the youth experiences in Zimbabwe to light.

Chapter breakdown

The book is divided into three sections. The first provides an overview of the period 1980 to 2020 and youth issues. It consists of two chapters. Chapter Two, by Michael Bourdillon and Ross Parsons, provides a sketch of Zimbabwe's history from 1980 to 2020. In doing so it touches on some of the main themes of youth and youth experiences in that 40-year period that are explored in more detail in the chapters that follow. Chapter Three, by Tony Reeler, offers a demographic overview of Zimbabwe and uses the Afrobarometer surveys to investigate young Zimbabweans' views on the state, political participation, and social relations. It explores how these views are different from those of older generations, and also reveals how the youth engage as citizens.

The second section looks at education in Zimbabwe since independence. Education provision and literacy rates have constantly been hailed as one of ZANU-PF's triumphs, regardless of other political and social failings. However, the two chapters in this section investigate this assertion and find that the reality was a little more complicated than often portrayed. The first, by Brian Raftopoulos and Rory Pilossof (Chapter Four), looks at education provision from 1980 to just after the turn of the millennium. The second, by Felix Maringe and Alfred Masinire (Chapter Five), covers the period from 2000 to 2020. Together they show how education provisions were often inadequate and failed the pupils and families they were supposed to help. While education expanded rapidly, the training of teachers, the infrastructure, and the curriculum taught were often insufficient or poorly planned. In addition, the prospects of finding waged work once students graduated from secondary or tertiary education diminished consistently over this period. Both chapters illustrate that the growing number of qualified school leavers found very few opportunities in the formal economy due to a lack of employment creation and escalating economic crises.

The third section looks at youth, society, and the state. The chapters in this section review a range of issues youth negotiate in dealing with the state, surviving the surrounds they find themselves in, and dealing with social and cultural norms. Ivo Mhike (Chapter Six) provides a history of state youth programmes and shows how the youth were politicized and used as frontline troops to push ZANU-PF's political agenda. This chapter is a timely reminder of the violent nature of such organisations, particularly as in April 2021 the government approved the re-establishment of the National Youth Service Programme, in preparation for the 2023 national elections. Timothy Scarnecchia and Erik Makombe's chapter (Chapter Seven) provides an overview of urban experiences of youth in Zimbabwe from 1980. They focus on issues of economic mobility, and the survival strategies employed by the youth to negotiate the economic crises. They also look at housing issues and how these affect family relations in urban centres. Finally, they provide an insight into the new urban cultures that have emerged in Zimbabwe and how these are often at odds with the ruling party and the social norms of older generations. Simbarashe Gukurume and Marjoke Oosterom (Chapter Eight) look at youth politics in Zimbabwe. Rather than focusing on the official youth wings of either ZANUP-PF or the opposition, they explore more informal avenues of political engagement and expression. In doing so they highlight the tensions between 'born frees' and the ruling elite, and how a limited civil space has often led to the youth participating in informal street mobilisation and protest. As Mhike's chapter makes apparent, the youth have been politicised by the state since independence, and the following chapters by Scarnecchia and Makombe and Gukurume and Oosterom show how this has played out in different settings. Finally in this section, Ngonidzashe Muwonwa's chapter (Chapter Nine) looks at concepts of sexuality and identity for young women in Zimbabwe. It analyses sexual expressions and activities in the post-colonial state and how various laws and policies have sought to police the sexual activity of the youth. Here the focus in mostly on women, and the chapter provides important insights into yet another controlled space many youth have to negotiate in Zimbabwe.

The fourth section looks at work and employment options. As the previous sections make clear, finding work and formal employment for the vast majority of Zimbabwean youth has been a challenge throughout the post-colonial period. Economic stagnation resulted in the loss of many jobs and the country's economy was unable to provide the employment opportunities to the country's youth, whether they had education or not. Eve Chandaengerwa and Michael Bourdillon's chapter (Chapter Ten) on artisanal mining illuminates the dangers many youths have to negotiate to find alternative forms of livelihood. While artisanal mining has offered many Zimbabweans wealth and income that was unattainable in formal employment, this has come with risks and dangers. The chapter provides an insightful background to mining in Zimbabwe and the growth of artisanal activities since the mid-1990s. It the focuses on gold mining in Chiweshe and how young people navigate both mining and the industries that emerge around mining centres. In Chapter Eleven, Toendepi Shonhe and Rangarirai Gavin Muchetu look at another key rural activity for the youth – agriculture. On the back of an intersectoral household survey carried out in Mvurwi, Goromonzi and Hwedza farming districts, they show that many youth straddle multiple livelihoods. Indeed, many still face challenges in accessing secure land to farm and manage, and Shonhe and Muchetu outline how these affect youth participation in agriculture. Importantly, Shonhe and Muchetu explore differences between successive generations of youth in their research areas, and are able to differentiate between 'old' and 'new' youth and their agricultural pursuits.

The last two chapters in this section look at other forms of informal work that youth have been engaged in. Rekopantswe Mate (Chapter Twelve) investigates sexuality, gender relations and paid sex work. It offers a background to youth and social change in Zimbabwe, and shows how unemployment and informal work intersect with paid sex in times of economic crisis. The chapter includes observations across several different locations, such as Mutare, Beitbridge and Victoria Falls. The final chapter, Chapter Thirteen, by Simbarashe Gukurume and Marjoke Oosterom, looks at the growth of the informal economy from 1980 to the present. It shows how the informal economy has moved from the periphery to the centre of the country's economic landscape, and how many young people have negotiated this shift. Key to the chapter are insights into the resilience of the youth, and how they have found ways of navigating uncertainty; as the previous chapters illustrate, uncertainty has been an ever-present theme in Zimbabwe since 1980.

Along with uncertainty, there are several other themes that cut across the entire collection. Migration, in various forms such as rural to urban, urban to rural, and out of the country, is a key one. Many of the chapters note how many young people have left the country due to the political and economic crises. In addition, many of the informal livelihood choices necessitate movement to new areas to find land, minerals, and employment. Trauma, both physical and mental, is another facet of the youth experience that cannot be ignored. This is directly addressed in the chapters on the urban experience, youth brigades, and sex work, but is an issue that deserves more considered investigation across the spectrum in Zimbabwe. Finally, many of the chapters make obvious the resilience and agency of many of Zimbabwe's youth. During the past 40 years there has been no shortage of challenges to navigate. Many of these have had severely detrimental effects on the health, education, livelihoods, and possible futures of many Zimbabwean youth, yet at the same time, the resilience shown by many of them has been remarkable.

2

Young Postcolonials: Youth in Zimbabwe 1980-2020

Michael Bourdillon and Ross Parsons

What is youth?

This book is about the experiences of youth in the first 40 years of
Zimbabwe's postcolonial history. This introductory chapter considers
how we can usefully think about the very different experiences of
young people in a variety of situations and over these changing years.
Youth is a time of relatively malleable psychosocial development, in
which young people acquire an imprint of the past as the basis for
their own exploration of new forms of living. On the one hand, they
depend on the environment in which they are growing up, which can
be constraining and cause much suffering, but which can also open up
opportunities for growth and development. On the other hand, as they
grow, they respond to this environment and its past in ways that can be
innovative and unexpected. To understand the experiences of youth, we
need to consider not only the history of their changing environment, but
also their creative responses to this environment. These can sometimes
result in benefits both to themselves and society, but they can also be
disruptive – exacerbating differentials and exclusions– and even create
new faults in the social fabric.

'Youth' is a term that defies clear definition. It includes children and adolescents, but also young people who have reached the age of majority, and are therefore legally adults, while still very much in their formative years and heavily dependent on their elders. For statistical purposes, youth is often defined as including young people up to the age of 35. Indeed, this is how the Zimbabwean government defines 'youth'. However, any clear cut-off point has its dangers. Ideally a person should continue to develop mentally and socially throughout life: there is no age at which this stops. On the other hand, given the appropriate circumstances and expectations, even children can begin to take responsibility for the communities in which they live and can contribute towards their development. Our focus in this book is the changing situation of young adults in their formative years from roughly the age 15 to 35.

A key element of the environment is the history of the peoples and the country. The period we consider in this book starts at a time where the dominant thought was on breaking with the colonial past. This came formally in 1980 after a long and bitter liberation war. We start this introduction with a reminder of how things generally appeared for youth at that time. The legacy of colonialism, and of resistance to it, continues into the present, but it affects contemporary youth differently, as they never experienced the social, economic and political dominance of colonial power directly. We start with the war and the early independent years of the 1980s, and then we outline key events and processes that affected youth in the various periods leading to the very different situation of youth in Zimbabwe and the world in 2020.

With a picture of the changing forces acting on youth in the 40 years after independence, we can begin to understand their varied and changing responses over this period. Their perspectives on such things as education, government, and even their own well-being, change as the world in which they live changes, and their responses vary with their specific situations in this world. Young people in Zimbabwe are not a monolithic bloc.

Leading to independence

Prior to the period under consideration in this volume, the country had been under colonial domination or settler rule for nearly a century. During this period, the population increased around ten-fold due to a variety of contributing factors, including relatively stable government, more secure nutrition, and improved health facilities. But racial differentials grew also. The colonial settlers had taken over much of the prime agricultural land. Apart from areas designated for national purposes, agricultural land was divided such that half was owned by whites, who never numbered as much as 10% of the population. Only half was designated for ownership, for the most part communal ownership, by the black populations. Many people were forcibly moved away from their ancestral land to be confined to less fertile and smaller areas. Urban areas were segregated, with the wealthiest suburbs and many facilities reserved for whites. The black population was oppressed, and politically suppressed.

The black youth were at a double disadvantage. Schools were also segregated, with black children having very limited opportunities for quality education, especially at the secondary level. Employment opportunities on leaving school were also restricted. In their more traditional homes they were constrained by a patriarchal society, with older men controlling land and wealth. Young people often sought to escape domination by their elders through migration for work in farms, mines and urban areas and in neighbouring South Africa (Grier 2005). A minority found independence through education and professional careers. Many others were attracted by facilities and lifestyles at their places of work, and never returned to their rural homes. The few who benefitted from the wealth and improved livelihoods of the colonial era gave to all a taste for new ways of living.

The colonial era ended after 15 years of violent civil war. Young people were notable for their committed activity in the war, which was frequently willing, but sometimes taken on under a degree of coercion. Guerrilla fighters were known as the *vakomana* (boys). Children and youth who assisted on the home front were called *majibha* (singular *mujibha* – male collaborator) and *zvimbwido* (singular *chimbwido* – female collaborator). Even young children played active roles as scouts, spies and guides. Contact with the fighters, usually secret and nocturnal, freed young people from many constraints imposed by tradition and by their elders. It also gave them power to denounce individuals in the community as sell-outs and thus to seriously challenge traditional patriarchy (Kesby 1996).

Young people also paid a direct price for their involvement in the war. Fighters gave up their education for the liberation struggle. The collaborators suffered at the hands of colonial forces. These sacrifices were deemed by many to be a price worth paying for liberation, and there were promises that those who sacrificed themselves for the war effort would be suitably rewarded in independent Zimbabwe. Questions over whether these promises were kept have been a recurring theme in much subsequent political and economic debate. The guerrilla war was fought largely in the rural areas: rural families and their children lived on the frontlines (for a brief account, see Mtisi et al. 2009). Rural communities frequently suffered brutal treatment, from both the colonial forces, under suspicion of collaborating with the guerrillas, and from the guerrillas, under suspicion of collaborating with government. Normal life was severely disrupted, with schools and health services particularly affected. Many people witnessed traumatic violence. Torture, summary execution and death were common. Sometimes children and youths were compelled to watch the brutal punishment of community and family members. The long-term effects of such everyday violence and mass bereavement have been insufficiently studied.

The guerrilla war also brought international isolation to the colonial state and its increasing imbrication in the proxy politics of the global cold war. Besides direct implications for the flow of trade, sanctions brought a real sense of global exclusion. One effect of this was to complicate the movement to new ways of life, in which youth had always been in the vanguard. Education, wage employment, urbanisation, and even the political project of nationalism were all elements of a movement away from past ways and towards an association with the wider 'modern' world. For most of the colonial era, young people had been key actors in such social change.[1]

Independence promised a break from this disruptive past as a new era dawned. But these historical events left a range of negative effects, including a draconian state apparatus that demanded conformity and allegiance to the ruling elite, a highly extractive economy, and the long-term consequences of war. Such consequences included the displacement of whole communities, injuries, deaths, and a lasting aversion to public political speech (see Chapter 3).

---

1   For an illustration how youth can lead creatively in culture change, see Mitchell (1956).

From 1980s onward

It was against this background that political independence was achieved in 1980. This event was a marked rejection of colonial control, but not of modernity. It was a period of great hope for a new beginning socially, politically, economically, and racially. The new state was explicitly non-racial and, for the first time, white and black children encountered each other in some classrooms. Two major political projects of the time greatly affected young people: the rapid expansion of high quality education and of health services.

The expansion of educational services was especially important. Apart from disruptions to the rural schools, many young people had missed out on much of their schooling in order to enter into the war. As well as the expansion of regular schools for the young, a system of schools for the older youths was established under the title of *Education with Production*, in which young people were involved in building the schools in which they were to learn. These learners were also supposed to finance them through productive work, offering a chance to catch up on missed years of formal school, and the chance to acquire practical livelihood skills (McLaughlin et al. 2002). However, such schools were not without problems; as pointed out in Chapter 4, one was that it reminded many parents and teachers of attempts by the colonial administration to force vocational education on poor black communities which inhibited paths to tertiary and further education.

The combination of war and international economic isolation disrupted the country's economy, and consequently livelihoods broadly. This disruption was exacerbated by severe drought in 1982-3, which diminished agricultural production. Nevertheless, in the early years of independence, jobs expanded in industry and in the civil service and minimum wages rose. There were promises of land reform that would make good quality farmland available to rural populations. At a development conference in 1981, donors (especially Britain and USA) pledged Z$1.3bn (equivalent to US$1.45bn) in grants and loans, which helped to keep alive the optimism that a new and better era was beginning (Dougherty 1981).

Despite a strong political rhetoric of self-reliance, the expansion of government services and a reliance on donor funding created a paradox of expectant dependency on state and international donors. At the same time, an abiding belief in unlimited economic growth was reinforced.

Further major social change for young people in this period was also visible in shifting gender relations. The overt roles of girls and young women in the liberation war, and their visibility after independence, fuelled a welcome change in gender relations in the new state. A growing awareness of the oppression of women led to legal changes in the status of women, and the expansion of education included that of girls. The marked patriarchy of Zimbabwe did not disappear, but it was more commonly challenged by a Zimbabwean feminism. Young women became more visibly engaged in economic activity and political activism. However, there needs to be a note of caution in regard to the extent of changing gender relations. Many women avoided publicly talking about their role in the struggle because of the general belief that women were largely 'prostitutes' in the camps. Changes in women's status caused social unease, as they challenged a profound patriarchy (see Chapter 9). There were state crackdowns on a claimed increase in prostitution, and a focus on 'baby dumping', with young women being accused of abandoning newly born infants (although it remains unclear how widespread the practice was or the degree to which it was a response to social pressures).[2] The paths to greater gender equality were not smooth, and remain uncompleted, as Chapter 12 illustrates.

Towards the end of the first decade after independence and into the second, it was clear that wealth was becoming more available to the black population. But there were signs of wealth being siphoned into the hands of influential people at the expense of the country and the larger population, typified by the Willowgate scandal, which broke in 1988 and revealed senior government officials involved in corruption in the motor industry.[3] Meanwhile, jobs remained scarce for the poor and unskilled. Settlements of homeless people living in makeshift, plastic-covered huts began to appear in and around major cities. Children living and working on the streets of cities became ever more noticeable; living on the streets left many young people without the protection and support of elders, and at the same time freed them from patriarchal authority and constraints. The response of municipal and state authorities was to destroy the shelters, and to round up and detain children on the streets.

2   'A Zimbabwe Issue: Killing of Babies', *The New York Times*, 17 May 1987.

3   See 'Revisiting history: Sandura commission – early signs of a flawed justice system', NewsDay, 10 January 2017. See also Chapter 8, which discusses the role of university students in objecting to the Willowgate scandal.

These urban experiences are explored further in chapters 7 and 8 (see also Bourdillon 1991, 1994).

The repressive legislation through which the colonial state tried to contain opposition to its rule remained largely intact, and it soon became clear that the postcolonial state was also inclined to curtail political freedoms. In the mid-1980s, the state committed major atrocities in southern Zimbabwe with the events of Gukurahundi, with mass violence against the Ndebele people (Werbner 1991; CCJPZ 1990). It became apparent that the government had inherited its predecessor's more violent and draconian forms of social control in an effort to undermine democracy and perpetuate its own political power. It had also perpetuated its own tendencies to violence as demonstrated in the liberation war, where summary violence was meted out to those considered 'sell-outs' to the colonial regime. Young people again bore the brunt of state violence. Schools and clinics were destroyed, and communities laid waste. Mass graves from this period remain unexhumed and the political promises of independence, democracy and freedom, shown to be highly vulnerable. Free political activity and speech were shown again to the young to be highly dangerous.

Global events impinged on Zimbabwe again in this period with the advent of the HIV pandemic. The region came to dominate global infection rates. HIV is a sexually transmitted disease which, until the arrival of anti-retroviral drugs around 2000, was incurable and largely untreatable. Health services and social structures were placed under enormous strain. Children born HIV-positive were likely to die within five years, and non-infected children were likely to suffer the loss of carers and the diminishment of family networks (Parsons 2012). The disease generated a demographic shift as it affected the sexually active population of the young and middle-aged adults. The social and sexual conservatism of Zimbabwean society hindered the provision of sexual health education and services. This placed increased demand on state and international funding. After the rollout of effective anti-retroviral treatments, the disease could be managed but not cured. A vaccine remains elusive. Infection rates continue to remain high. HIV in Zimbabwe is now a disease of the poor. Pandemics always reveal the fractures and inequalities in societies, as the current COVID19 pandemic continues to demonstrate (Chigudu 2020).

By the mid-1990s Zimbabwe was experiencing major economic

difficulties. These were exacerbated by drought 1991/1992, which cut the staple maize production by around 75%, followed by less severe droughts in 1993 and 1994. A strong political opposition emerged to challenge the ruling ZANU-PF party, in power since 1980, and the beleaguered government turned to international neoliberalism in the form of a World Bank structural adjustment programme, with dire effects on spending for educational and health services. This programme was unpopular, and the consequent loss of jobs and deepening poverty contributed to wider social disaffection (Raftopoulos 2009). In this context, war veterans (the young of a previous generation) emerged as a powerful political voice challenging the ruling party. Social unrest, once again led by the young, strengthened. So did state oppression and violence, sometimes involving youth groups of the governing party. Politics for the young – outside of co-option into the ruling party's activities – remained a dangerous activity.

Another important way in which Zimbabwe followed global trends was the rapidly rising power and visibility of churches. Since colonial times, churches had been important, particularly in the mission-based provision of health and education services. Especially in rural areas, their services provided glimpses of different life in the wider world, widely perceived as 'modern'. By the late 1990s, Pentecostal and charismatic churches had flourished, with large congregations and politically influential leaders. Mainstream political figures from all parties found it expedient to declare their religious affiliations publicly. Sundays provided social gatherings at churches, which invariably included large numbers of youth.[4] Churches continued to be perceived as modern social projects, and as honest and safe places in contrast with the more problematic nature of political activity. In Zimbabwe, as in much of the global south, neither modernity nor the postcolonial state are associated with secularism (Maxwell 2006; Parsons 2012).

By 2000, Zimbabwe looked very different from how it had looked in 1980. Poverty had risen dramatically and state services had crumbled. Education had once promised wage employment and a steady rise to the urban middle classes, but now no longer promised either of these. Chapter 6 shows how education provision has suffered since 2000 and

---

4   While we do not have accurate figures for church participation or age groups, ZimStat (2017: 6) shows 84% of the population identifying themselves as Christian, suggesting churches to be a significant part of the self-identity of many Zimbabweans.

how the crises have forced many teachers and young people out of the country. Those who came of age in the heady dawn of independence were now more likely to be alienated and disaffected. Every family carried severe, cumulative grief from HIV. Their own children faced very uncertain futures, with the majority of jobs being in the informal sector. The social and economic problems apparent in the 1990s were to be exacerbated in the new millennium by a series of political crises.

Into the twenty-first century

At the turn of the millennium, Zimbabwe entered what might be called a perfect political and economic storm. Widely referred to in the academic literature as a 'crisis' (Hammar et al. 2003), long simmering discontent with the absence of serious land reform (specifically the problem of the best agricultural land still remaining in the hands of white farmers), together with broader demands of rural people for improvements to their lives, resulted in invasions of farms that were mostly owned by whites. The process was chaotic and in defiance of the law, and it remains unclear who benefited from the wholesale process of redistribution. These processes were endorsed by the state to counter the growing unpopularity of the ruling party, and to offer white farmers as scapegoats to a restive population. Land 'reform' was both popular and politically expedient.

The ruling party attempted to energise its rural support through these events, and leaned heavily on its liberation credentials to do so. The land reform process was titled the 'Third Chimurenga', which implied blaming the current ills of the country on the lack of change since 1980. The Third Chimurenga would finally bring about the necessary revolution. The war veterans were a powerful force in the land occupations at this time. The rhetoric employed harked back to the liberation war, during which many of the current rulers were youthful fighters, but it stood in obvious contrast to the current comfort of ruling elites.[5] It is debatable whether such rhetoric was persuasive to younger generations who had not experienced the war. The state also galvanised the national youth militia, known colloquially as the Green Bombers (see Chapter 6). It has proved difficult over the subsequent years to

---

5   For an account by a participant war veteran, who had been a youth in the liberation war, and who discusses continuities and discontinuities between the liberation war and the land invasions, see Sadomba 2008.

research these groups in any systematic way, but it is clear that they were central (along with other security forces) in policing all forms of political opposition, through the widespread use of state sponsored violence. Such violence included beatings, torture, rape, killings and abductions (Hammar et al. 2010). Both rural and urban populations experienced mass displacements. In 2005, a nationwide displacement and destruction of poor urban communities, Operation Murambatsvina, was officially depicted as slum clearance, but was widely interpreted as the ruling party's response to urban electoral support for the opposition a few months earlier. The operation heightened the sense that all social groups thought to be supporting political opposition were under sustained attack (Vambe 2008; also see Chapter 7).

Indeed, the political opposition had cohered into a formidable force under the aegis of the Movement for Democratic Change (MDC). The MDC showed itself to be particularly strong in all urban areas, and had a broad spectrum of support across class, gender and generational divides. The ruling party, however, remained firmly in control of rural areas. It remains unclear the extent to which this difference in support for the ruling party results from the different interests of the rural populations or from more effective state coercion in the rural areas. Elections throughout the 2000s lacked transparency and democratic legitimacy, and were accompanied by high levels of state violence. As noted in Chapter 3, such realities have directly affected the political participation of youth in Zimbabwe.

A major feature of this period was the flight of a large number of Zimbabweans into exile and the formation of a large diaspora. Since the 1990s, net annual emigration has reached between two and three million (approaching 20% of the current population of the country).[6] Young adults despaired of their political and economic prospects, and sought relief in countries that were perceived to be better off. Neighbouring South Africa was most accessible, but historical links and educational opportunities drew many to the UK and USA. Families took their young children with them when possible, but quite often children and parents were separated for long periods of time as children stayed with other

---

6   Using World Bank figures, and allowing for an estimated death rate of 1.25% p.a., the accumulated net emigration figure comes to 2.7m, or 18% of the current population. Calculated from https://www.macrotrends.net/countries/ ZWE/zimbabwe/net-migration and https://data.worldbank.org/indicator/SP.POP. TOTL?locations=ZW (accessed 12 March 2021)

family members. Zimbabweans in the diaspora, including young adults, often lead the lives of undocumented migrants (Bolt, 2012). They are also assiduous in sending money home to family members still in the country, and these remittances have become a formidable economic force in alleviating poverty.[7] As a consequence, the ruling party has denied political rights to those in the diaspora, who are assumed to be opposition supporters.

The Zimbabwean crisis had powerful international effects, with the systematic abuse of human rights drawing strong international condemnation. This affected the country's ability to access funding for development, and as a consequence, essential services in health and education continued to be underfunded. The gains of the 1980s were reversed and often lost. For example, pass rates in national school examinations have seen a steady decline, and even university graduates struggle to find paid employment (see Chapters 4 and 5). With the failings of the formal economy, many young adults still rely on small-scale agriculture for sustenance, and others have moved into the sometimes lucrative but often dangerous arena of artisanal gold mining (see Chapters 10 and 11). Nonetheless, young people in the informal sector have shown remarkable entrepreneurial spirit, sometimes in the face of constraining interventions by the state (see Chapters 12 and 13).

In the 2000s, Zimbabwe experienced hyperinflation at astronomic levels, further eroding the real value of incomes and savings. Shops emptied, basic commodities became very scarce and parallel or 'black' markets emerged. A period of dollarisation under a brief government of national unity stemmed the tide of rapid economic collapse and the further flight of capital and populations (Raftopoulos 2009). However, the situation continued to decline.

In November of 2017, elements in the army supported a faction in the ZANU-PF leadership to remove President Mugabe from power. While many who had lived through the 1980s were cynical about a change in leadership without structural change in the system of government, younger people who had been born since Zimbabwe became independent, and who had no direct experience of the hopes

---

7   Since personal remittances are not always sent through official channels, accurate statistics are hard to come by. In 2019, they were estimated to amount to $636m, roughly 3.5% of GDP, rising to just over $1bn in 2020, about 7% of a lower GDP. https://www.techzim.co.zw/2021/01/remittances-to-zimbabwe-increased-by-over-42-in-2020/ (accessed 9 March 2021).

of the 1980s and the disappointments that followed, were caught in a brief and febrile elation. With the coup came hopes of a new beginning and a joyful party atmosphere on city streets, with civilians celebrating casually with army personnel.[8] Afterwards, there was some attempt to open up the economy, but it soon became apparent that rather than 'open for business', the new government's adopted moto, it was 'business as usual'. Corruption, nepotism and abuse of state machinery continued apace. Repression and assaults on opposition figures and detractors was heavy-handed and often violent. A disputed national election in August 2018 returned the ruling party to power. After this election, protestors in Harare were shot by security forces. Up to this point President Mnangagwa and the new regime had been welcomed on the international stage. Yet, immediately after this obvious display of state violence and abuse, international opinion changed, and Zimbabwe was once again isolated.[9] By 2020, Zimbabwe's crisis appeared intractable and the young who were now coming of age carried all the consequences forward into their adult lives.

Forty years on: 2020

Pessimism dominated Zimbabwe in 2020, contrasting starkly with the optimism of the early 1980s.

A severe drought had followed previous seasons of low rainfall, exacerbating the collapsing economy and resulting in a severe food crisis, with estimates reporting over half the population of the country as food insecure and in poverty towards the end of 2019. Less than half the men of working age, and just over a quarter of women, were in employment; of these roughly a third were in formal employment, a third in informal employment and a third in the household sector (ZimStat 2020: 51, table 4.1; 68, table 4.11). In March of 2020, cases of Covid-19 arrived in the country and the government responded with a lockdown that restricted travel and prohibited most informal trading, which severely disrupted the meagre incomes of the majority of the population. In April, the UN World Food Programme estimated that over four million Zimbabweans (roughly 25% of the population) were acutely food insecure, dependent on help coming

---

8   'Zimbabwe's military takeover was the world's strangest coup', *CNN,* 21 November 2017.

9   'President Mnangagwa claimed Zimbabwe was open for business. What's gone wrong?' *The Conversation,* 31 January 2021.

from outside the country.[10]

Government health facilities had long been struggling with inadequate resources for drugs and equipment, and poorly paid staff. Fears of transmitting Covid-19, together with increasing demands on medical services, stretched the facilities further. Inadequate protective equipment of health workers led to repeated strike action.

Institutions of learning were closed. While well-resourced private institutions and several tertiary institutions were able to introduce on-line teaching methods for their pupils, the vast majority of schools lacked the resources, and pupils lacked adequate access to the internet. When schools partially re-opened towards the end of the year, many teachers were unwilling to work for low wages and without adequate protection from the virus.

The change of political leadership in the country in 2017 had not produced the improvement in the economy that people had hoped for, nor an end to the suppression of political opposition. Rules for the prevention of transmitting Covid-19 included a prohibition on large gatherings and made political protest even more difficult. Indeed, as elsewhere in the world, it has been argued that the government has used the pandemic to tighten its control over the population (Rivers and Ndlovu 2020). By-elections for vacant parliamentary seats were not held, and the chances of serious change seemed remote. Whereas in 1980, young people were returning to their newly independent country, in 2020 young people wishing to improve their lives frequently looked for opportunities outside it.

While there has been a suggestion that the optimism of the 1980s led to the growth of unhealthy dependency, crises can teach people not to wait, and not to rely on state support. Private initiatives to feed the hungry have been reported, as have initiatives to help children out of school to continue their learning.[11] For many, however, life is dominated by the struggle for survival. Consideration of the development of one's country or community gives way to what one can do to make one's own

---

10 'Urgent international support needed to prevent millions of desperate Zimbabweans plunging deeper into hunger', UN World Food Programme, 8 April 2020.

11 Many such initiatives are very local and small in scale, and knowledge of them comes by word of mouth. For an example, see '"We can't turn them away": the family kitchen fighting lockdown hunger in Zimbabwe', The Guardian, 20 May 2020.

life liveable, perhaps outside the community and even the country.

The world itself had changed. Through the development of information technology, Zimbabweans are now much more aware of different lives and lifestyles in the wider world. Although such knowledge may be limited and distorted by the glamour and flaws of popular media, it results in young people looking at other lives and values. Changes in the wider world relate to changes in Zimbabwe. One topic that has changed in Zimbabwe and in the wider world is how colonialism is perceived and how people relate to the colonial past.

By 2020, the youth of 1980 who saw the last days of colonialism in the country had become elders, with the promises and disappointments of independence behind them. The youth of 2020 have no direct experience of formal colonialism, though it remains part of their consciousness through the culture in which they live and what they have learned at school. However, the version of both the colonial past and the processes of liberation from it, as offered in school curricula and state media, are highly idealised. Divisions within oppositions to colonialism, and the contribution of other social groups to national development are all erased in this version of history, whereby the ruling party claims ownership of the anti-colonial struggle and the benefits of independence.

In practice, the repressive colonial regime has been replaced by one that is repressive in its own way. A ruling Shona elite has established a hegemonic control of all political power and economic benefits. A recent report outlines how the Zimbabwean state has been captured by powerful cartels of wealthy elites in the country and regionally, which siphon much wealth into private pockets at cost to the state and its people.[12]

The bleak experiences of postcolonialism are not unique to Zimbabwe. Many countries in Africa have struggled to maintain social and political order after liberation or the coming of majority rule. Theories of postcoloniality have emerged and grown with the eclipse of the major European colonial empires. In part, postcolonial theory points to persistent ways in which postcolonial states remain tightly linked economically to the previous colonial powers. However, they also point to other processes. Franz Fanon (1961), a founding theorist

---

12 'How cartels operate – and their impact on the people of Zimbabwe', *Maverick Citizen*, 9 February 2010.

of postcolonialism, believed that the process of decolonisation was inevitably a violent one. New elites replaced old ones, and the lot of the poorest remained little changed. The violence of colonialism, and decolonisation, was both direct and indirect. Elites assumed the superiority of previous (racialised) elites. This chapter has pointed to such processes in Zimbabwe.

More recently, Achille Mbembe (2001) has suggested that the postcolony in Africa is marked by 'contemporaneousness'. This refers to a process of adaptation to continued states of social, political and economic crisis in which temporality itself is affected. Both past and future recede and the demands of the present become all-consuming. What does this mean for the young in Zimbabwe? On the one hand it recognises that energies must go into the demands of the day. Most Zimbabweans produce what they need to survive within very small timeframes. On the other hand it highlights the extraordinary creativity of people in adapting to harsh realities. For example, the ever expanding informal sector is a demonstration of such creativity and adaptation.

Conclusion

In considering the young in Zimbabwe between 1980 and 2020, the paucity of research becomes starkly apparent. Many of the issues discussed in this chapter are not underpinned by good research findings, either quantitative or qualitative. There are reasons for this state of affairs. The political and economic crises, and the land question, have dominated scholarly interest in Zimbabwe. Behind the large, significant events, many of the more intricate processes have been understudied. Social researchers have been severely hampered by the political climate in which people asking questions in communities attract hostile attention from ruling party officials, supporters and militias. Even where such interviewing and observation can proceed unhindered, informants often receive unwelcome visits and questions in their wake. Thus, research activities become unsafe for researchers and informants alike. Furthermore, even indirect methods of inquiry must be carefully scrutinised. For example, the use of national statistics as collated by the state should be viewed with caution, since they have too often been used and misused for narrow political purposes.

This chapter has reviewed how the postcolonial history of Zimbabwe has affected lives of young people in varied ways over the 40-year period.

It shows that the fate of young people during this time has not been a happy one: the country has failed to substantiate the initial optimism that came with liberation from the oppression of colonial rule. Since then, young people have not only suffered from a declining share of national resources (reflected particularly in declining health and educational services), but they have also suffered increasingly restricted personal freedoms – restrictions on the expression of views, limited opportunities in the face of general economic stagnation, and interspersed periods of extreme political violence. We have remarked that youth have not simply suffered passively under the oppressive situations they have faced: they have responded, sometimes creatively, to make new and different lives for themselves, and sometimes independently of their communities. In the twenty-first century of the wider world, we see young people actively striving to rectify the political and environmental messes that previous generations are passing on to them. The hope for Zimbabwe must lie in the ability of its youth to fend for themselves and to discover and implement new directions for their future in the context of the future of their country.

References

Bolt, M. (2012) 'Waged entrepreneurs, policed informality: Work, the regulation of space and the economy of the Zimbabwean-South African border', *Africa*, 82(1).

Bourdillon, M. (1991) *Poor, Harassed, But Very Much Alive: An Account of Street People and their Organisation.* Gweru: Mambo Press.

———— (1994) 'Street children in Harare', *Africa*, 64(4), pp. 134–152.

Catholic Commission for Justice and Peace in Zimbabwe (CCJPZ) and Legal Resources Foundation (1997) *Breaking the Silence, Building true Peace: A Report on the Disturbances in Matabeleland and the Midlands, 1980 to 1988.* Harare: CCJPZ and LRF.

Chigudu, S. (2020) *The political life of an epidemic.* Cambridge: Cambridge University Press.

Dougherty, E. (1981) 'Zimcord Conference Documentation', *A Journal of Opinion*, 11(3/4), pp. 51-53.

Fanon F. (1961) *The wretched of the earth.* London: Penguin.

Grier, B.C. (2005) *Invisible Hands: Child Labour and the State in*

Colonial Zimbabwe. Portsmouth, NH: Heinemann.

Hammar, A., B. Raftopoulos and S. Jensen (eds) (2003) *Zimbabwe's unfinished business: rethinking land, state and nation in the context of crisis*. Harare: Weaver Press.

Hammar, A., J. McGregor and L. Landau (2010) 'Displacing Zimbabwe: crisis and construction in southern Africa', *Journal of Southern African Studies,* 36(2), pp. 263-284

Kesby, M. (1996) 'Arenas for control, terrains of gender contestation: guerrilla struggle and counter-insurgency warfare in Zimbabwe 1972-1980', *Journal of Southern African Studies*, 22(4), pp. 561-584.

Maxwell, D. (2006) *African Gifts of the Spirit: Pentecostalism & the Rise of a Zimbabwean Transnational Religious Movement*. Oxford: James Curry.

Mbembe, A. (2001) *On the Postcolony*. Berkeley: University of California Press.

McLaughlin, J., V. Nhundu, P. Mlambo and F. Chung (2002) *Education with Production in Zimbabwe: The Story of ZIMFEP*. Harare: Zimbabwe Foundation for Education with Production (ZIMFEP) and Foundation for Education with Production (FEP).

Mitchell, J.C. (1956) *The Kalela Dance: Aspects of Social Relationships among Urban Africans*. Rhodes-Livingstone Papers. Manchester: Manchester University Press.

Mtisi, J., M. Nyakudya and T. Barnes (2009) 'War in Rhodesia, 1965-1980', in B. Raftopoulos and A. Mlambo (eds), *Becoming Zimbabwe*. Harare: Weaver Press.

Parsons, R. (2012) *One day this will all be over: growing up with HIV in an eastern Zimbabwean town*. Harare, Weaver Press.

Raftopoulos, B. (2009) 'The crisis in Zimbabwe, 1998-2008', in B. Raftopoulos and A. Mlambo (eds), *Becoming Zimbabwe*. Harare: Weaver Press.

Rivers, M., and P. Ndlovu (2020) 'COVID Raises the Stakes for Zimbabwe's Civil Society Movement'. Washington, DC: United States Institute of Peace.

Sadomba, W.Z. (2008) 'War Veterans in Zimbabwe's Land Occupations: Complexities of a Liberation Movement in an African Post-Colonial

Settler Society'. PhD thesis, Wageningen University.

Vambe, M. (2008) *The Hidden Dimensions of Operation Murambatsvina in Zimbabwe*. Harare: Weaver Press.

Werbner, D. (1991) *Tears of the Dead*. Edinburgh: Edinburgh University Press.

Zimbabwe National Statistics Agency (ZimStat) (2017) *Inter-Censal Demographic Survey, 2017*. Harare: ZimStat.

———— (2020) *2019 Labour Force and Child Labour Survey.* Harare: ZimStat.

3

Born free, but everywhere in chains:

What has happened to the youth of Zimbabwe

since 1980?

Tony Reeler

Introduction

In 1982, shortly after independence, Zimbabwe's population was slightly more than seven million. By 2017, it had doubled to 13.5 million with 40% under the age of 15, but with 74.4% under 35. The demographic shift to a very young population is, of course, not unique to Zimbabwe and is a characteristic of many African countries, but the very large 'youth bulge' brings with it many attendant risks. Following Huntington (1996), countries with such large youth segments are argued to be at serious risk of civil unrest and high rates of criminality, especially when their economies are unable to meet the employment needs of the youth. This is a view echoed more recently by Urdal (2004, 2006) and Cincotta (2008). It is this perspective that informs this chapter.

Zimbabwe, in common with most countries in Africa, has a significant youth bulge that it has maintained since 1982. There is a slight downward trend, but this matters little against the very large number of young persons, and this is unlikely to change in the next decade or two. United Nations projections suggest that Zimbabwe's population will reach 20 million in 2028.[1]

At independence, therefore, Zimbabwe was a country with a small population, but well-endowed with natural resources and good infrastructure. Against the background of state failure in so many African countries, the aspirations for Zimbabwe were very high: Julius Nyerere, for one, called Zimbabwe the 'jewel of Africa'.[2] A young person in the 1980s could look to the prospect of becoming educated in one of the most developed education systems in Africa, and to the prospect of getting a good job as a result. Thirty years later, a young person could still look forward to becoming educated to secondary school level and beyond, but with virtually no prospect of any employment other than in the informal sector, and hundreds of thousands had left the country in search of a reasonable and dignified livelihood.

Other chapters will unpack the failures of the state, but here the focus is on the youth as citizens and how this changed over the past 40 years: from the energy and enthusiasm involved in the 1980s for building a new country to the disillusionment and despair of the 2000s. This is examined through the lens of seven surveys carried out from the end of the 1990s to the recent past, 2017.

The Changing Landscape

As indicated briefly above, Zimbabwe is hardly the same country as it was in 1980. The 1980s were a decade marked by important social progress, driven by significant state investment in education, health, and social services. It was also a decade in which the region was struggling for an end to colonial domination, marked by violent struggles for independence in Angola, Mozambique, Namibia and South Africa, and followed by brutal civil wars in Angola and Mozambique. Zimbabwe came of age in a very dangerous neighbourhood, and did not escape unscathed. The 1980s saw violent low intensity conflict in the southern half of the country, involvement in the Mozambican civil war, and violent interventions by South Africa in Zimbabwe. However, there was universal primary school education, relatively easy access to secondary school education and access to health in what many regarded as the most developed and successful health care system in Africa. A young citizen

---

1 'Zimbabwe Population. 1950-2021', *Macrotrends*.
2 'Robert Mugabe, Zimbabwe's independence leader, 1924-2019', *Financial Times*, 6 September 2019.

had much to be grateful for, and much to hope for in his or her future.

When the low intensity conflict in Zimbabwe ended in 1987 (*Gukurahundi*, a very one-sided conflict that some would characterise as a crime against humanity, or even genocide), the country entered a long period of relative peace, apart from violence during elections in 1990 and 1995. It was also a period when the government reversed its socialist policies, implemented an Economic Structural Adjustment Programme (ESAP), and borrowed heavily from the International Monetary Fund. This changed the possibilities for many young people, as 'cost-recovery' became a new constraint. Whilst primary education remained largely free, there were costs for secondary and tertiary education that now had to be borne by families. The increasing hardship under ESAP, as well as the more open public arena after the repeal of Emergency Powers, led to the growth of a much more assertive civil society. Students and the women's movement became an important part of this assertiveness. The students had become a critical voice even in the 1980s, a position that strengthened in the 1990s, and thereafter (Hodgkinson 2013). Many of the student leaders of the 1990s became central figures in both the National Constitutional Assembly (NCA) and the original Movement for Democratic Change (MDC). This was the beginning of deep polarisation, with the country divided between supporters of the two main political parties, ZANU-PF and the MDC, as well as a growing rift between rural and urban areas. By 2018, Zimbabwe was the most polarised of 34 African countries (Bratton and Masunungure 2018).

The growing political and economic discontent resulted in a changed perspective of the youth. Whereas they were celebrated as the leaders for social change in the 1980s, building on the role that the young had played during the liberation war, as *mujibhas* and *chimbwidos*, the young became an increasing enemy for the ruling party. This was particularly emphasised by the support base for the MDC, and the threat of the young forced the government into creating an alternative youth base through the National Youth Service Training Scheme (SPT 2003). This scheme rapidly gained a reputation for being a violent youth militia, with many reports of their participation in political violence, especially during the elections in 2002 and 2005. Serious as this was, the Youth Service scheme only engaged a small proportion of the youth population, with most actively avoiding being involved. A report by ActionAid (2013) claimed that only 9% of young respondents would retaliate with violence if attacked by the supporter of another political party.

Nonetheless, youth became a site for contestation, and were feared for different reasons depending on the viewer's political affiliation. For ZANU-PF they were the threat at the polls due to the size of the youth demographic, and, for the MDC, they were the 'green bombers', a violent youth militia intent on the disruption of any election campaigning. Most young people found ways to avoid the political spaces altogether and were very adept at so doing (Osteroom and Pswarayi 2014).

The one reality that no young person could avoid was the declining economy and its effects on their present and their future. As pointed out above, Zimbabwe had *ab initio* a strong commitment to education, and, despite ESAP, this continued through the 1990s and 2000s, particularly with the establishment of multiple universities. Zimbabwe inherited only one university at independence in 1980, which was inadequate both for the needs of the country and the very large numbers of young people completing secondary school education. A second university was established in 1991, and, over the next two decades, ten state universities were established, as well as a further seven private universities. However, the downside to having a very large number of graduates is the need to find them jobs, and the need to grow the economy at a rate sufficient to the supply. This has proven to be impossible for the government, resulting in the migration of tens of thousands, some suggest millions, out of the country.

Having such a large cohort of well-educated young people with little chance of their aspirations being met is argued by some to be a recipe for civil conflict (Urdal 2004, 2006; Cincotta 2008). This view is given further force by the revolutions in North Africa (Masoud 2011), and how these compared with the so-called 'colour' revolutions in the Balkans (Way 2011). The argument that frustrated, educated youth, and particularly young men, are likely to be trouble is contested as well. Some argue, on the basis of looking at 40 developing countries, that youth unemployment is more likely to be a symptom of political instability than the cause (Azeng and Yogo 2015), but generally the evidence does support the view that unemployment and political violence are related. This is modified by the finding that level of education lessens the effect: developing countries with higher proportions of well-educated young people will see proportionately less engagement in political violence.

This is also the conclusion of the 2013 ActionAid study.

Looking at Zimbabwean youth over time, from 1999 to 2017, there is data on seven youth cohorts, each of which came of age during very different socio-political circumstances, and gives an opportunity to examine what effects each short period had on the beliefs and attitudes of these cohorts.

Methods

The Afrobarometer is a valuable resource in understanding the attitudes of African citizens. It now provides regular surveys of 34 African countries. The data not only provides the basis for comparisons of citizens' views over time, but also allows for more nuanced analyses within countries. Too frequently the only use that is made of it, concerns narrow political questions, particularly about party affiliation and elections. However, the richness of the data can give a much better understanding about all manner of important socio-political issues.[3]

The Afrobarometer has been conducting surveys of Zimbabwean citizens since 1999, with Zimbabwe amongst the first countries to be surveyed. A total of seven major surveys have been carried since then, as well as several others (mostly focused on elections), and, excluding Round 1 (1999), the six surveys gave a potential pool of nearly 9,353 respondents over almost 30 years. This is a large sample, with 4,956 youth under the age of 35. Of course, it was a different youth cohort for every survey, but, nonetheless, for every one of the seven surveys there is a youth cohort. For the purposes of this study, we defined youth as any respondent between the ages of 18 and 35 years.

Not every survey in Afrobarometer series asks the same questions, but enough of the questions are repeated in every survey for the purposes of comparability. In order to compare the youth over the years the same questions were used, and a number of comparable

---

3   A recent analysis of the 34 participating countries included questions about climate change, a reality that will probably affect the African continent more severely than other continents (Selormey et al. 2019). The study showed that a small majority of Africans (58%) had heard of climate change and, surprisingly for such a developed country in Africa, much less than half (41%) of South Africans had. It also demonstrated that rural people, women, the poor, and the poorly educated were less aware than other groups. This kind of data is helpful in addressing the problem of climate change – i.e. which groups in a country need special attention – and can also be used in understanding other socio-political issues.

measures constructed.[4] In addition to these variables, there were a number of demographic variables: age, obviously, but also education, employment and residence (rural or urban). Political affiliation was included as well, but not direct questions about actual political party support, rather whether the respondent was close to a political party or not. The rationale here is that Zimbabweans are sometimes cautious about disclosing their political affiliation, and many will not answer the question or claim that they have none. This group is termed 'reticent' by other researchers (Bratton and Masunungure 2018).

The results are reported separately in two sections. The first is the obvious contrast between the young and the old, using the entire sample of 9,353 respondents: simply because it is important to know whether the young and the old are any different. The second analysis involved the central question about whether the youth have changed over the past 28 years. As pointed out earlier, Zimbabwe has changed dramatically over this period, with serious adverse consequences for the youth, with the likelihood that this reflected many of the views of the various youth cohorts.

One issue regarding the use of survey data is the frequent criticism that respondents in Zimbabwe will show a reluctance to be honest if they suspect that they might get into trouble for their responses, especially on questions that are politically sensitive. (RAU and MPOI 2017). A recent study showed that older, rural and less educated Zimbabweans were more likely to perceive the sponsor to be the government and have trust in the president (Moyo-Nyede 2020). This was tested by looking at the comfort that the respondents had during the interview, as rated by the interviewers, and whether the respondents think the government was sponsoring the interview.

Furthermore, rural or urban residence is a sufficiently critical factor

---

4   These measures were used in other studies using the Afrobarometer, and the Research and Advocacy Unit (RAU) has used them in a wider variety of studies on Zimbabwean citizens. These studies have involved looking at the youth, women, political trust, social capital, religion, and even climate change.

All the questions were converted into binary variables (1 or 0), and analysed in the Statistical Package for Social Sciences (SPSS.20). All the measures are examined for their reliability and these were generally satisfactory, ranging from 0.55 for Lived Poverty to 0.99 for Anti-authoritarianism: *Lived Poverty (0.55); Social Capital (0.62); Access to Information (0.63); Social Participation (0.60); Political Freedom (0.79); Satisfaction with democracy (0.87); Political Trust (0.73); Service Delivery (0.73); Corruption (0.77); Ownership (0.63); Anti-authoritarianism (0.99)*.

in the polarisation in Zimbabwe, to be included as a variable. As seen in Figure 1, there are no real differences between the two groups in their levels of rated comfort during interview: both groups were, by a large majority, not ill at ease. However, this was not the case when asked who sponsored the survey, and the rural respondents were significantly more likely to believe that the government was the sponsor of the survey.[5] We therefore included some analysis of the residence variable in order to take account of this as a confounding factor.

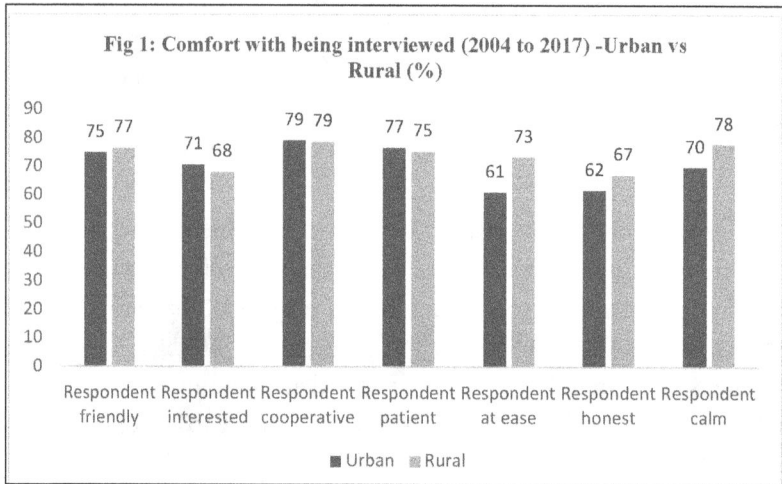

Fig 1: Comfort with being interviewed (2004 to 2017) -Urban vs Rural (%)

Results

Firstly, we examine the differences between the young and the old. This comparison uses the entire data set of 9,353 respondents, from every completed survey, without reference to time. Secondly, we examine the youth alone (4,956), and look at what changes, if any, occurred for each of the six periods. A working hypothesis here is that the older would have more positive views than the younger, having had better opportunities for good life experiences during the 1980 and 1990s.

Young versus old

The Young sample are those between 18 and 35. The Old were those older than 35, ranging from 36 to a startling 103, with a median of 48 years. On the first measure, *Lived Poverty*, there are no differences of any significance between the two age sets. The Young are more likely to report lack of access to medical care than the Old, and both groups have large numbers experiencing a lack of cash income. Poverty or lack of it has affected both groups similarly. There are also few differences between the two groups when it comes to *Ownership* of various items (radio, TV, computer, etc.), and the trend is the same for both. However, it is evident that ownership, apart from owning a radio, is extremely low for both groups, and this over a very long period.

Access to Information does show a difference between the two groups, with the Young expressing greater frequency of access than the Old to radio (59% v 50%), TV (40% v 28%), and newspapers (22% v 14%). Since there is no difference in ownership, the difference would seem to be due to the greater interest of the Young. Newer forms of media could not be tracked over the period as internet or cell phones have only become more widely available recently.

The idea that the Young have a greater interest in accessing information does not however translate into participation, or *Social Capital*. As can be seen in Figure 2, the Young are much less likely to attend community meetings or join others to raise an issue. This is interesting because the period covered by the Afrobarometer data sees the emergence of strong civic and political party opposition to the ruling party, ZANU-PF.

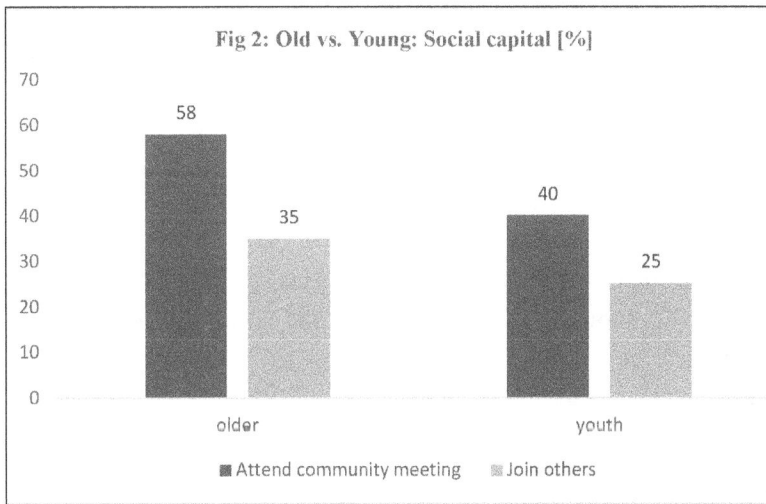

Fig 2: Old vs. Young: Social capital [%]

The emergence of the NCA and the MDC is usually attributed to their having strong support from the youth, but this was not widespread. The youth and the women's movement undoubtedly offered crucial support for both, but the Afrobarometer data suggests that this should not be overestimated. It is also important not to lose sight of the fact that Zimbabwe is not merely polarised politically, but also that rural or urban residence is a significant factor in the shaping of opinions and beliefs. Neither should the effects of patriarchy and culture (including respect for age) be ignored.

For example, both patriarchy and age play a strong role in determining the participation of young women in political life. Studies of young women's participation in elections show that both these factors have strong inhibitory effects. In 2018, a majority (71%) of young women reported a lack of support from older women, and 64% reported being affected by the 'pull her down' syndrome, whilst only 31% reported that culture forced them to concentrate on domestic duties (RAU 2018). In the 2013 elections, women identified the same factors, with 58% claiming that the 'pull her down' syndrome was a factor in why there were so few female politicians, and only 38% of rural women and 21% of urban women felt that older women had done a good job in supporting younger women (RAU and TWT 2014).

Read together with the findings on *Ownership* and *Access to Information*, it seems clear that *Social Capital* amongst the Young is subject to wider influences, and this is borne out further by the findings on *Social Participation*. Older persons are more likely to contact duty bearers than the Young, but this is in the context of extremely low rates of *Social Participation* generally. As seen in Figure 3 (overleaf), the vast majority on Zimbabwean citizens, young and old, do not engage duty bearers. Zimbabweans vote, and in large numbers, but are not politically active by any other measure. The relationship between state and citizens is remarkably absent.

Hoping that the state and its agents are more efficient and effective is obviously not creating much pressure for accountability, and, if the Old are not doing it, then this is not much of a model for the Young. There may be other factors explaining the absence of *Social Capital* and *Social Participation*. Zimbabwe over this entire period has been characterised by considerable political violence, especially around elections, and has become the most politically polarised African country of the 34 surveyed by the Afrobarometer (Bratton and Masunungure 2018). The fear generated by this political violence is the most commonly evoked explanation for the 'apathy' of the Zimbabwean citizenry.

It is evident that Zimbabwe has an unenviable reputation for political violence, so the view above is certainly credible. This violence is particularly severe during elections, but, notwithstanding this,

Fig 3: Old vs. Young: Social Participation [%]

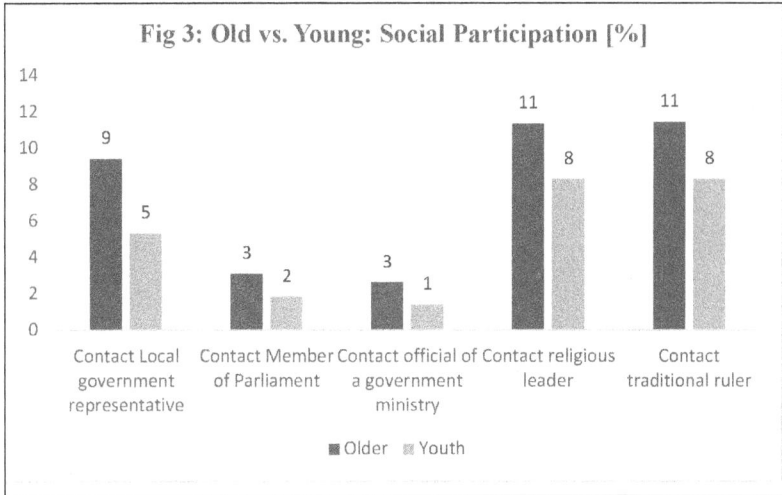

Fig 4: Old vs. Young: Freedoms [%]

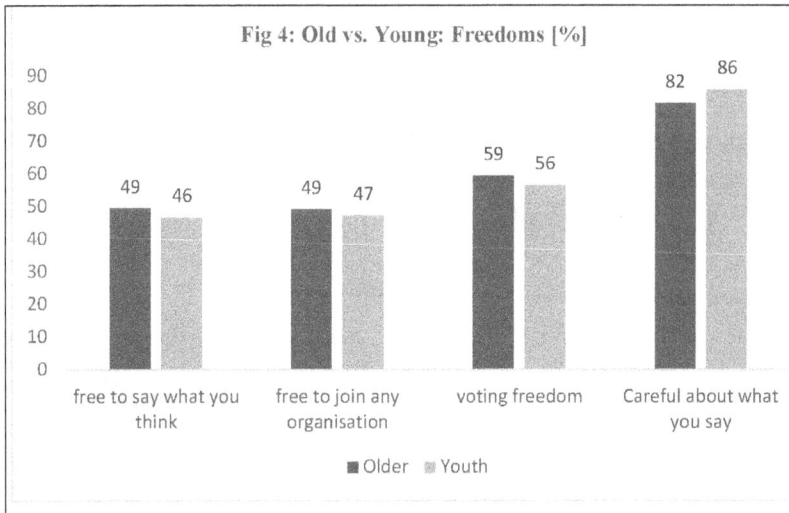

Zimbabweans generally vote in large numbers, and even more when the processes for registering as a voter are made easy. For example, in 2018, when registration was simplified, the youth registered in greatly increased numbers, and presumably voted in equally large numbers according to the increased turnout: 4.7 million in 2018 as opposed to 3.4 million in 2013. Figure 4 shows the lack of *Political Freedoms*, where over 80% of both Old and Young say they are careful about what they say in public, and about half say that they are not free to say what they think, about which organisation they can join, or for whom to vote. Clearly, the political environment is adverse, irrespective of age.

Zimbabweans have generally been the most supportive amongst Africans of the value of democracy (Figure 5), and there has been a steady increase in this support over the years since 2004, despite all

Fig 5: Old vs. Young: Democracy [%]

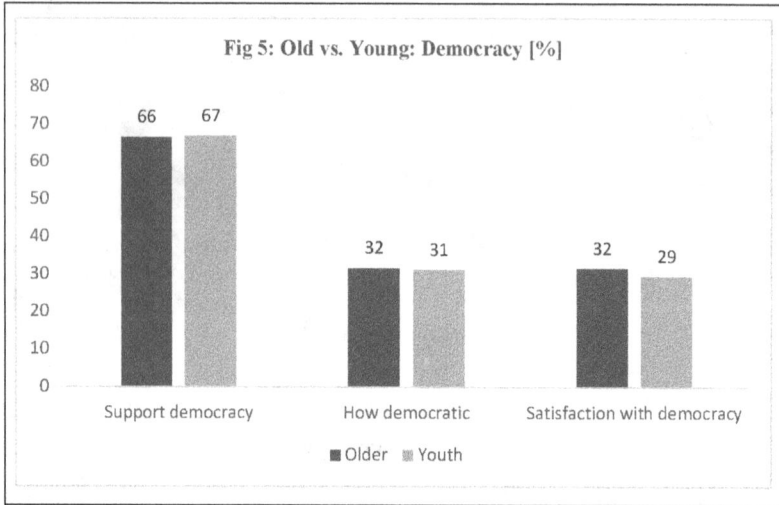

vicissitudes they have experienced at the hands of the state. It reached a peak during the life of the Inclusive Government (2009-2013), and declined slightly thereafter. For example, in 2004, only 48% of the Young expressed *Support for Democracy,* 79% did in 2012, and this dropped to 75% in 2017. When combining the data for all the years, all the six rounds since 2004, there is still a majority that support democracy, but no difference between Young and Old. Both Young and Old are equally unhappy with the Zimbabwe variety of democracy: two-thirds of each do not see Zimbabwe as a democracy, nor are they satisfied with Zimbabwean democracy. Citizens want democracy, but do not think that they are getting it.

The pessimism about Zimbabwean democracy has political consequences: if citizens believe they are not living in a democratic state that obviously says something about how they feel they are governed, and a crucial factor here is political trust. *Political Trust* in the state has been very low since 1999, and probably before, but there is no survey data prior to this date (RAU 2019b). As seen in Figure 6, less than half of the Old and Young express *Political Trust* in a range of duty bearers, political parties and public figures.

What is interesting is that the Old express greater *Political Trust* than the Young, and in significant numbers. Neither the Young nor the Old have much trust in opposition political parties and the Young

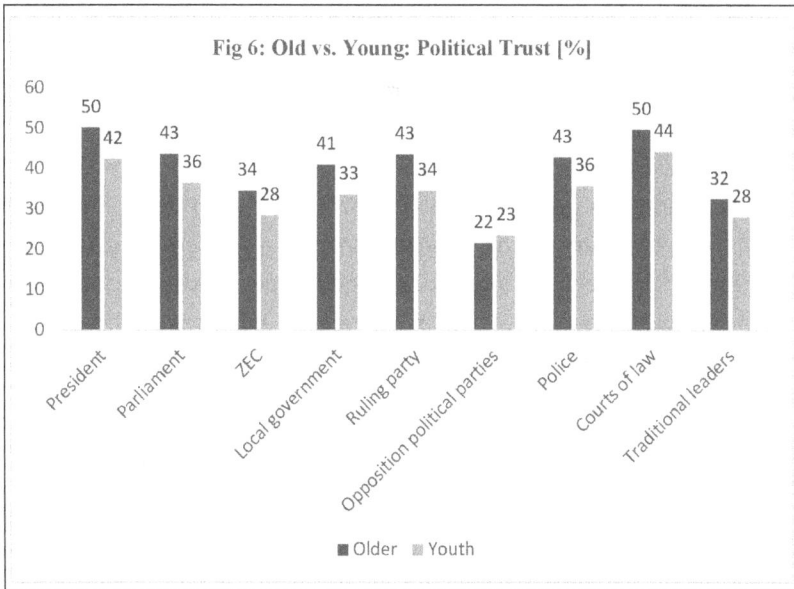

Fig 6: Old vs. Young: Political Trust [%]

have significantly less trust in the ruling party. The main point here is that *Political Trust* is a diminished commodity in Zimbabwe, and, commented on elsewhere, this is exacerbated by the lack of trust that the government has in its citizens: calling supporters of other political parties 'enemies' and resorting to coercion as a major strategy for enforcing political power is hardly likely to increase political trust. One other factor, added to the resort to coercion by the state, that is likely to reduce *Political Trust* is the effectiveness and efficiency of the delivery of public goods and services by a government.

It is evident that Zimbabweans do not have a high opinion of the government's ability to deliver public goods and services (*Service Delivery*). Less than 20% of both groups feel that the government is doing a good job in creating jobs, or narrowing wealth gaps, and less than half (43% and 45% of the Old and Young respectively) think that the government is keeping prices stable. There is an additional point in relation to government and service delivery and this relates to which problems the citizens think that the government should be addressing. Here it might be expected that the Old and the Young might have very different opinions.

As it turns out, there are differences. The Young, unsurprisingly in the economic decline that has marked the past two decades, see unemployment as a much more serious issue for government to address than the Old. The only other difference is the higher frequency of the Old who think that farming needs addressing, but in fairness, and despite all the rhetoric about land reform, neither Old nor Young see farming and land as important. Only 10% of the Old see farming as an important need, and only 5% of the Young do.

Corruption is a prevalent problem in Zimbabwe, ranked the 154th most corrupt country in the world (Transparency International 2019). Corruption has become a bigger and bigger issue over the period of the Afrobarometer surveys, but neither Young nor Old have real differences of opinion. They both see the police as the most corrupt, and religious leaders and NGOs as the least. It is also clear that Corruption is largely a high-level, elite practice, and hence it might be another factor limiting Political Trust, and also trust in the government.

Finally, there is the issue of Political Affiliation, which is important in a country that is so polarised. The question about political affiliation revealed some interesting differences between Young and Old. The Old are more likely to support a political party than the Young, although half of the Young do. However, nearly 40% of the Young, and significantly more of the Old, are not close to a party.

This lack of political interest by the Young must be read together with the findings that they have less Political Trust, Social Participation and Social Capital. These are all important factors that are critical to agency and good citizenship, and, whilst there are many similarities between the Young and the Old, the findings suggest that the Young have, and at least by 2017, participated less in the socio-political life of the country. It also suggests caution in calling the youth 'apathetic', unless we understand apathy to mean a disinterest in socio-political life due to very clear factors, and factors, that were they addressed coherently, would see a non-apathetic youth.

Finally, and for completeness sake, we report on the findings from testing the differences between Young and Old. Note that many of the differences were largish, five percentage points or more, and this generally implies a statistically significant difference. Explicitly testing this, these differences were in fact significant.[6]

---

6   All differences commented upon were statistically significant *[t=2.96 (Ownership)*

The Young were significantly more likely to be urban, educated, have better access to information, and more likely to reject authoritarianism. The Old, by contrast, were more likely to be male, have lower lived poverty, more social capital, more likely to participate socially, believe that they have freedoms, have greater political trust, be close to a political party, and have greater ownership. There were no differences due to employment, service delivery or beliefs in corruption.

Simply put, the Young are actually different from the Old, as might be expected, but this does not suggest how they might behave differently. Being better educated, rejecting authoritarianism, and having little political trust in the context of low employment and economic adversity might suggest trouble brewing in the future. It also seems that the working hypothesis is confirmed: the Old, having had more positive life experience, and hence greater possibility of developing agency, do have more positive views and attitudes about life than the Young.

Youth from 2004 to 2017

The comparison above involved a contrast between Young and Old by aggregating all the data from six survey rounds. This could not easily show changes that might have taken place over time, and, furthermore, always involved a different youth cohort. Those who were 18 years old in 2004 were 31 in 2017, still within the youth cohort, but with very different life experiences from those who turned 18 in 2016-2017. The 2004 cohort had lived through violent elections, hyperinflation, and Operation Murambatsvina, and have probably never had formal employment. This suggests that the 2004 cohort might have more jaundiced views about life in Zimbabwe, and this can be examined through contrasts with the more recent cohorts. A working hypothesis would be that the older youth groups – 2004 to 2009 – should have more negative views about the country than the more recent groups.

This next section thus looks at the youth alone, and using all the same measures, examines whether there were changes over the period. Here, rather than using the individual questions and frequencies, the measures are compared over time. The mean scores for each measure are used for the comparison.

The first comparison over time was that between Lived Poverty and Ownership. Logically, we might expect Ownership to increase as Lived

---

to -22.19 (Education); p=0.001].

Poverty decreases, as is the case here. Ownership stayed static from 2005 to 2012, but Lived Poverty deceased very slightly during the life of the Inclusive Government, decreased again between 2012 and 2015, and rose again by 2017.

Most likely, Lived Poverty has risen again by 2020. This seems corroborated by a small study of young women that showed large rises in Lived Poverty between 2017 and 2020 (RAU 2020a).

The information sphere has changed dramatically over the past 14 years with the accessibility of electronic media. Unfortunately, questions about social media (internet and cell phones) were not included in the earlier surveys as these media were not available at those times. There has been radio ownership over the period, but a big drop in 2017 from 2015 presumably reflects the increased interest in social media devices. There is also the suggestion, from the drops in 2009 and 2017, that economic factors are playing a role.

When the various types of information are combined in a single score, it is evident that Access to Information is getting worse over time. The trend is towards the youth having decreasing access to radio, TV and newspaper. This would seem to be a function of the economy and increasing poverty, as well as a switch to social media.

Political Trust was increasing from 2005, but on the decline after 2015, and most have little political trust over the decade or so. Furthermore, most see Corruption as a problem, and one that has worsened since 2005.

Social Capital and Social Participation are very low, and have remained that way since 2004. As was seen in the previous section, this is not unique to the youth, and is characteristic of Zimbabwean citizens as a whole. However, the youth are less engaged with the social world, and this has changed not at all over the years.

What is also evident is that both Social Capital and Social Participation are on downward trends, with a very small rise in 2017. The country's situation has worsened considerably since 2017, and in 2020 has worsened further due to the Covid-19 pandemic. The pandemic will undoubtedly worsen this as both Social Capital and Social Participation are affected directly by the lockdowns and the regulations for social distancing. We can confidently predict that these will not have improved when the pandemic eases and in the data provided by the next Afrobarometer survey. It is evident that youth over time have rejected all forms of authoritarianism: they are consistently anti-authoritarian. The mean scores are also very close to the maximum, three, and have changed minimally over the thirteen years. They are not strongly supportive of democracy, but this needs brief explanation.

This index comprises three questions.[7] The youth consistently feel that Zimbabwe is not much of a democracy, but are also strongly in favour of democracy as the correct model for the country. Apart from 2004, when only 48% of the youth felt that democracy was the best, 75% were supportive of it thereafter.

This is encouraging from the perspective of youth not becoming victims of what John Gay (2003) called the 'vicious cycle'. Gay theorised that those who were amongst the most deprived in a society would tend to be less supportive of democracy and more supportive of authoritarianism. This thesis does not appear to hold for Zimbabwean youth; a previous study found that the big differences were due to residence, between rural and urban citizens (RAU 2020b). This rural/urban factor does still play a role for the young. The negative views about the supply and extent of democracy are amplified by the youth's views on Political Freedoms. There are three questions here, each dealing with one aspect of freedom.[8] Their views are very negative in 2005, the year in which Operation Murambatsvina took place, and have declined again in 2017.

The steep decline in 2005 is found in other studies; for example, in a study on 'risk aversion' it was found that Zimbabweans declined dramatically from previously being risk taking to being risk averse (Masunungure et al. 2016). In 2005, only 13% of Zimbabweans are risk taking, down from 89% in 1999 and 72% in 2004.

This is turn is given emphasis by what can be described as Political Fear, measured through a question that asks about the caution that people have in expressing their opinions in public.[9] It is evident that the majority of the youth have such caution and it was worst in 2012, presumably because of a forthcoming election, but nonetheless more

---

7   The three questions are as follows: *Democracy is preferable to any other kind of government; In your opinion how much of a democracy is Zimbabwe today? Overall, how satisfied are you with the way democracy works in Zimbabwe?*

8   The three questions are as follows: *Freedom to say what you think; Free to join any organisation; Free to vote.*

9   *In your opinion, how often, in this country: Do people have to be careful of what they say about politics?*

than 80% always or often are careful in expressing their views.

One final issue is relevant, and this is the matter of the delivery of public goods and services, or Service Delivery. Political trust in the government and state is generated by the extent to which these meet the aspirations of citizens (RAU 2019a). There is a complex relationship between political trust (the views and attitudes of the citizens) and the 'trustworthiness' of the government. As Levi and Stoker (2000: 493) point out, 'all agree that government officials who act in a trustworthy manner are more likely to elicit compliance, and virtually all agree that government regulators who trust the people that they are regulating are more likely to evoke trustworthy behaviour and compliance'. This shifts the problem of political trust away from the attributes of the citizen to the character and behaviour of the government, government officials and politicians.

Zimbabwean youth do not think that the government is doing a good job in delivering public goods and services, which is hardly surprising given the parlous state of the economy. It is also the case that, in addition to failing the citizenry in the area of their livelihoods (and worse for the youth), the government scarcely shows any trust in its own citizens. The government particularly distrusts urban youth as the likely supporters of opposition political parties.

The Zimbabwean context is one in which the government distrusts the youth, fails them in their aspirations for careers and livelihoods, and too frequently resorts to coercion as a mode of persuasion. In line with the general 'youth bulge' thesis, are Zimbabwean youth more likely to become militant, even violently disruptive? One way to examine this is to look at their political affiliations. As was seen in comparing the young and the older, the youth are less likely to claim political affiliation. There is a consistent pattern since 2004: half of the youth are 'close to a political party' and a similar proportion say that they are not. This has not changed over 13 years, but it is important to deconstruct what this might mean.

One way to understand this is to note the previous findings from comparing the young and the old, and the finding that the main difference in the youth was that they were urban, educated, had more frequent access to information, and were more rejecting of authoritarianism. Is this then a difference within the youth population? Are there differences due to residence, rural or urban, a difference noted in many studies of the Zimbabwean citizenry?

On statistical testing, residence, rural or urban, makes a significant difference.[10] Rural youth have greater Social Participation and Political Trust, are more content with Service Delivery and are close to a political party. The question about which political party, was not used, but a fair guess is that this closeness is to ZANU-PF. Urban youth, on the other hand, are more educated (secondary school or higher), more likely to be employed, and have some form of ownership. They also have greater social capital, better access to information, are more anti-authoritarian, and see corruption as more prevalent. Thus, this demographic variable is clearly important, and the two worlds in which the youth live should be thought about very carefully when planning interventions.

Conclusions

At the outset, the issue of the risks behind the 'youth bulge' in Zimbabwe was raised, and, in the context of great impoverishment in the country, there is the associated concern about whether the youth will become disruptive and violent. Whilst the demographic bulge is obvious, it is another step to suggest that Zimbabwean youth resemble their peers in North Africa, or any other part of the world where such youth bulges are evident.

This analysis reveals some interesting facts about Zimbabwean youth. Firstly, they are different from their elders in many respects, but not dramatically different. The youth, unsurprisingly, are better educated, make more use of sources of information, and reject authoritarianism more strongly than their elders. In 2017, the youth were five times more likely to use social media, three times more likely to use the internet, and more likely to own a computer. The percentages were low, but the direction was clear.[11]

The older group is significantly more likely to have more social capital, social participation, believe that they have political freedom, have greater political trust, be close to a political party, and have greater ownership. However, neither the young nor the old believe that Zimbabwe's form of democracy is satisfactory. They also believed that

---

10 All differences commented upon were statistically significant *[t= -3.75(Age) to 42.4 (Access to Information); p=0.001]*.

11 Afrobarometer Online: Use of internet – under 35 years (14%), over 35 (3%); Use of social media – *under 35 years (11%), over 35 (3%); Own computer – under 35 years (15%), over 35 (11%)*.

many duty bearers are corrupt and that the government is doing poorly in terms of service delivery. The broad conclusion from this contrast is that the youth have comparatively less agency than their elders, which is not surprising since so few will have had employment, and have probably been reliant on their guardians and elders for daily existence.

The studies on risk taking amongst Zimbabweans demonstrated several things. The older (over 41 years) were more likely to be risk taking than younger age groups by 2014, reversing a trend seen in 1999 and 2004 (Masunugure et al. 2016). It was argued that this shift was due to the better life experiences of the group that came of adult age in the 1990s, who had experienced relatively better conditions in the country. The group that was now 41 years old or more in 2020 had developed agency and maintained this through all the vicissitudes from 2000 onwards.

This would seem the plausible explanation for the current findings: the older group has had better life opportunities, and more opportunity to develop agency. The young cohorts have had no such opportunity, rather experiencing the opposite and increasing adversity. Even the cohort that came of age in 2004 was still within the youth demographic (under 35). It is easy to describe the youth as 'apathetic', as is frequently done in respect of registering and voting in elections, but this is a very crude characterisation and disregards the adversity with which youth have had to contend with since 2000. Of course, this comparison of the young and the old is also rather crude and is only quantitative, but it does suggest the need for more careful research into understanding the youth. For example, whilst it is evident that the youth are not violent generally, it is only studies examining why this is so that can allow the development of appropriate policies (Osteroom and Pswarayi 2014).

The second points made are about the youth themselves. The youth are not a homogeneous group; it is plain, and generally obvious to all. The significant differences between rural and urban youth are important for any policy. Urban youth show many more characteristics of agency than their rural counterparts; they are better educated, more likely to be employed, have more forms of ownership, greater social capital, reject authoritarianism more strongly, and see corruption as problem. However, rural youth have greater political trust and social participation, see the government doing well in service delivery, and are more likely to be close to a political party. These differences speak to the political polarisation in the country, a division based on the importance of the rural areas for the maintenance of political power for the ruling party, ZANU-PF. However, it is also heartening that both groups have remained supportive of democracy over the past 13 years.

The question remains, about the extent to which rural views, in particular, are just reflective of the social and cultural differences between rural and urban areas, or are a manifestation of the dual effects of patronage and political fear in the former.[12] We noted earlier the generally hostile attitude of the government to the youth, and more so towards the urban youth, and research elsewhere has noted the very different political pressures that can be applied to rural youth (Osteroom and Pswarayi 2014). For example, as these authors point out, it is more difficult for rural youth to avoid political co-option, given how important positive affiliation to ZANU-PF is for safety and livelihood opportunities.

One of the most important issues to address for the future will be the restoration of political trust in the youth. More recent data indicates that most (60%) of them have little interest in engaging in politics or believe that voting has any value (British Council 2020). Unfortunately, this study did not undertake any formal contrast between rural and urban youth, so does not allow any conclusions to be drawn about the differences between the two populations. Nonetheless, if extrapolated to the youth demographic, 60% represents an enormous group of disengaged citizens, approximately four million, and probably not a group that will forever remain resigned to their fate. It is also a huge youth dividend in a potentially wealthy country, and can be the force to change the country's trajectory.

References

ActionAid (2013) 'Eager or Slumbering? Youth and political participation in Zimbabwe'. Denmark: ActionAid.

British Council (2020) 'Next Generation'. Harare: British Council.

Azeng, T.F. and T.U. Yogo (2015) 'Youth Unemployment, Education and Political Instability: Evidence from Selected Developing Countries 1991-2009'. HiCN Working Paper 200. Sussex: Institute of Development Studies.

---

12 Always careful what you say (rural v. urban): *t-test – t=4.19 (p=0.000)*.

Bratton. M. and E. Masunungure (2018) 'Heal the beloved country: Zimbabwe's polarized electorate'. Afrobarometer Policy Paper No. 49.

Cincotta, R.P. (2008) 'How Democracies Grow Up: Countries with too Many Young People May Not Have a Fighting Chance at Freedom', Foreign Policy, 165, pp. 80-82.

Chikwanha, A. and E. Masunungure (2007) 'Young and Old in Sub-Saharan Africa: Who are the Real Democrats?' Afrobarometer Working Paper 87.

Gay, J. (2003) 'Development as Freedom: A Virtuous Circle?' Afrobarometer Working Paper 29.

Hodgkinson, D. (2013) 'The "Hardcore" Student Activist: The Zimbabwe National Students Union (ZINASU), State Violence, and Frustrated Masculinity, 2000–2008', Journal of Southern African Studies, 39(4), pp. 863-883.

Huntington, S.P. (1996) The clash of Civilizations and the Remaking of World Order. New York: Simon & Schuster.

Levi, M. and L. Stoker (2000) 'Political Trust and Trustworthiness', Annual Review of Political Science, 3(1), pp. 475-507.

Masoud, T (2011) 'The Upheavals in Egypt and Tunisia. The Road to (and from) Liberation Square', Journal of Democracy, 22(3), pp. 20-34.

Masunungure, E., A. Reeler, R. Kokera, D. Mususa, S. Ndoma and H. Koga (2016) 'Are Zimbabweans Revolting?' Harare: MPOI and RAU.

Moyo-Nyede, S. (2020) 'Fear and Trust: Explaining professed popular trust in Zimbabwe's presidents'. Afrobarometer Dispatch, No. 399.

Osteroom, M. and L. Pswarayi (2014) 'Being a Born-free. Violence, Youth and Agency in Zimbabwe'. Research Report No. 79, Institute of Development Studies.

RAU (Research and Advocacy Unit) (2018) 'Political participation by young women in the 2018 elections: Post-election report'. Harare: RAU.

——— (2019a) 'Political Trust in Zimbabwe over time'. Harare: RAU.

——— (2019b) 'Political trust, social trust and trustworthiness in Zimbabwe?' Harare: RAU.

——— (2020a) 'The Gender Lens: Women's Views on Zimbabwe in

2020'. Harare: RAU.

———— (2020b) 'Vicious and Virtuous Cycles: Development and Freedom in Zimbabwe'. Harare: RAU.

———— and MPOI (2017) 'Are Zimbabweans "Poll-arised" by opinion polls?' Harare: MPOI and RAU.

———— and TWT (2014) 'Do elections in Zimbabwe favour the rural woman? Analysis of a survey on women's participation in the 2013 elections'. Harare: RAU and The Women's Trust.

Reeler, A.P. (2017) 'Operation Murambatsvina and its effects on political participation'. Harare: MPOI and RAU.

Selormey, E.E., M.Z. Dome, L. Osse, and C. Logan (2019) 'Change ahead: Experience and awareness of climate change in Africa'. Afrobarometer Policy Paper No. 60.

Solidarity Peace Trust (2003) National Youth Service Training – 'Shaping Youths in a Truly Zimbabwean Manner'. An Overview of Youth Militia Training and Activities in Zimbabwe, October 2000–August 2003', Harare/Johannesburg: Solidarity Peace Trust.

Transparency International (2019) 'Global Corruption Barometer 2019. Citizens' Views and Experiences of Corruption'. Transparency International.

Urdal, H. (2004) 'The Devil in the Demographics: The Effect of Youth Bulges on Domestic Armed Conflict, 1950-2000'. Conflict Prevention and Reconstruction Series, CPR14. Washington, DC: World Bank.

———— (2006) 'A Clash of Generations? Youth Bulges and Political Violence', International Studies Quarterly, 50(3), pp. 607-629.

Way, L.A. (2011) 'Comparing the Arab Revolts. The Lessons of 1989', Journal of Democracy, 22(4), pp. 13-23.

4

Education in the First Two Decades
of Independence

Brian Raftopoulos and Rory Pilossof

Introduction

One of the central features of educational policy in Zimbabwe from 1980 to 2000 was the shift from the mass provision of education to a more instrumentalist concern with the relevance of educational provision to employment. This change took place within the context of a declining economic environment and subsequently a decreasing availability of revenue for public expenditure. The policy shift also coincided with an increasing lack of state legitimacy, and a global neoliberal orthodoxy, which provided fewer options at a national policy level.

In the immediate post-independence period, the mass provision of education was largely driven by the political demands of the electorate and the expectations of immediate changes by the African majority. As Dzvimbo (1991: 282) observed, education was used 'primarily to redress the imbalances in educational provision that existed before independence due to the racist policies of successive colonial regimes'. Such a policy was also consistent with human capital theory, which justified the mass expansion of education as an investment that increased the capacity of labour to produce material goods and thereby contribute to economic growth.

With the coming of the Economic Structural Adjustment Programme in the 1990s the sustainability of the mass expansion of education in the 1980s was brought into question. Concerns were raised about the financial viability of such education provisions, the value of continued quantitative expansion, and the relevance of the curriculum provided. Discussion focused on the rate of return on education, or to put it differently, the provision of a market-compatible rationale for educational expenditure. The discussion on rate of return analysis was strongly influenced by the World Bank, and the main features of its policy implications have been summarised by Bennell:

> First, education at whatever level is a relatively attractive investment not only for individuals but also for government. Second, with certain caveats, 'in most developing countries primary should receive the highest priority, followed by secondary education.' Third, government subsidisation of higher, and to a lesser extent secondary, education is excessive given the large differentials that exist between private and social [rate of returns]. To remedy this misallocation of resources students should be made to contribute significantly more to the costs of education (Bennell 1996: 183).

The Zimbabwean state was in a position where there was a growing tension in its education policy between, on the one hand, the need to provide mass education as 'an ideological arm of the state, reinforcing and reproducing the social structure', and on the other, the possible negative effects that the expenditure involved in such a policy could have on economic growth (Carnoy 1985: 164). Moreover, this policy tension began at time when the Zimbabwean state's legitimacy was declining, as the incumbent (ZANU-PF party was facing serious political challenges for the first time. These problems of policy making were compounded by the incapacity of most civic actors to intervene in educational policy, as indeed in policy issues generally. According to Dzvimbo:

> Education policy making in Zimbabwe since the colonial period has always been dominated by a minority. First it was dominated by a small white minority and now it is dominated by an educated African elite who form the cabinet and the top echelons of the ruling party (Dzvimbo 1991: 48).

Thus, the late 1990s education policy was caught between the demand for further democratisation of access to education, and the imperatives of macroeconomic stabilisation. Caught in this policy vice, the discussion around the relevance of educational content reached a crescendo by the time of the publication of the Government's Commission of Inquiry into Education and Training in 1999. After 2000, in the context of deepening political crises, a series of highly politicised problems emerged in the educational sphere, and which remain problematic in the current context. These problems have centred around: the 'disciplining' of teachers for their support for the opposition party, the Movement for Democratic Change (MDC); the militarisation of youth centres; the struggle by teachers for better conditions of service in a rapidly declining economy; and struggles over the curriculum, in particular the teaching of history.

This chapter is divided in to four parts. Part One will deal with the developments in primary and secondary education between 1980-2000. Part Two will provide an overview of vocational training during the same period. This will show the overall shifts in education provisions, and will also provide insights into how these changes affected the youth in Zimbabwe in the first two decades of independence. Part Three will look briefly at the employment context in which these developments have taken place, while the last section, Part Four, will discuss the educational problems that have resulted from the political crises the country experienced from the turn of the millennium until 2003.

Part One: Educational policy in the primary and secondary sectors, 1980-2000

One of the most celebrated successes of the ZANU-PF government was the massive quantitative expansion in educational provision during the first two decades of independence. Such an expansion was dictated by the pressures of popular demand for education from the African majority who had provided the support base for the anti-colonial struggle. As a consequence of this expansion, primary enrolment increased from 819,586 in 1979 to 1,235,994 in 1980, rising to over 2,223,000 by 1989. In the 1990s enrolment reached a peak of 2,493,791 in 1996, before falling to 2,460,669 in 2000 (see Table 4.1)

Table 4.1: Primary School Enrolment 1980-2000

YEAR	Male	Female	Total	% Male	% Female
1980	647,761	588,233	1,235,994	52.41	47.59
1981	892,680	822,489	1,715,169	52.05	47.95
1982	991,111	916,114	1,907,225	51.97	48.03
1983	1,060,154	984,333	2,044,487	51.85	48.15
1984	1,101,899	1,030,405	2,132,304	51.68	48.32
1985	1,142,480	1,074,398	2,216,878	51.54	48.46
1986	1,160,166	1,104,887	2,265,053	51.22	48.78
1987	1,146,361	1,104,958	2,251,319	50.92	49.08
1988	1,122,662	1,089,441	2,212,103	50.75	49.25
1989	1,131,986	1,091,185	2,223,171	50.92	49.08
1990	1,073,452	1,046,429	2,119,881	50.64	49.36
1991	1,168,460	1,126,484	2,294,944	50.91	49.09
1992	1,162,568	1,143,200	2,305,768	50.42	49.58
1993	1,258,465	1,178,206	2,436,671	51.65	48.35
1994	1,202,569	1,163,651	2,366,220	50.82	49.18
1995	1,259,891	1,222,686	2,482,577	50.75	49.25
1996	1,265,891	1,227,900	2,493,791	50.76	49.24
1997	1,259,888	1,231,473	2,491,361	50.57	49.43
1998	1,265,177	1,223,762	2,488,939	50.83	49.17
1999	1,251,533	1,208,790	2,460,323	50.87	49.13
2000	1,251,921	1,208,748	2,460,669	50.88	49.12

Source: Nherera 2000

At secondary level the expansion was even more impressive. Enrolment increased from 66,215 in 1979 to 148,690 in 1981, reaching 670,615 in 1989. In the 1990s enrolment reached 710,619 in 1991 rising to a peak of 844,187 by 2000 (see Table 4.2.) While this growth has been impressive there were several problems which confronted the nature of educational development in Zimbabwe over this period. These included: the absence of a comprehensive policy framework; limited access and gender equity; relevance of the curriculum; the problem of school dropouts, and crippling financial issues. Each of these will be dealt with in turn below.

Table 4.2: Secondary School Enrolment 1980-2000

YEAR	Male	Female	Total	% Male	% Female
1980	42,132	32,189	74,321	56.69	43.31
1981	86,550	62,140	148,690	58.21	41.79
1982	134,084	93,563	227,647	58.90	41.10
1983	187,583	128,855	316,438	59.28	40.72
1984	248,116	168,297	416,413	59.58	40.42
1985	287,061	194,939	482,000	59.56	40.44
1986	320,788	216,639	537,427	59.69	40.31
1987	354,175	250,477	604,652	58.58	41.42
1988	373,026	267,979	641,005	58.19	41.81
1989	386,928	283,687	670,615	57.70	42.30
1990	381,030	291,626	672,656	56.65	43.35
1991	397,954	312,665	710,619	56.00	44.00
1992	368,070	289,274	657,344	55.99	44.01
1993	355,262	284,890	640,152	55.50	44.50
1994	361,835	296,083	657,918	55.00	45.00
1995	386,775	324,319	711,094	54.39	45.61
1996	404,405	346,944	751,349	53.82	46.18
1997	421,039	367,565	788,604	53.39	46.61
1998	442,226	387,751	829,977	53.28	46.72
1999	442,226	391,813	834,039	53.02	46.98
2000	448,981	395,202	844,183	53.19	46.81

Source: Nherera 2000

The absence of a comprehensive policy framework

It is clear that, apart from a general commitment to rapid expansion of educational enrolment, the government had no provisions for a long-term comprehensive policy framework. As was noted in a joint paper by the Ministry of Education, Sports and Culture, and the Ministry of Higher Education and Technology in 1998:

> There is no comprehensive policy document on education and training. The absence of such a document has lead [sic]

to periodical political announcements, policy circulars and Chief Education Officer circulars that are at times conflicting sources of direction to the sector.

This lack of clarity created confusion on the ground that affected teachers, learners, school leavers and parents. These problems were exacerbated by the sheer volume of students now attending public institutions, as will be touched on below.

Limited access and gender equity

While overall enrolment expanded after independence, there remained problems of unequal access and gender equity in the 1980s and 1990s. Many children in the communal areas, resettlement areas and commercial farming areas remained out of school, due to the under-provision of educational facilities, poor infrastructure, and long walking distances to the nearest school. Approximately 15% of children remained out of school at the turn of the millennium (Nherera 2000: 11). Moreover, there was a shortage of school places in urban high-density areas because parents often moved their children from poor rural district schools to the better equipped urban schools (Nherera 1998: 51). With regard to gender equity, it can be seen from Tables 4.1 and 4.2 that at primary level there was a fair degree of gender parity. At secondary level the gender inequality is more apparent, as evidenced in Table 4.3.

Table 4.3: Drop-out Rates by Grade and Gender: 1990-1998

YEAR	Grade 1	Grade 2	Grade 3	Grade 4	Grade 5	Grade 6
	Male/ Female	Male/ Female	Male/ Female	Male/ Female	Male/ Female	Male/ Female
1990	4.5/7.1	0.9/0.1	2.1/0.5	2.8/1.4	6.2/6.1	1.5/2.8
1991	14.3/10.3	5.5/3.9	6.0/4	5.4/2.7	3.2/0.7	6.9/8.1
1992	10.3/11	3.5/4.2	3.7/3.3	2.8/3.1	0.4/1.1	7.1/2.3
1993	14/14.3	6.3/5.8	6.3/5.6	5.3/6.2	3.7/5	3.2/6.3
1994	8.5/8.9	2/0.5	0.8/0.3	1.2/1.1	4.2/4.2	2.4/16
1995	11.5/12.3	4.9/4.6	4.3/3.8	3.1/1.7	1/0.2	2.5/3.4
1996	12.2/13.2	5.2/3.3	4.8/3.5	3.4/2.6	0.6/1.4	5.5/4.6
1997	12.1/13.2	4.4/3.3	3.4/3.7	1.9/2.5	0.2/1.1	5.9/8.7
1998	12.87/12	4.77/4.1	4.25/3.59	3.3/2.92	1.28/1.38	5.46/8.28

Source: Kanyenze 1999 and 2000

School drop-outs

As Table 4.3 shows, the drop-out rate was highest at Grade One and higher among girls than boys. Moreover, the rate peaked in 1993, probably as a result of the disastrous drought of the previous year. At secondary level the highest drop-out rate was at Form 4 level after the 'O' Level exams. (Table 4.4 overleaf) This problem of drop-outs was (and is) directly related to the general problem of poverty in the population. In a poverty assessment study survey carried out in 1997, it was found that 61% of Zimbabweans are poor (UNDP 1998). With more specific reference to drop-outs, a study of social policy under structural adjustment conditions carried out in 1997/98 found that the major reason for children dropping out of school was 'unaffordability' (Mukotekwa et al. 1999: 29).

Poverty had knock-on effects with regard to education. Families' need for income often meant that child labour or work for the household was a necessity, rather than allocating resources to education. Families had to choose which children would go to school, and other income generating activities like agriculture, mining, or sex work became central to the experience of many youth. The lack of formal work opportunities, combined with crippling poverty, negatively impacted both access to education and belief in the need to stay in education. The shortage of work opportunities will be expanded in this chapter, and others. What is clear, is that there is a critical lack of studies into the education experience of Zimbabweans in the first two decades of independence. Important questions about what students went through, their thoughts and ideas about schooling and the role of education need more research. The role and motivations of parents, and their attitudes to education, also need more investigation. It is often presumed that there is a strong belief in the importance of education, but there has been little investigation into this and the differences between rural and urban populations, provincial experiences and gender biases.

Relevance of school curriculum

As the squeeze on state budgetary resources became a central aspect of the macroeconomic debate, so the debate on expenditure efficiency in educational provision and the lack of employment creation generated questions about the relevance of the curriculum. Thus, the Chief Economist of the Zimbabwe Congress of Trade Unions, has observed:

Table 4.4: Drop-out Rates by Form and Gender 1990–1998

Year	Form 1		Form 2		Form 3		Form 4		Form 5	
	Male	Female	Male	Female	Male	Female	Male	Female	Male	Female
1990	6.15	10.34	4.75	8.87	5	4.94	91.82	92.55	2.18	11.17
1991	14.85	15.58	10.88	14.77	13.36	20.4	93.36	95.11	383	23.33
1992	11.38	11.26	5.63	9.47	10.5	18.47	92.45	95.51	2.83	6.52
1993	8.12	9.71	3.68	9.69	7.99	14.64	91.65	93.09	1.33	5.22
1994	5.84	8.08	0.63	3.27	4.13	8.49	91.67	93.16	5.34	9.02
1995	7.66	9.13	2.66	5.81	6.11	11.14	91.44	93.07	1.71	0.28
1996	7.64	7.93	4.54	7.57	9.83	14.01	91.55	9279	4.84	8.57
1997	6.56	8.13	1.67	6.9	6.93	11.92	91.56	92.53	3.67	4.67
1998	6.12	7.8	4.8	6.61	8.35	13.52	95.3	95.93	9.68	15.3

Source: Kanyenze 1999 and 2000

The extent of the school-leaver problem is such that, of the estimated 200-300,000 school-leavers with secondary education entering the job market each year, the formal sector has only been able to absorb 20-30,000 of these. These school-leavers have no experience, no adequate practical skills. What they have is academic education, which has imbued them with high aspirations for white-collar jobs. What they need to improve their chances of (self) employment are opportunities for work experience on the labour market (Kanyenze 1997: 14).

The discussion about curriculum relevance had been going on since the colonial period, when government officials and missionaries debated the kind of education that would be most 'suitable' for Africans. Thus, in 1949, the chairman of the Federation of African Welfare Societies, Percy Ibbotson, advised that:

> The emphasis in the primary school in this country is far too much on the academic and not manual or industrial…I think the whole educational system of this country needs re-examination because education is not the mere acquiring of academic knowledge but equipment for life and we are turning out Africans who are totally unsuited to meet the demands upon them (NLAB 1949).

In 1966, the Rhodesian government introduced F2 schools for about third of African children entering secondary education. These schools were to provide children with an education more suited to their largely rural environment, and related to the requirements for semi-skilled labour in the colonial economy. Predictably, African parents regarded F2 schools as second-rate, and the pre-vocational courses offered were seen as providing few opportunities for substantive career development.

In 1980, the new government introduced a pilot project known as the Zimbabwe Foundation for Education with Production (ZIMFEP). This involved eight schools, and the result was that instead of ZIMFEP providing a model for the established school system, 'the pilot schools themselves were conventionalised' (Nherera 1998: 19). The reason for the failure of the experiment was that ZIMFEP reminded students and parents of 'colonial efforts to introduce vocational education which inhibited their children from proceeding to tertiary education' (Dzvimbo 1991: 292). Other attempts to introduce vocational courses in schools were attempted in the 1980s, particularly through the Zimbabwe

National Craft Certificate and the National Foundation Certificate. Both of these had limited successes (Nherera 1998).

In addition to the failures that characterised attempts to vocationalise the school curriculum, there remained a broad spectrum of opinion that was pressing for such reforms. Both Ministries of Education came out in favour of such a move, claiming that, 'The curriculum has remained unresponsive to the needs of the labour market and has failed to prepare the learners for the world of work and tends to promote rote learning' (ibid.). Academics, too, gave their support for this policy direction. Munowenyu (1999: 53) stated that:

> The present curriculum in Zimbabwe is failing, to a large degree, to help make school-leavers become better skilled, educated and confident problem-solvers. The solution is to introduce meaningful basic vocational education in schools.

The issue of the relevance of the school curriculum was thus viewed as a central aspect of confronting the crisis in the economy. These concerns have only increased since 2000, given the continued decay of the wage labour and the dramatic rise in the informal economy. The next chapter deals with this in more detail.

Finance

A report in 1999 pointed out that relative to comparable countries in the region Zimbabwe spent 'an unusually high share of national income on education'. For example, in the mid-1980s, Zimbabwe's budget allocation to the sector was more than twice the median of that spent by other low-income Anglophone countries, and exceeded the median for medium-income countries by about 22% (IRT Associates 1999: 13). Nevertheless, in the 1990s real per capita expenditure on education had fallen, with the total education allocation declining from 6% of GDP in 1986-87 to 4% in 1993-94. By 2000 real expenditure on primary education had declined to 2% of GDP (Nherera 2000). Moreover, about 97% of educational expenditure was allocated to salaries, leaving little for the provision of learning materials and equipment.

The most immediate problem facing children and families in high poverty areas is the low level of government funding available to support non-salary recurrent costs of education. Resources for teaching and learning materials, furniture and equipment, maintenance, consumables and other running costs are increasingly financed through fees and levies charged to parents. Poor communities were often unable to raise enough to meet minimum quality standards and, as a consequence, access to quality basic education was constrained. There was a clear tension between the need to increase private costs to improve quality and the adverse impact of higher fees on access (IRT Associates 1999: 21).

Table 4.5: Percentage of budget allocation for primary and secondary school during the fiscal year 1996/97

SECTOR	% Salaries	% Transport and subsistence	% School Services	% Grants, furniture and equipment
Primary	97.53	0.07	2.39	0.01
Secondary	87.81	0.14	8.23	3.83
Average	92.67	0.015	5.31	1.92

Source: Ministry of Education, Sports and Culture and Ministry of Higher Education and Technology (1998)

To sum up, it was clear by 2000 that, while there had been a remarkable expansion of educational enrolment in the first two decades of independence, this expansion intensified inequalities because of the different forms of educational provision and the problems of reduced financial expenditure that placed an increasing burden on poorer families. The youth, unsure about the long-term benefits of education, often sought other means to secure livelihoods. In addition, families often had to allocate resources elsewhere, particularly in rural areas. These choices were to be exacerbated by the political and economic crises post-2000, as other chapters will illustrate.

Part Two: Vocational training

We need to recall the reasons for state intervention in the area of human resource development in the 1980s: racial segmentation in the labour market; unequal wages structure; inequalities in access to training facilities; and trade union structures which favoured a minority labour elite. The imperatives of these conditions necessitated serious state intervention to rectify the imbalances of the past. Through one of the new ministries created in 1980, namely the Ministry of Manpower

Planning and Development, the government began instituting measures which would accord with the objectives of the new state. Such measures were part of the National Manpower Survey (1981-83), and included:

- The centralisation of apprenticeship training.
- Bonding of apprentices.
- Development of Vocational Training Centres.
- Introduction of the system of up-grading, through the trade testing of the many workers classified as semi-skilled in the colonial labour market.
- The development of pre-employment institutional training.
- Introduction of mechanisms to monitor private training institutions.
- The introduction of a 1% levy on the wage bill of firms in the private sector, in order to finance public training institutions.
- The creation of the National Manpower Advisory Council (NAMACO).
- The enactment of the Manpower Planning and Development Act to provide the legislative framework for these initiatives.

Predictably, these interventions caused a great deal of consternation at a time when the policy of reconciliation was still in its infant stages. Many in the private sector equated state intervention with socialism. In retrospect, these interventions were characteristic of the welfarism that has typified post-colonial states in the immediate period following independence, The weakness of the approach was its lack of clear objectives regarding the productive sector. As Bennell (1998: 5) has written of this problem more generally in Africa:

> There has long been widespread disenchantment with vocational training provision by government institutions in sub-Saharan Africa. The main concerns are that public sector training tends to be poorly related to (effective) demands for skills among producers, is "overextended" and has been strongly biased towards particular sectors (central government, parastatals and manufacturing) and groups (young, urban-based males in high-middle level occupations). Typically, public sector training has been poorly planned, managed and resourced, resulting in low quality but high-cost training.

Notwithstanding the achievements in training provision in the 1980s, government policy interventions resulted in several problems. First, the legislation gave rise to a rigid bureaucratic structure, with decision-making centralised in the ministry of Higher Education and Technology. Moreover, the centralisation did not result in better coordination. As Comninos et al. (1999: 18) observed:

> effective inter-ministerial coordination in respect of training provision is non-existent. Numerous ministries establish and provide training courses without reference to each other. Additionally, the advisory body provided for under the Manpower Act, namely NAMACO, proved to be a weak, government-controlled structure, unable to intervene substantially in policy issues.

Secondly, in the area of apprenticeship centralisation, the bottlenecks became apparent soon after implementation. The state took on an enormous and complex administrative task for what amounted to 'just a thousandth part of the formal economy' (King 1989: 23). Without the benefit of computers, the Registrar of Apprentices was simply unable to deal effectively with the large numbers of applicants, which reached up to 110,000 and more. Partly as a result of this centralisation measure, which led to increasing rigidity, the private sector withdrew from the utilisation of the apprenticeship system. In the words of King (ibid.: 25-26), the result was:

> with the reluctance of regular employers to recruit ... the state has felt it should intervene to continue the production of skilled labour in the event of a later recovery of demand. In the process, however, we can observe a shift from the older pattern of in-service training to something much nearer a vision of pre-service training.

The antagonism of the private sector towards the state's decision to remove the former's freedom to select and recruit apprentices resulted in an increasing retreat from the formal system of apprenticeship training (see Table 4.6). From a total intake of 1,816 apprentices in 1980, the figure dropped to an all-time low of 933 in 1988, rising again to 1,525 in 1995, and decreasing once more to 1,286 in 1997.

As one study observed about this trend:

The apprenticeship programme in the public sector has, in fact, been shrinking, with parastatals and government ministries alike facing increasingly hard budgets and retrenchments. In the private sector, recruitment of new apprentices has also declined in recent years. The centralisation of apprenticeship recruitment and the bonding of apprentices had a very negative impact on employer attitudes to apprenticeship training (Comninos et al. 1999:18).

Thirdly, the expansion of enrolment in Vocational Training Centres and Training Colleges, was confronted by a series of obstacles. A shortage of qualified and experienced technical trainers emerged because of deteriorating conditions of service, resulting in the under-utilisation of the institutions (Ministry of Manpower Planning and Development 1993). Those trainers who were appointed had inadequate training, largely because of the out-dated curriculum delivered by instructors who themselves lacked industrial experience. The largest increases in enrolment at the technical colleges was in the area of Business Studies rather than technical/vocational subjects (ILO 1993). In addition, gender dynamics remained problematic. Government training institutions did not seriously address disadvantaged groups such as women. Thus, as Table 4.7 shows, of the 1,678 apprentices in Harare, Bulawayo and Gweru in 1999, only 9.6% were female.

Fourthly, the attempt to develop Vocational Training Schools such as St Peter's Kubatana in Harare, demonstrated both conceptual and practical problems. One tracer study done on students at St Peter's noted that the programme had been 'neither effective nor efficient in training a core group of artisans during the 1980s' (Bennell and Nyakonda 1992).

Fifthly, the training levy provided for under the Manpower Act led to the establishment of the Zimbabwe Manpower Development Fund (ZIMDEF). The operation of this fund gave rise to a number of problems. An excessive percentage of the fund was utilised for the recurrent expenditure of training institutions, with a decreasing figure going to capital projects. As a result, insufficient funds were channelled towards the reimbursement of those institutions engaged in bona fide training. During the 1990s only 4% of total income went to rebates for employer training. Typical of many state initiatives in the second decade of independence, prohibitive bureaucratic procedures impeded the operations of the fund.

Table 4.6 a: Intake of Apprentices by Industry 1980-1988

Industry	1980	1981	1982	1983	1984	1985	1986	1987	1988
Aircraft	119	115	79	25	84	109	40	57	44
Construction	154	157	158	121	88	85	73	56	118
Electrical	392	350	391	260	269	279	302	216	225
Mechanical	641	797	478	511	472	582	456	372	351
Automotive	345	460	350	242	214	245	216	206	336
Printing	106	107	64	64	50	32	41	34	22
Hotel and catering	0	0	0	0	0	0	0	0	0
Hairdressing	59	58	29	8	47	64	17	37	37
Forestry	0	0	0	0	0	0	0	0	0
TOTAL	1816	2044	1549	1231	1224	1396	1145	978	1133

Source: Government of Zimbabwe 1999

Table 4.6b: Intake of Apprentices by Industry 1989-1997

Industry	1989	1990	1991	1992	1993	1994	1995	1996	1997
Aircraft	290	62	74	116	57	56	84	85	3
Construction	153	113	121	133	178	125	99	76	98
Electrical	271	365	424	430	383	232	285	232	211
Mechanical	556	555	813	665	556	412	465	437	333
Automotive	344	339	545	480	431	408	468	477	501
Printing	59	67	69	93	56	34	37	52	41
Hotel and catering	0	0	0	31	17	27	48	14	37
Hairdressing	54	40	26	26	32	46	39	53	58
Forestry	0	0	0	0	0	0	0	0	4
TOTAL	1727	1541	2072	1974	1710	1340	1525	1426	1286

Source: Government of Zimbabwe 1999

Lastly, there was increasing privatisation of training in the 1990s. In the previous decade there was a limited growth of private sector training institutions due to the state's opposition, and the limited amount of foreign exchange available for individuals to pursue courses leading to foreign qualifications. By the 1990s there was an explosion of private training institutions. This was also a consequence of the process of qualification resulting from the expansion of secondary and tertiary

Table 7: Apprentice intake by Region, Industry and Gender Order (1999)

	Harare			Bulawayo			Gweru			Total
	Female	Male	Total	Female	Male	Total	Female	Male	Total	
Aircraft	4	54	58				1	23	24	82
Automotive	10	325	335	4	106	110	3	66	69	514
Construction	6	106	112	3	27	30	3	34	37	179
Electrical	12	134	146	6	70	76	6	64	70	292
Hairdressing	58	18	76	5	7	12	15	2	17	105
Hotel and Catering	1	10	11	7	6	13				24
Mechanical	5	213	218	3	114	117	4	85	89	424
Printing	4	43	47		9	9	1	1	2	58
Total	100	903	1003	28	339	367	33	275	308	1678

Source: Kanyenze 1999

education. In the face of limited employment opportunities to meet this expanded output, school leavers 'sought additional professional and vocational qualifications that [would] enable them to compete successfully for the relatively few entry-level jobs in private sector enterprises' (Bennell 1998: 18-19).

Table 4.8 gives a breakdown of the number of students enrolled in vocational/ technical training in 1999, showing the bulk were enrolled in the fields of commercial, secretarial and computer studies.

Table 8: Enrolment in Vocational/Technical training in Government and Private Sector Institutions (P.S.I.): 1988

Vocational/Technical	Total
Gov. Vo. Tech	18,355
Apprentices	5,000
PSI registered	85,000
PSI registered	40,000
Correspondence Colleges	40,000
Sub-total	188,355
Source: IRT Associates 1999	

There is scope for more research into vocational training in Zimbabwe, to better understand how these schemes affected the lives and outlook of the youth. Sadly, the continued deterioration of the economy made much of this training meaningless, as formal jobs became more and more scarce.

Part Three: The employment environment

As the student output from the schools and private training institutions mounted, the problem of limited employment opportunities created more anxieties at the policy level. Additionally, the large numbers of students at university by the end of the 1990s (17,600 in 1998) highlighted the seriousness of the problem. Against this background the government instated a Presidential Commission of Inquiry into Education and Training in 1998, which set out to inquire into the 'relevance, quality and orientation' of the inherited system of education 'in a rapidly changing socio-economic environment.' Amongst the many findings of the commission were:

- The majority of students lacked 'relevant practical training skills since the curriculum was mainly academic and theoretical'. This problem was highlighted by the lack of a match between phenomenal educational expansion and low economic growth.

- The system was also unable to produce the 'complex skills' required by the growing demands of information technology.

- That twenty-first century education and training policy makers 'should bear in mind that the future will be dominated by globalisation and that Zimbabwe will be part of a global community'.

- The importance of 'participatory democracy in which citizens play a more active role in political, economic social and educational affairs'.

- The education philosophy should be based on Unhu/Ubuntu principles which emphasised a 'good person morally with such values as honesty, trustworthiness, discipline, accountability, respect for other people and elders, harmony and hospitality'.

- In terms of national culture, the report recommended a blending of traditional beliefs and institutions with a dynamic multiculturalism. Although the report recommended the inculcation of 'patriotism', it posed this issue in a tolerant way, emphasising also the importance of including human rights issues on the curriculum. This observation is particularly important given the form of intolerant state nationalism that emerged after the political crises of the 2000s (GoZ 1999).

The emphasis of the report was on a more relevant curriculum and philosophy of education, but one that also included a realistic assessment of the demands of globalisation. Moreover, the report stressed the need for a tolerant and democratically based education. The events of the early 2000s and beyond were to severely test the propositions of this Commission.

Part Four: Educational challenges from 2000-2003

The political and economic crises that unfolded from 2000 were complex and multi-layered and have been well documented. The education sector did not escape the fallout from these crises. In its attempt to deal with the economic disasters and the severe loss of political legitimacy that accompanied it, ZANU-PF carried out an authoritarian restructuring of the state, in order to consolidate its beleaguered position. In the process the judiciary was been severely undermined, the youth had been militarised, repressive legislation has been put in place to deal with political and civic opposition, and the ruling party attacked its own state structures, including those in the education sector. Moreover, this restructuring was carried out under the aegis of a selective and authoritarian nationalism. These developments affected the education sector in a number of ways.

First, teachers were targeted on a regular basis for their alleged support for the opposition MDC, because they were considered key informants and community leaders in the rural areas. As one human rights report observed about the attacks on the schools during the 2002 Presidential election:

> The Zimbabwe Government has consistently targeted schools as a locus of anti-government sentiment. There has been a campaign of terror and intimidation against teachers and principals at schools countrywide. In July 2001 Ministers Stan Mudenge and Samuel Mumbengegwi threatened principals and teachers at training colleges telling them that they could be killed for supporting the MDC. This threat was repeated by ZANU-PF MP Didymus Mutasa and the Minister of Justice, Legal and Parliamentary Affairs, Patrick Chinamasa, at a forced gathering of teachers, civil servants, community leaders and other state employees at Biriwi Business centre on 7 October 2001 (Zimbabwe Human Rights NGO Forum 2002: 20).

The Progressive Teachers Union of Zimbabwe (PTUZ) also documented what it referred to as the 'intimidation, harassment, detention, arrests, torture and the unprecedented unleashing of state security agents onto the schools' (PTUZ 2002). The Union noted that these attacks began after the 2000 referendum on the Constitution and continued during the 2000 general election and the 2002 Presidential election. As a result of the assault by state agencies, the PTUZ reported that in 2000-2002, 5 teachers were killed, 119 raped and 'many more were maimed, kidnapped, tortured and displaced' (ibid.).

Secondly, and more insidiously, large numbers of youth were sent to paramilitary national service training centres for 're-orientation' classes. These centres are also used to 're-orient' temporary teachers, as a precondition for going into the schools, in place of those considered enemies of the ruling party. At these centres, lessons focused on a narrow, party-oriented 'history of Zimbabwe, including the importance of the national flag, the formation of ZANU-PF and the Zanla forces, the Unity Accord between ZANU-PF and PF Zapu and why ZANU-PF deserves to be in power as long as possible' (*Daily News on Sunday*, 18 May 2003.) As Terence Ranger wrote, the state increasingly insisted on 'one particular narrow and nationalist version of the past'. He added that:

> Patriotic History is preached on television and radio. The new History syllabus in schools is based upon it. The Youth militia are taught 'patriotic history' by war veterans in their training camps and some in government have asserted that instruction in such history was the main purpose for which the camps were set up. Recently headmasters have been sent to the camps for crash courses in 'patriotic history'. In the future, it has been announced, every tertiary institution in Zimbabwe including universities will be obliged to offer courses in patriotism (Ranger 2004).

State violence against teachers, and the narrow nationalist approach to the teaching of 'patriotic history' are a long way from the tone of tolerance that characterised the 1999 Education Commission Report.

Thirdly, the state responded repressively to teachers' attempts to strike for better conditions of service. In October 2002, the PTUZ called on teachers to strike for three demands: 100% salary adjustment backdated to January 2002; a 100% cost of living adjustment backdated to June 2002; and an end to teacher victimisation. The state responded by driving the Union out of its offices, arresting senior officials and torturing the union president. In Mutare, ZANU-PF officials forced teachers to join an alternative union aligned to the ruling party.

Fourthly, food shortages and the highly politicised food distribution process have seriously affected schools. In Hwedza, Mutoko, Buhera, Rushinga, Mudzi, Murehwa and Mberengwa, teachers have been forced to register with ZANU-PF as a prerequisite for receiving food aid. By January 2003, 29% of the sites covered by the National NGO Food and Security Network had been affected by food insecurity, while 42% observed reduced enrolments and increased output in the new school term (FOSENET 2003).

Conclusion

Education provision has been lauded as one of the fundamental successes of post-colonial Zimbabwe. While many failings of ZANU-PF have been noted, the education sector appears to have maintained positive reviews. However, as this chapter has outlined, the reality on the ground was more complicated and problematic than one of continued success and improvement. Lack of clarity over education policy, diminishing state resources for education, high levels of school drop-outs and uneven access between rural and urban populations all had a serious impact on education provision.

Poverty directly affected the ability of many youths to access education. Those in rural areas were adversely affected as the state allocated resources elsewhere, and in turn, families and young people had to face hard choices about where to allocate their own time and money. These issues will be expanded upon, particularly in Chapter 5; despite the growing failings at schools, it is apparent that many parents and young people still believed in the promise that a good education could deliver a better future.

References

Bennell, P. (1996) 'Rates of Return to Education: Does the Conventional Pattern Prevail in Sub-Saharan Africa?', *World Development*, 24(1), pp. 183-199.

———— (1998) 'Vocational Education and training in Zimbabwe: The role of private sector provision in the context of economic reform'. IDS Working Paper 74.

———— (2018), 'Alternative Training Modes: Engineering Artisans in Zimbabwe'. Working Paper. Department of Economics, University of Zimbabwe.

———— and D. Nyakonda (1992) 'The Vocational Training School Fallacy Revisited: The Employment Experiences of Secondary Technical School Graduates in Zimbabwe', Working Paper. Department of Economics, University of Zimbabwe.

Carnoy, M. (1985) 'The Political Economy of Education', *International Social Science Journal*, 37(2), pp. 157-173.

Comninos, S., D. Lewis and R. Malvern (1999) 'How to Improve the Relevance of Technical Education and Formal and Informal Training'. Harare: GTZ Study.

Department of Manpower Planning and Development (1993). 'Report on the Study into the Provision and Utilisation of Facilities in Technical and Vocational Institutions'. Harare: Government of Zimbabwe.

Dzvimbo P. (1991) 'Education for Liberation and Development: A Comparison of Cuban and Zimbabwean Educational Practices', *Zimbabwean Journal of Educational Research*, 3(3).

FOSENET (2003) 'Community Assessment of the Food Situation in Zimbabwe', December 2002/January 2003. Harare.

Government of Zimbabwe (GoZ) (1999) 'Report of the Presidential Commission of Inquiry into Education and Training'. Harare: Government of Zimbabwe.

ILO (1993) 'Structural Change and Adjustment in Zimbabwe'. Occasional Paper 16. Geneva: ILO.

IRT Associates (1999) 'Education Transition and Reform Programme'. Harare: IRT Associates.

Kanyenze, G. (1997) 'Youth Unemployment in Zimbabwe'. Mimeo.

King, K. (1989) 'Inservice Training in Zimbabwe: An Analysis of the Relations Amongst Education and Training, Industry and State'. Occasional Paper No. 3. Human Resources Research Centre, University of Zimbabwe.

Ministry of Education, Sports and Culture and Ministry of Higher Education and Technology (1998) 'Issues in Education and Training in Zimbabwe'. Harare: Government of Zimbabwe.

Ministry of Manpower Planning and Development (1983) 'National Manpower Survey, 1981, Vol 3'. Harare: Ministry of Manpower Planning and Development.

Munotekwa, T., P. Gumbo and R. Kamidza (1999) 'Social Policy in an Economy under Stress: The Case of Zimbabwe', SARIPS.

Munowenyu, E. (1999) 'The Need to Offer Basic Vocational Education in Zimbabwe's Secondary Schools', *Zimbabwe Journal of Educational Research*, 11(1).

National Labour Advisory Board (NLAB) (1949), Vol 111, NAZ S2824/5/2.

Nherera, C. (1998) 'Education Provision in Zimbabwe'. Harare: Japan International Cooperation Agency.

Nherera, C. (2000) 'Current Issues in Education'. Mimeo.

PTUZ (2002) 'Report on the Teachers' Strike of October 200. Harare: PTUZ.

Raftopoulos, B. (1986) 'Human Resource Development'. in I. Mandaza (ed.), *Zimbabwe: The Political Economy of Transition 1980-86*. Dakar: CODESRIA.

———— (2003) 'The State in Crisis: Authoritarian Nationalism, Selective Citizenship and Distortions of Democracy in Zimbabwe', in A. Hammar, B. Raftopoulos and S. Jensen (eds), *Zimbabwe's Unfinished Business? Rethinking Land, State and Nation in the Context of Crisis*. Harare: Weaver Press.

Ranger, T. (2004) 'Nationalist Historiography, Patriotic History and the History of the Nation: the Struggle over the Past in Zimbabwe', *Journal of Southern African Studies*, 30(2).

UNDP (1998) *Zimbabwe Human Development Report*. Harare: UNDP.

Zimbabwe Human Rights NGO Forum (2002) 'Are they Accountable? Examining Alleged Violators and Their Violations Pre and Post the Presidential Election March 2002'. Harare: Zimbabwe Human Rights NGO Forum.

5

Selling a False Dream: Youth, Education and Employment in Zimbabwe

Felix Maringe and Alfred Masinire

Introduction

In 2020, Zimbabwe was still seen to have one of the best education systems on the African continent, competing strongly with Kenya, the Seychelles, Mauritius, Tunisia, Egypt and Algeria, This estimate was based on levels of skills development. However, we argue that the quality of education has been falling for several reasons and that the skills developed in schools are not finding expression in turning around the economic fortunes of the country. Zimbabwe's economic collapse has meant that most graduates from schools and tertiary institutions cannot enter the employment sector. Depending on who you ask, Zimbabwe's unemployment rate is quoted variously between 20% and 94% implying that even the government's conservative estimates suggest that the country is experiencing a substantial unemployment crisis. During the colonial era, school and tertiary graduates usually found it easier to break into the employment sector, and education was thus sold to the youth as the route out of poverty and underdevelopment. Today there is little or no guarantee of employment whatsoever for those who go through Zimbabwe's education systems, including those who graduate from its universities.

We argue that the dream of employment after schooling has outlived its purpose and that the education systems have to be redirected towards education for work rather than education for employment. We specifically argue for integrating entrepreneurial curricula through which youths are taught and supported at various levels to create working opportunities for themselves and others. The continued mis-selling of a dream of employment has substantial implications for building generations of unfulfilled youths who have the potential for negative social upheaval in the country. More specifically, we argue that the sharp decline of the economy following the controversial land redistribution between 1999 and 2020 has reduced Zimbabwe from a once-thriving economic giant in Africa to a state of financial ruin. The country cannot support and sustain decent livelihoods for its citizens. In this environment, the young people, who are supposed to be pillars of development, tend to vote with their feet. Although there are no accurate emigration figures of young people in Zimbabwe, it is estimated that approximately five million Zimbabweans have or are likely to have left the country by 2020 (Madebwe and Madebwe 2017). Amongst these are young professionals such as teachers, nurses, paramedics, engineers, doctors, and academics who have routinely left for greener pastures. The majority of Zimbabwean youths who leave the country go to South Africa and Botswana, but many have also left to Europe, the United Kingdom and the United States.

The chapter weaves through this discussion in three main sections. As education in the pre-independence period and the first twenty years following political independence have been covered elsewhere in this book (see Chapter 4), we begin our discussion in 2000. We specifically examine changes in the demographic dividend of the country during this period. In the second section, we focus on school dropouts, noting the gender disparities and rural-urban divide as the most visible signs of an ailing and unequal education system. We then examine the patterns and causes of emigration of young people as evidence of their voting with their feet. We focus on the broad arguments of the relationship between education and development, including the debates about what counts as quality in education and the nature and limits of Zimbabwe's employment sectors. We also argue for developing an entrepreneurial education system in the country. We end with a cautionary note on the need for a new national boldness, with specific recommendations for transforming the general philosophy of education, arguing for a shift from a focus on employment to a preoccupation with preparing learners for work. The entrepreneurial curriculum is suggested as key to this transformation. We thus turn to contextualise the discussion in debates about pre- and post-independence education in Zimbabwe in the first section.

A brief account of education in Zimbabwe after independence

A glorious narrative of education reform success pervades many accounts of the history of education in Zimbabwe after independence in 1980. What is not often acknowledged in these accounts is the ideological and policy contradictions inherent in the education transformation. The revolutionary struggle led by ZANU-PF was anxious to press on towards a Marxist-Leninist agenda of collectivism, productive work and egalitarianism vis-a-vis the realism of training a relatively wide range of manpower skills that the economy depended on (Atkinson 1984).

The shift from elite education provision to education for all, inspired by a populist-ideological rationale of egalitarianism, led to a huge quantitative increase in who received an education (Dorsey 1989; Nhundu 1992; Kanyongo 2005). A unitary national education system was adopted to cater to the large rural clientele, which made up approximately three-quarters of the population. Notwithstanding the challenges of quality posed by the inadequacies of infrastructure, qualified teachers, and learning resources, there was also the question of how to absorb the large number of students leaving the new secondary schools. There were not enough Sixth Form places for them, and neither were there enough jobs on the market. As noted by Atkinson (1984), and also supporting our claim of selling false dreams, the evidence of a causal link between education provision and economic development was already emerging. The large expenditure in education, that amounted to 23% of gross domestic product, was financed by a high tax regime leading to a lack of investor confidence, currency depreciation, high inflation, and a drastic shortage of materials. Nhundu (1992: 84) has noted some of the consequences and contradictions of education for all in Zimbabwe as the crisis of unmet expectations, rising unemployment, declining education quality, wastage, teacher shortages, an expensive education budget, and increased social differentiation. We argue below that an ailing education system, through which Zimbabwe nevertheless continues to sell a false dream to its youth, was only a symptom of a deeper crises in the country.

Conceptualising educational quality

Quality is a slippery concept whose definition often reflects the specific preferences of individuals, organisations and systems in a given context. However, there are at least two ways of looking at the idea of quality. The first is the notion of the agreed set of inputs assumed to drive acceptable standards in an educational system. The second is the notion of performance criteria that can determine and ascertain the quality of the outputs associated with an education system. These views provide us with what may be called input and output perspectives of quality (Sahito and Vaisanen 2017). Despite their importance, we argue that they represent an engineering/industrial model based on legacy conceptualisations of quality in manufacturing and product development. The focus is on maximising the inputs and measuring performance (Crosby 1979; Juran 1986). In education, especially as we deal here with human beings who are part of both the inputs and outcomes, it seems we need an additional view of quality that specifically relates to notions of equality and the equity of opportunities available to a wide range of learners to access the inputs and perform in ways that not only preserve human dignity but enable the learners to participate productively in economic development.

The input dimension of quality

Global and local conceptualisations of the inputs that contribute substantially to quality education include:

Well qualified and experienced teachers: Teachers contribute more substantially to school improvement and educational quality than any other factor (Hallinger and Heck 1999). After independence, Zimbabwe undertook an unprecedented expansion of its education system. The Zimbabwe Integrated Teacher Education Course (ZINTEC) (Chivore and Masango 1984) was a flagship innovation through which new teachers were trained in a rather unconventional way, which required trainees to spend substantially more time in schools as full-time teachers with shorter periods of on-campus training often provided during school holiday times. Evaluations to assess the ZINTEC teachers' effectiveness have tended to show that the new teachers were as effective as conventionally-trained teachers on most of the good teaching criteria (Chivore 1989). However, despite the good quality, it is estimated that more than 50% of the trained teachers in Zimbabwe migrated to neighbouring countries in search of better-paying jobs, political stability, and better prospects for their families (Weda and Lemmer 2014). Children, especially those from poor families, are left with inadequate numbers of fully trained teachers.

Effective and trained school leaders: Leadership is seen as the second most important factor contributing to the quality of education in any country (Bush and Glover 2021), but school leaders in Zimbabwe are simply appointed from the pool of experienced teachers and receive no training before enacting their roles in schools. Research shows that substantial school improvement is best delivered by leaders who have undergone formal training and who have substantial experience of working in schools (Barrett et al. 2008).

Educational resources: the nature, types, accessibility, utilisation, and maintenance of educational resources is considered as the third most influential group of factors contributing towards school improvement and the overall quality of education systems (OECD 2013). However, substantial research in Zimbabwe shows that most schools are ill-equipped and do not have supporting technologies to enhance the quality of teaching and learning, and where these resources are available, they are either in a state of disuse or malfunctioning due to poor maintenance (Ndlovu 2017).

Other inputs include teachers' pedagogical competences, home-school relations to support learning, and programmes for continuous professional development for teachers and school leaders.

The output dimension of educational quality

The output dimension speaks to evidence of performativity in education. In this regard, the focus is on issues such as learner outcomes, learner progression, efficiencies in times of transition, and efficiencies in retaining students and staff within the system as evidenced by trends in learner dropout.

Zimbabwe's education performativity data are highly variable depending on whether the schools are in rural or urban areas, private or public, or boarding or day schools. At Grade 7, the national pass rate since 1981 has been oscillating between 40% and 60% (Ncube 2004). In the last three years, there has been a noticeable decline in the rate, accompanied by a decrease in enrolments, perhaps due to increasing poverty and, more recently, the impact of the Covid-19 pandemic. The situation at O-level is roughly similar in terms of performance in different educational spaces and contexts. Interestingly, performance in indigenous languages is high compared to foreign languages. Performance in sciences and mathematics, which are critical subjects for entry into the labour markets and progression to higher levels of study in many disciplinary areas, tend to be on the lower end of the scale. A-level students' performance data provide a completely different picture, with a more than 90% pass rate nationally. However, this is due to the very stringent admission criteria; only the top 3-5% at O-level are admitted to A-level studies (Ncube, 2004). Educational wastage, especially in terms of non-completion and dropping out, also provides indicators of Zimbabwe's quality of education. Approximately 28% of primary school children do not complete the seven year primary school cycle, while close to 30% drop out before they write their O-level examinations, for a wide variety of reasons, including poverty, lack of school fees and examination fees, distances travelled to school, and teenage pregnancies (Ngwenya and Pretorius 2014). There is also a notable urban-rural divide in examination performances in primary and secondary schools, with some rural schools producing 0% pass rates in Grade 7 and O-level examinations. Almost 70% of the top-performing schools are in Harare and Bulawayo. Priscilla Misihairabwi-Mushonga, an MDC-T legislator, slated the government, urging it to allow learners in 88 mostly rural schools, to rewrite the Grade 7 examinations after recording a 0% pass rate.[1]

While in the early days of independence, a university education was almost a guarantee to a decent and well-paying job, today many university graduates remain unemployed. Also, universities generally do not teach students the self-employment skills required in the informal sector. For many reasons, the informal sector is generally shunned as the terrain for the less educated. Yet stories abound of university graduates

---

1 'Misihairabwi-Mushonga Fumes over 0% Grade 7 Pass Rate, Urges Rewrite', *New Zimbabwe*, 7 February 2020.

involved in menial tasks such as selling air-time and internet bundles in the city centres (Mazvarirwofa 2016).

The further dimension of quality in education focuses on epistemic/ cognitive justice, equality, and equity (Fricker 2007). At independence, Zimbabwe democratised its education system, creating opportunities for millions who were previously denied participation, hoping that these young people would use education as an escape route out of poverty. Today, however, the focus has to be on the extent to which this democratisation has uplifted the lives of the youth, whether opportunities have been created and distributed to different socio-economic groups equally and whether education had made a dent in ameliorating poverty.

Education post-2000

A number of significant disruptions conspired to weaken the education system in Zimbabwe in the wake of the land redistribution of the early 2000. Unlike in the past where most violence and unrest took place in urban areas, there was a period in the first decade of the 2000s when rural areas experienced severe violence. Organised youths, such as the Green Bombers, who were allegedly sponsored by the ruling party, were deployed against people suspected of harbouring anti-government sentiments. They were often mobilised in support of ZANU-PF during times of elections. Teachers in rural areas were also targeted, resulting in massive migration to urban areas and frequently out of the country.

The fast track land reform was the culmination of a long standing and deepening political crisis. As noted by Ndlovu-Gatsheni (2003) the country was beset by a serious crisis of governance, a crisis that has given birth to political, economic, social, ideological, educational, and humanitarian problems. For a government short of tangible political options, ZANU-PF intensified nationalist authoritarianism, violence, and intimidation during and after elections. Youth remilitarisation intensified after 2000, and particularly during the 2002 elections. The cost of the crisis has been felt heavily in nearly all sectors of society, including health and education (Mlambo 2013). Mlambo also noted that school attendance and enrolments declined, completion rates went down, and transition was low from primary to secondary levels. The situation was particularly serious in the newly established satellites schools in the occupied farms, where there was no infrastructure, learning materials or teachers.

Tables 5.1 and 5.2 present figures that characterise Zimbabwe's education after 2000.

Table 5.1 Primary school enrolment trends by sex, number and percentage change: 2014-2018

Year	Male	Female	Total	% Female
2014	1,344,234	1,314,456	2,658,690	49.44
2015	1,344,626	1,313,789	2,658,415	49.42
2016	1,344,538	1,317,472	2,662,010	49.49
2017	1,346591	1,329,894	2,676,485	49.69
2018	1,369,142	1,356,828	2,725,970	49.77

(Source MPSE 2019)

Table 5.2 Primary school enrolment trends by location, sex and grade: Zimbabwe 2018

	Rural Enrolment			% Female
Grade	Male	Female	Total	
1	177,179	171,541	348,720	49.19
2	161,761	16,002	321,763	49.73
3	150,875	147,925	298,800	49.51
4	141,801	139,962	281,763	49.67
5	139,514	137,518	277,032	49.64
6	133,137	131,868	265,005	49.76
7	124,036	125,567	249,603	50.31
Skills Orientation	2,752	1,902	4,654	40.87
Grand Total	1,031,055	1,016,285	2,047,340	49.64

(Source, MPSE 2019)

	Urban Enrolment			% Female	Grand Total
Grade	Male	Female	Total		
1	56,821	56,040	112,861	49.65	461,581
2	54,405	53,768	108,173	49.71	429,936
3	49,567	50,586	100,153	50.51	398,953
4	45,941	46,555	92,496	50.33	374,259
5	44,518	45,428	89,946	50.51	366,978
6	43,228	43,562	86,790	50.19	351,795

	Urban Enrolment			%	Grand
Grade	Male	Female	Total	Female	Total
7	41,756	43,387	85,143	50.96	334,746
Skills Orientation	1,851	1,217	3,068	39.67	7,722
Grand total	338,087	340,543	678,630	50.18	2,725,970

(Source, MPSE 2019)

Secondary school enrolment

Statistical comparison reflects a gradual increase in secondary school student enrolment since 1980. According to the Ministry of Primary and Secondary Education (MPSE 2019), by 2018 there were 1,093,550 students enrolled in secondary schools. This compares markedly with the 979,644 registered in secondary schools in 2014. While the numbers show a slight increase over the years, there is a disturbing gender gap. The number of female students begins to decline as one moves up the educational ladder. As noted by MPSE (2019), the proportion of females decreases with form, reflecting the gender disparities favouring males at higher levels of education.

The issue of female under-representation at higher levels of schooling is not unique to Zimbabwe. Globally, this gender disparity is acknowledged with female students under-represented in previously male-dominated fields of study such as engineering, medicine, and maths and science (Madara and Cherotich 2016). The trend of gender disparities in Zimbabwe is also confirmed by Runhare (2003) and Chivore (1992), who observed that gender inequalities in access to and achievement in mathematics, science and technical education were more pronounced at secondary and tertiary levels. What is equally significant is that even when they access higher education and these specialised fields of study, females experience exclusion practices, which make their persistence and achievement very low (Masinire 2015).

Rural-urban secondary enrolments

According to the MPSE report (2019), 68% of the Zimbabwean population resides in rural areas. As of 2018, there were 5,311 primary schools in rural areas representing about 84.46% of all the country's primary schools. Masvingo had the highest number of rural schools

Table 5.3 Secondary school enrolment trends by location, sex and grade: Zimbabwe 2014-2018

Grade	Rural Enrolment				Urban Enrolment				Grand Total
	Male	Female	Total	% Female	Male	Female	Total	% Female	
Form 1	97,897	100,117	198,014	50.56	34,730	37,178	71,908	51.70	269,922
Form 2	93,243	94,636	187,879	50.37	33,885	36,044	69,929	51.54	257,808
Form 3	94,943	90,041	184,984	48.68	36,231	37,748	73,979	51.03	259,863
Form 4	71,638	64,867	136,505	47.52	32,121	32,926	65,047	50.62	201,552
Form 5	13,593	11,695	25,288	46.25	12,949	12,294	25,243	48.70	50,531
Form 6	13,019	10705	23,724	45.12	11,329	11,176	22,505	49.66	46,229
Skills Orientation	244	246	490	50.20	195	138	333	41.44	823
Grand Total	384,577	372,307	756,884	49.19	161,440	167,504	328,944	50.92	1085,828

(Source: MPSE 2019)

in all the provinces, with 96.36% of the schools in the region being rural. Masvingo also had the highest number of rural secondary schools (94.13%).

Table 5.4 Number of teachers: 2014-2018

Year	ECD	Primary	Secondary
2014	12,124	74,129	43,361
2015	15,260	75,072	46,512
2016	14,006	72,410	45,326
2017	14,937	71,242	45,780
2018	15,086	72,512	46,160

(Source: MPSE 2019)

The figures in Table 5.4 include both trained and untrained teachers. However, the bulk of the untrained teachers are in the ECD phase, which has 58.45% qualified teachers compared to 86.47% and 97.14% at secondary and primary levels, respectively. Because more schools are in rural areas, we would also assume that most teachers serve the rural regions.

Table 5.5 Trends in school dropouts

Year	Primary			Secondary			Grand Total
	Male	Female	Total	Male	Female	Total	
2014	15,316	13,982	29,298	14,498	17,800	32,298	61,596
2015	16,905	14,882	31,787	19,534	23,810	43,344	75,131
2016	15,588	13,715	29,304	18,174	21,468	39,642	68,945
2017	14,941	12,708	27,649	19,687	23,272	42,959	70,608
2018	11,070	9,330	20,400	16,423	20,658	37,081	57,481

(Source: MPSE 2019)

Conventional thinking would suggest that school dropouts represent a significant waste for the nation. Wastage, in this case, is considered in terms of resources used but with no anticipated outcome. Another dimension of waste is that those who drop out would eventually become a national burden because they will not have developed the skills necessary to participate and integrate fully into the economy. However, given the context of the economic crisis currently facing Zimbabwe and the high unemployment rate of those who are dully qualified, the second dimension of waste appears irrelevant. Even those who are qualified and educated end up not significantly contributing to the national economy. It is at this level that the mismatch between education and development becomes apparent. At the same time, one would assume that the demand for education would decline given its lack of utilitarian value. Thus, the question of why people still invest in education in Zimbabwe would suggest an answer that disputes the education-economic development thesis.

Table 5.5 above, shows that more boys than girls drop out at primary school level while more girls than boys drop out at the secondary level. Tables 5.6 and 5.7 present reasons for this trend.

Table 5.6 Primary school reasons for dropping out by gender (2014-2018)

| Reason | Dropout Numbers | | | |
	M	F	Grand Total	Female %
Absconded	5,230	3,970	9,200	43.15
Death	651	503	1,154	43.59
Expulsion	61	51	112	45.54
Illness	320	322	642	50.16
Marriage	13	218	231	94.37
Other	1,195	969	2,164	44.79
Financial	3,569	3,148	6,717	46.87
Pregnancy	31	149	180	82.78
Grand Total	11,070	9,330	20,400	45.74

(Source: MPSE 2019)

Table 5.7 Secondary School reasons for dropping out by gender (2014-2018)

| Reason | Dropout Numbers | | | |
	M	F	Grand Total	Female %
Absconded	5,560	4,749	10,309	46.07
Death	308	246	554	44.40
Expulsion	95	47	142	33.10
Illness	167	236	403	58.56
Marriage	278	3,558	3,836	92.75

Reason	Dropout Numbers		Grand Total	Female %
	M	F		
Other	869	786	1,655	47.49
Pregnancy	51	2,861	2,912	98.25
Financial	9,095	8,175	17,270	47.34
Grand Total	16,423	20,658	37,081	55.71

(Source: MPSE 2019)

Case study research from specific provinces sheds light on why more girls than boys drop out of secondary school. Dakwa et al. (2014), Moyo et al. (2016) and Maramura and Mago (2017) noted that key factors were HIV/AIDS, financial constraints, negative attitudes towards education, traditional cultural practices, and religion.

The emigration factor in Zimbabwe

As the economy went into a downward spiral in the early 2000s, more and more youths began to emigrate. The main reasons were a lack of employment opportunities; lack of food supplies and other commodities; and an adverse political environment (UNDP 2010). It is estimated that almost five million Zimbabweans now live outside the country, mainly in South Africa and other neighbouring countries in the region, but also in Europe, primarily the UK, the USA, Canada, Australia and New Zealand (ibid.); almost 70% of them are 16-40 years old. (Makina 2010) We can conclude that Zimbabwe bleeds a substantial proportion of its young people to other countries and, therefore, can be said to be a cheap resource of intellectual and economic capital for other countries. The following tables provide illustrative statistics of the state of emigration in Zimbabwe.

Table 5.8 Estimated numbers of Zimbabweans in the diaspora by location

Country/Region	Estimated numbers of Zimbabwean emigrants
South Africa	2,120,000
UK	400,000
Botswana	200,000
Elsewhere in Africa	200,000

Country/Region	Estimated numbers of Zimbabwean emigrants
USA and Canada	50,000
Australia and New Zealand	20,000
Elsewhere in the world	50,000
Total	3,040,000

(Source: UNDP 2010: 9)

By 2010, over three million Zimbabweans had left the country for greener pastures, with South Africa alone receiving more than two million and the UK being the second most favoured destination. By 2019, the numbers were estimated to have exceeded five million.[2]

Table 5.9 Top ten countries supplying migrant teachers to South Africa

Country	Percentage supply of migrant teachers
Zimbabwe	61%
Ghana	9%
Nigeria	7%
Lesotho	5%
Democratic Republic of Congo	4%
Swaziland	3%
UK	3%
India	3%
Uganda	3%
Zambia	2%

(Source: Keevy et al. 2014)

Although teachers from Zimbabwe and elsewhere constitute a small proportion of the total number of teachers in South Africa (about 9,000 of a total of 410,000), their presence makes a substantial contribution towards closing the gap between supply and demand. Considering the huge government spend on teacher training and development in Zimbabwe, the country has become a cheap source of skills for the South African economy. The loss of teachers from Zimbabwe could also negatively impact the quality of teaching and learning in the country, which has a spiralling negative effect on the country's general economic performance (De Villiers and Weda 2017).

The invisibility of the entrepreneurial curriculum in Zimbabwe

The entrepreneurship curriculum is based on three important sets of assumptions. The first is that most countries are incapable of creating enough jobs for their citizens (Schumpeter 1947). This is largely due to rising population numbers, especially among the youth, poorly performing economies, the impact of disruptions such as climate change, wars and political hostilities, and, in the developing world, corruption, poor governance and lapses in accountability that tend to divert resources away from the majority to the pockets of a few well-connected people in society.

The second assumption is that a focus on the entrepreneurial curriculum swings the pendulum away from the narrative of employment, on which many students are fixated, to one of job creation. By their nature, entrepreneurs create work for themselves and others. If even half of the school population in any country leave school with skills to create employment for themselves and others, unemployment would be drastically reduced.

The third is that entrepreneurial curricula emphasise problem-solving skills, creativity and innovation, which are linked strongly to economic development (Audretsch et al. 2006).

Despite these assumptions, entrepreneurial curricula have not been successfully conceptualised and implemented in Zimbabwe. Key factors that would provide an impetus for the successful introduction of entrepreneurial education include: developing a register of successful entrepreneurs who could act as role models in delivering such curricula; creating and supporting strong entrepreneurial courses in universities, and especially in teacher education programmes, to support its implementation in schools; the use, adaptation and adoption of well-tested models as a basis for curriculum development, and financial support to grow creative and innovative ideas of young people at different stages of their education and careers (Boldureanu et al. 2020).

Zimbabwe's first decade of independence was marked by an unprecedented expansion in education provision, driven by a retributive social justice agenda (Dorsey 1989; Nhundu 1992) as well as meeting the human resources skills needs of an emerging economy (Atkinson 1984). The euphoria began to dissipate after 1990, bringing into doubt some of the normative discourse about the close and causal links between education, economic development and youth employment.

Several reasons are proffered to explain the mismatch between the increase in education provision and the declining economic development and high youth unemployment. Since the start of the millennium, the political milieu was marked by instability, resulting in a massive brain drain coupled with declining investor confidence. Also, land reform crippled the agricultural sector. The internal national context attracted global hostility, particularly from the West, leading to sanctions and calls for regime change amid allegations of human rights violations. Despite the unfavourable political and economic context, education has remained one of the trusted assets at both the individual and national level. Over the years, demand for education has led to reduced government financial support with individuals bearing the cost of schooling even at the university level. With the decline of the formal employment sector and the rise of the informal employment market, Luebker (2008) claims that the Zimbabwean unemployment rate matches international trends of below 10%. However, considering the varieties and forms of unemployment, Zimbabwe appears to fare badly on demand deficient employment and voluntary unemployment. This is because the economy has not grown to the level where it can absorb those who have the requisite skills, and at the same time, those who have the skills have been attracted by employers beyond the country's borders.

In the current context of Zimbabwe, education is still a valuable asset. Individuals' level of investment in education is high, despite the questionable quality of that education. But the dream of formal and local employment has faded.

Reimagining the future of the youth and education in Zimbabwe

The youth in Zimbabwe comprise more than 50% of the population. With an unemployment rate of approximately 90%, the potential for widespread disaffection and social upheaval is always a strong possibility.. Many of these young people have good educational credentials, but they are still trapped in a vicious cycle of poverty.

Outside of education, five fundamental interventions seem to be at the heart of any ambitions to change the narrative of a mis-sold dream.

1. With the strong support of the government, entrepreneurship has to become an integral part of all school and tertiary level curricula.

2. Greater government investment into curricula which prepare young people for self-employment.

3. There is a need to level the political terrain in Zimbabwe. Constitutional rights and freedoms need to be respected more than they currently are.

4. Greed, corruption and the looting of national resources have the potential to reduce the extent to which the government can provide adequate services to the people. This idea that 'it's our time to eat' must be replaced by the idea that 'it's our time to govern responsibly'.

5. Alongside a revitalised economic development plan should be a blueprint for reforming the so-called informal sector in Zimbabwe. Aspects of this sector need proper regularisation to allow and encourage sustainable growth of the sector. For now, the informal sector is just an escape from a false dream that young people have been sold.

We end this chapter with a brief outline of a proposal to transform the education system, which, to a large extent, is complicit in selling the false dream to the country's youth. We focus specifically on two aspects:

Towards an entrepreneurial curriculum in Zimbabwe

Entrepreneurship education (Audretsch et al. 2006) will mean that every student will exit the system with a set of skills to start a business venture and, more importantly, with a set of attitudes of self-determination rather than of dependence. By refocusing education towards work rather than employment, the expectation of dependency on government to supply jobs will diminish.

This goal permeates the other two reform proposals. We are not suggesting that the state should absolve itself of the responsibility for employment creation and economic development, rather that the idea of informal employment should be revisited. The concept of the informal or non-formal sector conjures up images of illegality, non-viability, insecurity, non-profitability and other negative associations. A refocusing on education for work rather than for employment (Herr 1987) will contribute to greater pragmatism, realism and expectation by school and university graduates towards more dignified lives, which depend not so much on the government's ability to create employment as on the abilities of graduates to eke out a living under the prevailing circumstances with adequate government support and encouragement.

Conclusion

Young people are the backbone and future of any country. In Zimbabwe, the youth are generally traumatised and are made to live a false dream for most of their lives. The future of the country belongs to these young people. The very least we can do is to allow them to dream realistically. Changes to our education, our politics, our ignominious appetite for selfish wealth creation and our trust in them as future leaders are part of the transformation. We need to let these young people dream again, properly and realistically. This requires boldness to change, politically, economically and educationally, without which, unfortunately, Zimbabwe will continue to be a cheap skills development space for other countries enjoying relative stability.

References

Atkinson, N.D. (1984) 'Education in Zimbabwe: The historical roots', *Paedagogica Historica*, 25(1), pp. 5-25.

Audretsch, D.B., M.C. Keilbach and E.E. Lehmann (2006) *Entrepreneurship and economic growth.* New York: Oxford University Press.

Barrett, S.B., C.P. Bradshaw and T. Lewis-Palmer (2008) 'Maryland statewide PBIS Initiative: Systems, Evaluation and Next Steps', *Journal of Positive Behaviour Interventions*,10(2), pp.105-114

Boldureanu, G., A.M. Ionescu, A.M. Bercu, M.V. Bedrule-Grigoruta and D. Boldureanu (2020) 'Entrepreneurship education through successful entrepreneurial models in higher education institutions', *Sustainability,* 12(3).

Bush, T. and D. Glover (2021) 'Research on School Leadership in South

Africa: A systematic review', in F. Maringe (ed.) *Systematic Reviews of Research in Basic Education in South Africa.* Stellenbosch: African Sun Media.

Chivore, B.R.S. (1989) 'Zimbabwe's experiences in the evaluation of distance education programmes', in M. R. Simonson and S. Zvacek (eds) *Proceedings of Distance Education Workshop*, Colleges of Education, Iowa State University.

Chivore, B.R.S. (1992) 'Technical Education in Post-Independent Zimbabwe: Conditions of Service', *Zimbabwe Journal of Educational Research*, 4(5), pp. 71-88.

Chivore, B.R.S. and B.B. Masango (1984) 'An assessment of distance education materials in ZINTEC'. Harare: Ministry of Education and Culture.

Crosby, P. (1979). *Quality is free: The art of making quality certain.* New York: McGraw Hill.

Dakwa, F.E., C. Chiome and R.A. Chabaya (2014) 'Poverty-related causes of school dropout: Dilemma of the girl child in rural Zimbabwe', *International Journal of Academic Research in Progressive Education and Development,* 3(1), pp. 233-242.

De Villiers, R. and Z.L. Weda (2017) 'Zimbabwean Teachers in South Africa: A transient greener pasture', *South African Journal of Education*, 37(3), pp. 1-9.

Dorsey, B.J. (1989) 'Education development and reform in Zimbabwe', *Comparative Education Review,* 33(1), pp. 40-58.

Dowrick, S. (2002) 'The contribution of innovation and education to economic growth'. Paper presented to the conference 'Towards Opportunity and Prosperity', Melbourne Institute.

Fricker, M. (2007) *Epistemic injustice: Power and the ethics of knowing.* Oxford: Oxford University Press.

Hallinger, P. and R. Heck (1999) Can leadership enhance school effectiveness?' in T. Bush, L. Bell, R. Bolam, R. Glatter, and P. Ribbins (eds), *Educational Management: Redefining Theory, Policy and Practice*. London: Paul Chapman.

Herr, E.L. (1987) 'Education as preparation for work: Contributions of career education and vocational education', *Journal of Career Development*, 13(3), pp. 16-30.

Juran, J.M. (1986) 'The Quality Trilogy: A Universal Approach to Managing for Quality'. Paper presented at the ASQC 40th Annual Quality Congress in Anaheim, California, May 20.

Karlsen, G.E. (2000) 'Decentralized centralism: Framework for a better understanding of governance in the field of education', *Journal of Education Policy*, 15(5), pp. 525-538.

Kanyongo, G.Y. (2005) 'Zimbabwe's public education system reforms: Successes and challenges', *International Education Journal*, 6(1), pp. 65-74.

Keevy, J., W. Green and S. Manik (2014) 'The Status of Migrant Teachers in South Africa: Implications for Policy, Research, Practice'. Waterkloof: South African Qualifications Authority.

Luebker, M. (2008) 'Employment, unemployment and informality in Zimbabwe: Concepts and data for coherent policy-making'. Integration Working Paper No 90. Harare: ILO.

Madara, D.S. and S. Cherotich (2016) 'Female Underrepresentation in Undergraduate Education: Case study in School of Engineering', *Research on Humanities and Social Sciences*, 6(14), pp. 157-175.

Madebwe, C. and V. Madebwe (2017) 'Contextual background to the rapid increase in the migration from Zimbabwe since 1990', *Inkanyiso: Journal of Humanities and Social Sciences*, 9(1) pp. 27-36.

Makina, D. (2010) 'Determinants of Return Migration: Evidence from Migrants living in South Africa'. Paper presented at the International Migration Conference, Trinity College, Dublin. 30 June - 3 July.

Maramura, T.C., & Mago, D. (2017). Girl-pupil school dropouts in secondary education in Masvingo District, Zimbabwe: Influencing factors and effects', *Journal of Social Sciences*, 13(1), 78-88.

Masinire, A. (2015) 'Teachers' perceptions and students' lived experiences in Vocational-Technical subjects in a rural high school in Zimbabwe', *Gender and Education,* 27(6), pp. 618-634.

Mazvarirwofa, K. (2016) 'Forced into Street Vending: Zimbabwe's Professional Class Struggles to Survive'. Special Report in the Global Press Journal.

Ministry of Primary and Secondary Education (MPSE) (2019) 'The Republic of Zimbabwe 2018 Primary and Secondary Education

Statistics Report'. Harare: Ministry of Primary and Secondary Education.

Mlambo, A.S. (2013) 'From education and health for all by 2000 to the collapse of the services sector in Zimbabwe, 1980-2008', *Journal of Developing Societies*, 29(40), pp. 335-378.

Moyo, S., D. Ncube and M. Khupe (2016) 'An assessment of the factors contributing to high secondary pupils dropout rates in Zimbabwe: A case study of Bulilima District', *Global Journal of Advanced Research*, 3(9), pp. 855-863.

Ncube, N.J. (2004) 'Managing the quality of education in Zimbabwe: The internal efficiency of rural day secondary schools'. Doctoral Thesis, UNISA, South Africa.

Ndlovu, N. (2017) 'School resources and student achievement: A study of primary schools in Zimbabwe', *Educational Research and Reviews*, 13(7), pp. 236-248.

Ndlovu-Gatsheni, S.J. (2003) 'Dynamics of the Zimbabwe crisis in the 21st century', *African Journal of Conflict Resolution*, 3(1), pp. 99-134.

Ngwenya, V.C. and S.G. Pretorius (2014) 'Parental involvement with Education in Zimbabwe within a Total Quality Management Framework', *International Journal of Educational Sciences*, 7(3), pp. 701-710.

Nhundu, T.J. (1992) 'A decade of educational expansion in Zimbabwe: Causes, consequences and policy contradictions', *Journal of Negro Education*, 61(1), pp. 78-97.

OECD (2013) 'Education at a glance 2013, OECD Indicators'. Paris: OECD Publishing.

Runhare, T. (2003) 'Women perceptions of "masculine" technical careers: A comparative study of women in "feminine" and "masculine" employment occupations in the city of Gweru, Zimbabwe', *Zimbabwe Journal of Educational Research*, 15(3), pp 133-150.

Sahito, Z. and P. Vaisanen (2017) 'The diagonal model of job satisfaction and motivation: Extracted from the logical comparison of content and process theories', *International Journal of Higher Education*, 6(3), pp. 209-229.

Schumpeter, J.A. (1947) 'The Creative Response in Economic History', *The Journal of Economic History* ,7(2), 149-159.

UNDP (2010) 'Human Development Report 20th Anniversary Edition: The Real Wealth of Nations: Pathways to Human Development'. New York,: UNDP.

Weda, Z.L. and E.M Lemmer (2014) 'Managing status: A grounded theory of teacher migration from Zimbabwe to South Africa', *Mediterranean Journal of Social Sciences*, 5(7), pp. 416-225.

6

The Post-colonial State and Youth Political Participation: the Case of State-run Youth Programmes, 1980-2017

Ivo Mhike

Introduction

In 1980, ZANU-PF began a simultaneous process of post-war reconstruction, economic restructuring and consolidation of political power. In order to achieve these goals, it created an intolerant and paternalistic party/state system to push the development agenda and control the national narrative by bringing all dissenting voices under its wings. Among the earliest examples of this were the youth programmes of the 1980s, which were platforms for youth mobilisation and guidance in the national political and development agenda. This chapter is a reflection on youth political participation and interaction with the state, in the context of these state-run youth programmes in post-independence Zimbabwe. I argue that the Youth Brigades movement of the 1980s and its successor, the National Youth Service founded in 2001, and various other youth economic empowerment initiatives, were attempts at social engineering by the state meant to create young citizens with an allegiance to a particular vision of the nation-state. I focus on these institutions in order to understand how the ZANU-PF party/state has used patronage politics, violence and coercion to control and define 'youths' as a political concept in order to sustain political hegemony. Over the past four decades, the youth have emerged as a significant factor in Zimbabwe's democracy and electoral process, and ZANU-PF, through party ideologies, has attempted to mobilise, indoctrinate and appropriate them.

African political upheavals in the new millennium have inspired the need to understand the relationship between the post-colonial state and the structure and forms of political participation by African youth. Since the turn of the millennium the category of youth on the African continent has emerged with renewed importance, influencing policy and academic research (Honwana and de Boeck 2005). Young people below the age of 30 constitute 70% of the continent's population and Africa is the youngest continent in the world (Oinas et al. 2018). This young population continues to demand better social services, jobs and political change from post-colonial states that are often incapacitated and lack the political will to reform (Honwana and de Boeck 2005). In the 2010s, the role of youths in social transformation and political democracies/dictatorships has been magnified by a recurrence of unrest, violent uprising and protest on the continent, from Nigeria's oil-rich Niger Delta, to the 'Arab Spring' in North Africa, and the more recent rise of Islamic insurgency in northern Mozambique (Osaghae et al. 2011; Morier-Genoud 2020). This significant altering of the socio-political landscape has elicited state intolerance and repression. It is, therefore, critical to understand the forms and scope of African governments' initiatives to retain power by controlling the aspirations of young people within and outside the formal political structures.

Zimbabwean youth experiences refract these state structures of control as well as the role of young people in post-colonial democracies and hegemonic political discourses of unity in repressive states. Youths often find themselves in circumscribed political spaces and are sometimes constrained to act against their will. Proponents of the Youth-Bulge theory aver that the underlying features of conflict are generational differences, but power relations create what appears to be a cohesive monolith of repression with shared ideologies between political parties and youths in state politics. The social changes in the post-colonial state have given rise to perpetual tension and vulnerabilities in groups, such as the youths, which are on the fringes of state power. In African economies such as Zimbabwe, basic survival and access to employment opportunities have become interwoven with political allegiances, and political affiliation is often a necessity, not a choice. In this respect, empirical realities and perspectives of youth in post-colonial Zimbabwe reflect an eclectic mix of experiences where the youth programmes emerged as a source of power, ambivalence and danger.

Independence, euphoria, and a hegemonic discourse of unity, 1980-1987

In 1980, Joice Mujuru was appointed Minister of Youth, Sport and Recreation at the age of 22. In 1982, the Legal Age of Majority Act was passed, which gave the youth full adult status at the age of 18. Prime Minister Robert Mugabe made impassioned speeches that recognised the importance of youths to the new nation state, not least because of their role in future economic development, but because they had also played an active role in the liberation war. Politically, the creation of a youth ministry and Mugabe's pulpit recognition of the young generation were potent signs of the importance of this constituency to Mugabe's political vision. In his quest for total control, Mugabe exhibited intolerance for political diversity and sought to build ideological consensus, or an illusion of it, through repression. He identified the youth as key to driving party programmes in ZANU-PF's hegemonic discourses. Although the youth had shared the ideas of revolution that underpinned the liberation war, their allegiance could not be guaranteed in light of the economic problems they faced. The Zimbabwean economy was beset by structural unemployment affecting youths from the late 1950s and the situation was much worse by the late 1970s. Political independence brought hope to the young generation but the economy lacked the capacity to absorb the thousands of unemployed at the required rate. The economy witnessed very little radical or structural reform in the 1980s, employment creation was slow, and unemployment continued to grow (Muzondidya 2009). The average annual economic growth rate was 1.3% while the population grew at 3.3% per year (Stoneman 1988). In real terms, 10,000 jobs were created annually against an annual rate of 100,000 school-leavers by the mid-1980s (Chung 1988). In this respect, the government had to prioritise youth affairs to maintain political stability.

ZANU-PF's anxiety about the youth 'problem' was informed by the history of youth agitation in Zimbabwe's political history dating back to the early years of nationalism. The City Youth League, later called the African National Youth League, formed in 1955, was among the first organisations with a nationalist approach to politics. In 1956, it organised the Salisbury bus boycott in protest against high bus fares which successfully brought the operations of urban transport services to a standstill (Manganga 2011). The boycott was one of the watershed moments of African nationalism and a glaring feature of the boycott was the violence that introduced youths onto the political scene (ibid.). Subsequently, youth unemployment in the late 1950s and 1960s provided political capital for nationalist movements – the National Democratic Party, Zimbabwe African People's Union (ZAPU), ZANU – and violent youth agitation in the urban areas forced the Rhodesian government to promulgate the Law and Order (Maintenance) Act of 1960 (Alexander 2012). The National Union of Rhodesian Students, formed in 1963, engaged in student and nationalist agitation (Makunike 2015). In the 1970s, students at the University of Rhodesia and Nyasaland staged several anti-state and often violent demonstrations challenging the racial order in higher education which resonated with wider politics of African nationalism (Mlambo 1995). Young people also fought in the war of liberation; many left school at a very young age to fight, while some were coerced into joining the war. Armed youth violence was a feature of the latter stages of the war as they terrorised communities and murdered 'collaborators' and 'sell-outs' (Kriger 1988). At independence, ZANU-PF mobilised young people to be harbingers of its political ideologies and as agents of persuasion, violence and various forms of coercion.

The Youth Brigades of the 1980s were an offshoot of the National Youth Service provided for by the National Service Act of 1979, which set the criteria for who could be incorporated into the Zimbabwe National Youth Service and the military. The institution drew more than 300,000 into its ranks over a period of seven years across the country's provinces (Vezha 1987). The government praised the institution as a model of progressive and patriotic young citizens who contributed to the development agenda (ibid.). Youth Brigades ostensibly took a civilian structure to 'meet the needs and aspirations of unemployed youths,' but in practice they retained the command structure and authoritarian aspects of the politics of the liberation war (ibid.). The government claimed that the Brigades were there to offer the youth 'proper guidance' and the 'orientation relevant to the needs of the country'. Discipline was a key element of Brigades' culture and the youth worked according to instruction. More crucially, ideas of unity were loosely framed to mean acceptance of the governing party's political vision to enable total control of the state. The Brigades were framed in national discourse as encapsulating civic duty and youth citizenship in the new Zimbabwe. Youths who wanted to act in the 'national interest' had to mobilise and join the Brigades. The government also preached the idea of service to the nation as a quality that all the youth had to possess in order to contribute to national development. To prove one's citizenship, one had to serve in the Brigades, where the youths were fed on revolutionary ideology and the central role of ZANU-PF.

The command structure of the Brigades entailed instilling discipline in young people. There was no room for debate, and party elders provided 'guidance' on the party's ideological foundations (*gwara remusangano)*, an element which would emerge more clearly in the 1990s. This structure derived from the social position of youths as a category below adulthood and a symbol of the future. More crucially, decision making was the prerogative of elders, not the youth. This structure of conduct incubated the politics of gerontocracy – rule by the elderly – which took root and thrived. The concept of gerontocracy features in much of the analysis of African politics, pointing to the ways in which young people are systematically denied access to political power or economical resources by older generations (Oinas et al.: x). Party leadership and ideological guidance was not only about hierarchical position but was also determined by age.

The Brigades helped tame the aspirations of the thousands of unemployed youths and school dropouts to align them with the government's ideas, but the more urbanised youths and those in schools were able to circumvent this form of institutionalisation. First, the hordes of unemployed youths could not be allowed to roam the streets, and the rigid system of the Brigades occupied their time. Second, the government used activities in the Brigades to guide the understanding of development, which was largely what ZANU-PF framed as the 'priorities' and 'needs' of the country. Projects such as the construction of classroom blocks, clinics and the rehabilitation of roads were presented as essential activities for the youth and central to national development.

The Brigades had a curriculum by which the idea of 'progress' among the youth was controlled. In this way, the government was able to frame the development agenda for the youths and tie their aspirations to those of the state. A patronage system therefore emerged where young people were provided with employment in the Brigades as a reward for participating in government programmes. Even the aspirations of the more educated students in university and other tertiary institutions were tied to the state. At independence, student representative bodies ceased to be part of a political vanguard contesting state authority in order to become part of the project of national healing, reconstruction and development (Makunike 2015: 36). Students from the University of Zimbabwe, like most groups, operated under the fold of the state which supported tertiary education with student grants and loans. In this respect, ZANU-PF's increased economic and political capacity as the government enabled the creation of patronage politics based on economic incentives.

Another incarnate feature of the party/state was that the Brigades could not be separated from the ZANU-PF youth wing, and youth leadership straddled both party and state programmes. This way, party ideologies were effectively implemented using state machinery. For example, Brigades and the ZANU-PF party youth wing were central in mobilising support for the governing party in the run-up to the 1985 elections and both were implicated in acts of violence against PF-ZAPU supporters (CCJPZ and LRF 1997). The party had also used political violence and intimidation in the 1980 election before the Brigades were formed. In the 1980s, youth violence became a feature of Zimbabwe's electoral system, which helped cultivate a culture of political intolerance of alternative voices often regarded as dissent and discord. Acts of violence were committed by the youth in the name of 'defending the revolution' as defined by ZANU-PF and carefully woven into state ideas of development. The Brigades emerged as the civilian arm of a repressive state machinery which also included the Central Intelligence Organisation (CIO), the military and the police. Despite these efforts, the government's political ideas and coercive nation building met with limited success, as racial, gender, ethnic and geographical divisions continued to frustrate plans for a cohesive and subservient nation-state (Mandaza 1986).

One could argue that the youth were trapped in a liminal space in which they genuinely sought to express their patriotism and good citizenship by joining the Brigades, but without making a conscious choice they parroted and enforced ZANU-PF ideologies. In this regard, political space for the youth was circumscribed, only existing within the confines of the Brigades and the party's youth wing. Alternative voices were either drowned by the dominant narrative or brutally crashed. ZANU-PF nationalist, Nathan Shamuyarira, boasted that, 'violence is an area where ZANU-PF has a strong, long and successful history' (Meredith 2007: 241). Muzondidya (2009) argues that the post-colonial state was authoritarian and repressive and it used both violence and a hegemonic discourse of unity on its official opposition, workers, students and youth groups. Indoctrination in the Brigades created a group mentality among the youths, who felt duty bound to 'defend the nation'.

End of honeymoon and divergence, 1988-1999

The late 1980s saw the emergence of new alliances and the collapse of old ones. The Unity Accord between ZANU-PF and PF-ZAPU in December 1987 secured political hegemony in ZANU (PF) and ended one of the most polarising episodes of Zimbabwe's political history. The Brigades, which had been established partly to crush opposition, now lost relevance. State heavy-handedness began to taper off, paving the way for an environment relatively tolerant to the emergence of alternative voices. The Zimbabwe National Students Union (ZINASU), led by the Students Union of the University of Zimbabwe, formed in 1989 to advocate good governance, human rights and empowerment of the youths, emerged as a powerful political force (Hodgkinson 2013). University education came with social respect and an elite status, so ZINASU's criticism of government policy had greater impact than that of the newly formed political party, the Zimbabwe Unity Movement, led by Edgar Tekere. The nadir of state-student relations came with the adoption of ESAP in 1990 which forced cuts in government expenditure, severely reducing students' loans and grants. The erosion of students' material condition fit awkwardly with their self-conscious elitism, and their social prestige began to dissipate. This sparked violent anti-government demonstrations and long-running battles with the police at the University of Zimbabwe. Students blamed the government for failing to meet their needs and threatening their livelihoods. In their sense of self-entitlement, university students felt that ZANU-PF corruption and poor economic choices had combined to pauperise them. Although dissent to ZANU-PF policies had existed both within and outside of the party in the 1980s, the student movement morphed into a powerful opposition force outside of the traditional political structures and its activities were unequivocally confrontational.

Student activism brought a new form of politics that directly questioned the moral authority of political leaders, in contrast to the politics of the 1980s that deified them as revolutionaries and visionaries. According to Brian Raftopoulos (2001), by the mid-1990s student activism led by the Student Representative Council (SRC) of the University of Zimbabwe had 'shattered the mould of reverence to leadership'. However, Dan Hodgkinson traces the process to a much earlier period beginning with the Willowgate scandal of 1988 when the then president of the SRC, Arthur Mutambara, criticised the national leadership for 'betraying the revolution' (Hodgkinson 2013: 871). In 1989, students at the University demonstrated violently against corruption and forced the institution to close following a brutal state crackdown which Mutambara (n.d.) described as 'state terrorism', claiming that the country's leaders had 'completely lost legitimacy'. In 1993, Mugabe refused to attend May Day celebrations at the University for fear of ridicule by the students. Students had perforated the façade of an invincibly strong leadership and forced it to answer to the people. According to Hodgkinson (2013), student activism 'represented the first moment when young, largely male, student activists cultivated a political identity at odds with the ruling party that heckled national leaders and influenced opinion in the press'. Students' claims of 'defending academic freedom' while dealing with national political issues was as much a threat to ZANU-PF as any other political formation.

The state's response to student demonstrations and criticism was typically paternalistic. It sought to rein in the students and re-establish control by appealing to a gerontocratic and traditional discourse of authority, where the authority of 'elders' was firmly established against their 'children'. In this vein, President Mugabe and Vice President Joshua Nkomo referred to the students as 'school children' exhibiting behaviour that was 'not Zimbabwean' and patently 'childish' (ibid.). Government officials appealed to the waning discourses of unity and patriotism they had espoused in the 1980s. In the Youth Brigades, the government had controlled the policy agenda and national leaders were revered. The new forms of youth political participation that were outside strict state control proved problematic for ZANU-PF, which gave little room for democratic values or the youth voice to thrive either within the party structures or more widely. Students' refusal to acquiesce to state bullying and paternalism represented the limits of state power to supress alternative political voices in the 1990s. The new resistance movements of the early 1990s became synonymous with student struggles.

Students emerged as the 'voice of the people' in the shifting political discourse of the 1990s. They were the intelligentsia which articulated the national struggles of the peasants and workers who were burdened by poor economic performance under ESAP. The Zimbabwe Congress of Trade Unions (ZCTU) was organisationally weak in the 1980s but a change of leadership later in the decade, together with retrenchments and worsening poverty, reshaped and emboldened the movement to confront the government. The government estimated that by the mid-1990s over 20,000 workers had lost their jobs but the ZCTU pegged the figure at 30,000. Unemployment had risen from 36% in 1990 to 44% in 1993 (Mlambo 1997). The share of wages in the economy dropped from 54% in 1987 to 39% in 1997 (Raftopoulos 2009: 202). Students swelled the ranks of the jobless and often turned out in their numbers at ZCTU gatherings in solidarity with the working people. They were central to a new alliance of 'critical civil society groupings campaigning around trade union, human rights and constitutional questions' against an intransigent ZANU-PF government (ibid.). The failure of the neoliberal policies in the mid-1990s and the emergence of a strong social movement saw the government lean further towards authoritarianism. For example, the state crackdown on the food riots of 1998 signalled ZANU-PF unwillingness to negotiate a social consensus despite the clarion calls for dialogue. This social impasse culminated in the political formation of the Movement for Democratic Change (MDC) in 1999, an alliance that brought together the ZCTU, ZINASU, the National Constitutional Assembly (NCA), civil society and other pressure groups. Significantly, many student leaders formally joined the new political formation which represented the hopes of the workers and the young people for prosperous and democratic Zimbabwe.

Rupture and the resurgence of the authoritarian state, 2000-2017

Zimbabwe's multiple crises of the late 1990s worsened with the turn of the new millennium. In 2000 the government tried to quell the growing political opposition to its rule through a constitutional referendum but suffered a major blow when its proposal was rejected. The MDC and civil organisations had campaigned for a No vote which appealed to a predominantly young population, many of whom were unemployed and were suffering economic hardships. In the parliamentary vote of the same year, the MDC garnered 57 of the 120 seats with 47% of the popular vote and ZANU-PF got 63 seats with 49%. This was ZANU-PF's heaviest loss of parliamentary seats since independence. It came as no surprise that the 2002 presidential election was marred by political violence against MDC supporters by state agents and the ZANU-PF party youth wing. The government became more 'radicalised' and utilised 'patriotic history' to re-establish its political hegemony (Ranger 2004). The party's liberation struggle credentials were enmeshed with the Fast Track Land Reform Programme and it claimed to be fighting neoliberal imperialism in the form of the 'western sponsored' MDC party. These 'local agents of imperialism' were, therefore, 'sell outs' bent on reversing the gains of independence. The Mugabe regime created a narrative which glorified ZANU-PF as the 'revolutionaries' and all opposition to its political and social agenda as western sponsored 'sell outs' (ibid.: 223).

The student movement of the 1990s had represented what ZANU-PF had feared in an 'ungoverned' youth. The MDC electoral successes of the early 2000s illustrated its popular youth support and an active mobilisation by ZINASU at tertiary institutions. In line with its post-2000 political rhetoric, the government moved to create 'patriotic youths' through a formal state-run institution of mobilisation and indoctrination as a counterbalance to the 'unpatriotic' opposition youth groups. The Ministry of Gender, Youth and Employment introduced a National Youth Policy in 2000, which was designed to protect 'vulnerable' youths. It then launched the National Youth Service (NYS) in 2001. The NYS targeted those between the ages of 15 and 35, loosely called the *born-free generation*, for political orientation on national identity, unity, discipline, and self-reliance with a strong leaning toward a patriotic history which legitimised ZANU-PF's 'sacrosanct' and uncontested rule of the country (GoZ 2001). Participants in the NYS were unemployed males and females mainly from the embattled rural peasant households and resettled farming communities, comprising school-leavers, dropouts and the underqualified (Mhike 2018). The urbanised youths were generally safe from NYS conscriptions. The state-run NYS with its partisan philosophies targeted the youth because their demographic composition of 60% of the population was a critical factor in the elections (ZimStat 2012). The NYS started a few months before the 2002 presidential election which Mugabe won amid violence and the torture of MDC supporters by the NYS, the ZANU-PF youth wing and the CIO.

The NYS revealed a striking element of ZANU-PF politics, namely youth violence. Between 2001 and 2007, the NYS graduates, who were pejoratively called 'Green Bombers', went on a rampage of terror disguised as a political 're-education' exercise of the masses. For many in the rural areas, joining the NYS was the only way of guaranteeing individual and family safety from violence, and being labelled as 'sell outs'. At this point, the ZANU-PF government lacked a clear strategy to deal with urban youths, many of whom resorted to migrating into the region and beyond in search of better job opportunities. NYS youths were implicated in murder, rape, torture and other forms of coercion against real and suspected opposition supporters in the 2002, 2005 and 2008 elections (CSVR 2009). Their operations meant that ex-farming and rural areas became 'no-go' areas for MDC supporters. In the 2000s, the NYS was at the forefront of the politics of intolerance and bore a striking resemblance to the Brigades of the 1980s as it emerged as a tool to forestall opposition support in the rural areas. This helped confine the MDC to the urban centres.

Following the mould of the Brigades, the NYS helped texture the concept of youth in politics as one of violence. It represented how youths were appropriated, through state institutions, to act as 'defenders' of partisan ideologies often against their will. In addition, youths have figured prominently in the ZANU-PF political crisis management systems since the liberation war. They became central to the political crises of the 1980s and after 2000 by violently controlling opposition to ZANU-PF.

Political violence permeated Zimbabwe's political process so much that state repression bred a 'confrontational assertiveness' not only in student activism but in the opposition political formations such as the MDC. While ZINUSU leaders were engaged in running battles with the police on university campuses and on the streets, the MDC organised its youths to defend themselves against ZANU-PF attacks. ZANU-PF youths' attempts to disrupt MDC political meetings sometimes met with equally menacing groups, but it was usually the latter who were arrested for violent conduct. Tonderai Ndira, a 32-year-old member of the MDC security operations was abducted and murdered by a state 'death squad' in 2008. His life and political activities have come to symbolise the MDC youth organisational abilities to resist a persistently repressive state (Wilkins 2013). The CIO and the police continued to abduct, harass and beat ZINASU members. In 2008, ZINASU president Clever Bere was arrested and beaten in police custody and later released without charge. Students dealt with state brutality in a number of ways including verbal confrontation (shouting obscenities) and pelting police with stones during demonstrations. The strategy of security in numbers during demonstrations was threatened when the CIO targeted individual student leaders for abduction and torture. Often, student leaders on the state 'hit list' would go into hiding.

Patronage and coercion were at the heart of the NYS mobilisation. The state used the NYS as a *de facto* 'rite of passage' for youths' access to tertiary education, jobs in the civil service and state funded economic empowerment programmes. NYS candidates were presented in the media as willing agents and perpetrators of violence, mobilised as part of a repressive state (Mhike 2018). In reality, many of these youths were unwilling but active agents of a brutal system, who joined the institution in an endeavour to navigate economic and political constraints. By 2008, Zimbabwe's hyperinflation had reached a record 230 million percent and the 2006 GDP per capita was 47% lower than 1980 levels. Unemployment was above 80% (Raftopoulos 2009). NYS graduates had a better chance of admission into technical and vocational training institutions as well as jobs in the civil service. Therefore, an NYS certificate became a necessity, not a choice, for the thousands of school-leavers and job seekers. NYS graduates were also rewarded through youth economic empowerment programmes in the form of loans to start projects in their communities. In 2006 the National Youth Fund was created to provide loans for such projects. Between 2009 and

2013 youth empowerment was placed under the broader Indigenisation and Economic Empowerment Act.

The run-up to the 2013 election saw ZANU-PF shift its political messaging to identify more and more with the young people in the hope of winning their votes. This new thrust came against the backdrop of the 2012 national census that pegged the youthful population above 60%. Subsequently, Mugabe was cast as a leader who identified with the needs of young people and even appeared in some of the party sponsored youth musical videos. Although ZANU-PF was not committed to meaningful leadership renewal to accommodate the young people, the demographic realities forced it to focus on them. In 2016, Mugabe began to conduct *Youth Interface* rallies across the country. This trajectory was accompanied by economic incentives specifically for youths. A Youth Development Fund was established and ran under the Zimbabwe Agenda for Sustainable Socio-Economic Transformation policy culminating in the 2017 establishment of EmpowerBank with a US$12m capitalisation focusing on funding youth-led businesses. These state-run youth economic empowerment vehicles firmly operated within ZANU-PF structures to reward party affiliated youths. However, they tended to benefit the more urbanised youths at the expense of those in the rural areas. The financial institutions were in the urban areas and the urban youths had greater organisational capacity to apply for loans. Ironically, ZANU-PF has relied more on the rural youths for political support than it has on the urban youth vote.

The political violence in the 2008 election and allegations of massive rigging in favour of ZANU-PF, damaged the credibility of elections to bring about a democratic transition in Zimbabwe. ZANU-PF rhetoric that *'nyika haitorwe nebhiro'* (the ballot will not bring about change of government) and allegations of rigging has partly worked in discouraging the youth vote in the past three elections. Some young people felt it was useless for the opposition to contest in 'predetermined' elections and this caused youth voter apathy in the 2013 and 2018 elections. For example, in the 2013 elections, of the 5.9 million registered voters (with youth in the majority) only 60% turned out to vote. In addition, poor education about elections, corruption, poor infrastructure and an informal economy made voting a secondary priority for many youths who could not link the electoral process with their daily struggles to make ends meet.

The coup of November 2017 epitomised the youth 'problem' in ZANU-PF. The G40 faction, comprising the younger members of the party who advocated renewal in leadership to meet the demands of a young generation, found themselves at odds with the gerontocratic politics that the organisation had espoused since the 1980s. Following the coup, the Lacoste faction, consisting of the old guard and the military, purged G40 members from government and the ZANU-PF youth wing. Some have argued that the 2017 events might be considered as a lost opportunity for the party and nation to recognise the voice of the young generation in providing a vision for national development. This notwithstanding, the removal of Mugabe brought a genuine but misguided hope that political change was going to bring a new future. Many youths were won over by Mnangagwa's 'New Dispensation' rhetoric which promised renewal and progressive politics, but inside two years the 'new' hope was dashed by state militarisation and authoritarianism, a failing economy and little leadership renewal to accommodate youths. Zimbabwe's ageing presidium has perpetuated gerontocratic politics and illustrated the lack of belief in young leaders. In 2018, Mnangagwa's 20-member cabinet contained only one young person, the 35-year-old Kirsty Coventry as Minister of Youth, Sport, Arts and Recreation.

Conclusion

The experiences of Zimbabwean youths highlight the predicament of young people in the African post-colonial state. The ZANU-PF party/state manipulated youth economic vulnerabilities to advance politics of patronage and state coercion of opposition political groups and dissenting voices centred around youth violence. The Youth Brigades of the 1980s and the National Youth Service of 2001 were vehicles of control and a form of state sponsored youth violence. State programmes limited the space for youth political participation and young people struggled to articulate a national objective to shift the country's political discourse. Although student activism in the late 1980s brought about a new form of politics that upended the culture of deifying political leaders, this confrontational form of politics perpetuated the culture of youth violence dating back to the 1960s. Invariably, the capacity of the opposition political parties to wrest political power from ZANU-PF was enhanced by their ability to mobilise the youth vote and the youth as agents of political violence. The ZANU-PF state has attempted to tie youth aspirations to its own social and political agendas by rewarding allegiance to the party. Job opportunities and state funded youth economic empowerment programmes in the post 2000 period were firmly controlled from within ZANU-PF party structures making political affiliation a necessity rather a choice. Ironically, state structures that should guarantee youth social protection for the youth have been used by the party/state to entrench the very vulnerabilities they were designed surmount.

References

Alexander, J. (2012) '"Hooligans, spivs and loafers"?: The politics of vagrancy in 1960s Southern Rhodesia', *The Journal of African History*, 50(3), pp. 345-366.

Anderson, C.W. (2013) 'Youth, the "Arab Spring" and Social Movements', *Review of Middle East Studies*, 47(2), pp. 150-156.

Catholic Commission for Justice and Peace in Zimbabwe (CCJPZ) and Legal Resources Foundation (LRF) (1997) *Breaking the Silence, Building True Peace: A Report on the Disturbances in Matabeleland and the Midlands, 1980 to 1988.* Harare: CCJPZ and LRF.

Centre for the Study of Violence and Reconciliation (CSVR) (2009) 'Subliminal Terror? Human Rights Violations and Torture in Zimbabwe during 2008'. Johannesburg: Centre for the Study of Violence and Reconciliation.

Chung, F. (1988) 'Education: Revolution or Reform', in C. Stoneman (ed.), *Zimbabwe's Prospects: Issues of race, class, state and capital.* London: Macmillan.

Government of Zimbabwe (GoZ) (2001) 'National Youth Service Manual'. Harare: Government of Zimbabwe.

Hodgkinson, D. (2013) 'The "Hardcore" Student Activist: The Zimbabwe National Students Union (ZINASU), State Violence, and Frustrated Masculinity, 2000–2008', *Journal of Southern African Studies*, 39(4), pp.863-883.

Honwana A. and F. de Boeck (2005) *Makers and Breakers: Children and youth in postcolonial Africa.* Oxford: James Currey.

Kriger, N. (1988) 'The Zimbabwean War of Liberation: Struggles within the Struggle', *Journal of Southern African Studies*, 14(2), pp.304-324.

Makunike, B. (2015) 'The Zimbabwe student movement: Love-hate relationship with government?', *Journal of Student Affairs in Africa*, 3(1), pp.35-48.

Mandaza, I. (ed.) (1986) *Zimbabwe: The political Economy of Transition, 1980-1986*. Dakar: CODESRIA.

Manganga, K. (2011) 'Masculinity (dodaism), gender and nationalism: The case of the Salisbury bus boycott, September 1956,' in S. Ndlovu-Gatsheni and J. Muzondidya (eds), *Redemptive or grotesque nationalism? Rethinking contemporary politics in Zimbabwe*. Oxford: Peter Lang.

Meredith, M. (2007) *Mugabe: Power, Plunder and the Struggle for Zimbabwe*. New York: PublicAffairs.

Mhike, I. (2018) 'Political Violence in Zimbabwe's National Youth Service, 2001–2007', in O.E. Oinas, H. Onodera and L. Suurpää (eds), *What Politics? Youth and Political Engagement in Africa*. Helsinki: Helsinki Institute of Sustainable Science.

Mlambo, A. (1995) 'Student protest and state reaction in colonial Rhodesia: the 1973 Chimukwembe student demonstration at the university of Rhodesia', *Journal of Southern African Studies*, 21(3), pp. 473-490.

————— (1997) *The Economic Structural Adjustment Programme: The case of Zimbabwe, 1990-1995*. Harare: University of Zimbabwe Publications.

Morier-Genoud E. (2020) 'The jihadi insurgency in Mozambique: origins, nature and beginning', *Journal of East African Studies*, 14(3), pp. 396-412.

Mutambara, A. (n.d.) *In Search of Meaning and Significance: An Autobiography of Thought*. Unpublished ms.

Muzondidya, J. (2008) 'From Buoyancy to Crisis, 1980-1997', in B. Raftopoulos and A.S. Mlambo (eds), *Becoming Zimbabwe: A History from the Pre-colonial Period to 2008*. Harare: Weaver Press.

Oinas, O.E., H. Onodera and L. Suurpää (2018) 'Evasive Youth, Oblique Politics,' in O.E Oinas, H. Onodera and L. Suurpää (eds), *What Politics? Youth and Political Engagement in Africa*. Helsinki:

Helsinki Institute of Sustainable Science.

Osaghae, E.E., A. Ikelegbe, O.O. Olarinmoye and S.I. Okhomina (2011) 'Youth Militias, Self Determination and Resource Control Struggles in the Niger-Delta Region of Nigeria'. Dakar: CODESRIA Research Reports: No.5.

Raftopoulos, B. (2001) 'The Labour Movement and the Emergence of Opposition Politics in Zimbabwe', in B. Raftopoulos and L. Sachikonye (eds), *'Striking Back': The Labour Movement and the Post-Colonial State in Zimbabwe 1980-2000*. Harare: Weaver Press.

——— (2009) 'The Crisis in Zimbabwe, 1998-2008', in B. Raftopoulos and A.S. Mlambo (eds), *Becoming Zimbabwe: A History from the Pre-colonial Period to 2008*. Harare: Weaver Press.

Ranger T.O. (2004) 'Nationalist Historiography, Patriotic History and the History of the Nation: The Struggle over the Past in Zimbabwe', *Journal of Southern African Studies*, 30(2), pp. 215-234.

Stoneman, C. (1988) 'The economy: Recognising the reality', in C. Stoneman (ed.), *Zimbabwe's Prospects: Issues of race, class, state and capital*. London: Macmillan.

Vezha, O. (1987) *The Youth Brigade Movement in Zimbabwe as a strategy for meeting the needs and aspirations of unemployed youth: A case study of Kaguvi Youth Training Centre*. Harare: University of Zimbabwe Publications.

Wilkins, S. (2013), 'Ndira's Wake: Politics, Memory and Mobility among the Youth of Mabvuku-Tafara, Harare', *Journal of Southern African Studies*, 39(4), pp. 885-901.

Zimbabwe National Statistics Agency (ZimStat) (2012) 'Census 2012: Preliminary Report'. Harare: Zimstat.

7

A Brief History of Urban Youths in Zimbabwe: 1980-2020

Eric Makombe and Timothy Scarnecchia

Introduction

The urban youth in Zimbabwe have for a long-time presented a complex challenge to family, community, and the state. Colonial authorities largely despised the presence of youths in the urban spaces because they interfered with the envisaged labour reserve model by adding to the costs of labour reproduction. Likewise, parents were hesitant to bring up their children in the urban areas. Again, this was informed by the huge costs of maintaining a nuclear family in the urban areas. As a result, various family agglomerations, such as commuter households, emerged, during colonialism as families fashioned their daily lives to minimise the costs of urban living.

In their original design, colonial officials deliberately recruited single male labourers from Nyasaland (Malawi) and Northern Rhodesia (Zambia) to work in the urban areas of Umtali (Mutare), Salisbury (Harare), and Bulawayo. This was done to circumvent the possibility of family units (i.e. women and youths) settling in urban spaces. Indeed, Malawian male migrants constituted the largest group of migrants before the 1920s (Yoshikuni 2007). However, in the post-World War Two years, local Africans began to dominate numerically as they moved into the cities in greater numbers owing to increasing rural pressures. Barnes (1999) has shown that women were able to circumvent urban controls in the 1940s and 1950s despite colonial restrictions. Thus, although permanent homeownership was illegal for urban Africans until independence, family residence emerged in Rhodesian urban areas from the 1960s onwards (Schlyter 2006). Over time, and regardless of how they came to be in the urban areas, the different ethnic groups would through intermarriage and socialisation produce a truly dynamic and distinct urban culture.

The marginal success that the colonial authorities and parents registered in making the urban spaces youth-free came undone as the liberation struggle intensified in the 1970s.[1] The war forced many rural villagers to migrate to the cities for safety. For instance, the population in Zengeza – some 20 miles south-east of Salisbury – grew rapidly after it was set up in 1976 to house an estimated 15,000 people (Dambudzo 1979). People who had been internally displaced by the war added to the country's de facto urban population at independence in 1980 which experienced a further surge as the new government lifted any vestiges of influx-control laws.

The pre-1980 period had long registered a growing number of unemployed youths. The 1969 national census recorded over 750,000 idle school leavers who had no inherent desire to be in the rural areas but could not find openings in the wage sector (Whitsun Foundation 1978: 6). By 1974, the total African urban population increased by 23%, but African employment in all sectors other than agriculture had only increased by 15% (Kay 1971: 25). The urban areas were, therefore, not simply growing, but their character was also changing and the proportion of the urban population that were formally employed was also declining.

Based on World Development Reports data, Zimbabwe's urban population grew from 1,657,383 (22% of total population) in 1980, to 29% in 1990, 34% in 2000, 33% in 2010, and 32% in 2019. The total urban population was said to be 4,717,305 people in 2019. The post-2000 trends are contrary to developments in most African nations where urban population growth continues.[2] The severe economic and political

---

1   This is no way implies that there was an unholy alliance between the colonial state and (African) parents against (African) urban youths but just a congruence of goals.

2   For example, in 2019, Zambia's urban population grew at a rate of 4.15%, Tanzania

shocks of the 2000s, as well as out-migration, may have contributed to this flattening out; it could also reflect undercounting of some urban populations living in informal settlements.

Nuclearisation and new parent-child power relations

The attainment of independence in Zimbabwe in 1980 was met with a mounting problem of rural to urban migration by people who had long been constrained by the colonial administration. Urbanisation led to a greater proportion of children being brought up within the nuclear family, which not only influenced the parent-child relationship but also redefined childhood more narrowly and away from traditional society's extended family definitions (Ncube 1998: 23). The shift was brought about by the necessity of more prolonged, complex training needed to prepare youths for adulthood, and this training often extended beyond the legal age of the majority (i.e. 18 years) (Ncube et al. 1997). Ncube (1998: 24) asserted that this intensified the youth's economic and social dependence on adults. This fuelled a more aggressive assertion of parental authority over children, as parents invested more in their children's future and raised their expectations of substantial returns for their investment. This in turn put increasing pressure on children to perform well at school and brought about a much more competitive world with the possibility of frustrated expectations.

The new parent-child power relations created serious challenges and disharmony. Owing to the escalation of the liberation war in the 1970s, many schools were forced to close, reopening only after independence. As such, the median age for grade one pupils was much higher than the envisaged six years. According to Ncube (1998: 24), in the African cultural context, there are certain 'inter-generational obligations of support and reciprocity' that come with age. However, many youths attained adulthood at essentially the same time that they were still undergoing training to be able to perform expected adult responsibilities.

Not all urban youths had such encounters, as differences in economic class afforded some better-off youths more privileged experiences in the 1980s. As Wild (1992: 20) wrote, 'At the time of Independence, the [economic] gap between Lovemore Sibanda, the cobbler under a tree in Chitungwiza, and Paul Matambanadzo, the leading African

by 5.0%, whilst Zimbabwe's urban growth rate of 1.42% was the second-lowest in Africa. Zambia also overtook Zimbabwe in terms of the urban percentage of total population starting in 2000.

bus operator, had become too wide to be glossed over'. Paul's son, Tich Mataz (born Tichafa Matambanadzo) who was born in 1969 in Highfield, used the freedom afforded by independence to visit the United Kingdom. 'I probably visited the UK alone at about fifteen/ sixteen [at the time Zimbabwe was still in the Commonwealth] all you needed was an air ticket'.[3]

Apart from the economic gap, better-educated African professionals advanced upward in urban society. Many of them moved out of the high-density areas (former African Townships – hereinafter HDAs) to reside in the former white-only suburbs. Their children moved from former Group B schools to multiracial former Group A schools. Mataz recalled that 'Lord Malvern [his school in Harare] had a lot of access to sporting facilities and different environments we couldn't find in the Group B schools and also the friendships.[4] As such, the experiences of youths in the middle-income suburbs stood in stark contrast to those in the HDAs.

In the HDAs, however, life translated to a tough balancing act of attending night-school while simultaneously working during the day to meet some of the reciprocal social obligations placed on young adults. Zimbabwean author, Charles Mungoshi (1980: 98) captured such family strife in a 1980 short story:

> Hell, man, hell! And what has ever got me anywhere in this rotten world? Third division in Form Four and everyone at my neck saying I wasn't applying myself. Four years tramping around the country, knocking on every goddam door for any kind of job, and being shoed [*sic*] off with a boot in my ass and at home my old man out for my scalp telling me I am not searching hard enough.

Zimbabwe's economic and social problems were already getting worse owing to a 3% yearly population growth rate. Youth unemployment dominated unemployment data because of the high mobility that characterises this age group. In 1984 there were some 71,014 students in the Lower 6 class yet the economy was only able to generate a minimal increase of just 10,700 jobs (GoZ 1985). As a result of unemployment and poor prospects for the future, the youths became increasingly restless.

---

3 TichMataz with So Profound: https://www.youtube.com/watch?v=PQ_
   NqR8SDZI&t=102s 99 Lives: The TichMataz Story | Episode 1- Fiyo (Highfield).

4 Ibid.

The new government and youths

The immediate post-independence Cabinet in 1980 was relatively young, with one Minister, Joyce Mujuru, being just 22 years old. Perhaps not coincidentally, Mujuru was also the first Minister of Youth, Sport, and Recreation. Beyond Mujuru, several other Ministers and Deputy Ministers were still in their 30s. This, in some respect, fostered a sense of inclusion among the youth in the state-making and state-building decisions of the post-colonial order. Indeed, as part of post-colonial rhetoric, the government highlighted the importance of youth in economic development through the establishment of ministries of Youth, Sport and Recreation, and Health and Child Welfare.

However, as Mhike et al. (2018) rightly argued, the 'ZANU-PF government's seemingly broad and accommodating construction of youth in the 1980s masked narrow conceptions of the idea of progressive youth, citizenship, belonging and the overall development approach'. The ZANU-PF government had its roots in the liberation struggle, but its mutation into a political party in 1980 was by no means a smooth transition. The 'liberation narrative' continued to figure strongly in its claims to legitimacy and in shaping the new socio-economic order that it envisioned for the country. Similarly, the discourse and framing of youth throughout the 1980s and 1990s remained closely entwined with the liberation ideology (Kriger 2005).

Further, the Marxist and Pan-Africanist ideologies espoused during the struggle continued to shape the country's post-colonial agenda. Marxist-Leninist dogma informed the conflation of the ruling party and government and the subservience of the latter to the former. As such, a curious mixture of socialism, cultural idealism, Pan-Africanism, and an anti-western agenda dominated public discourse and praxis. For example, Mujuru was put in an invidious position when her ZANU-PF party directed her to ban beauty pageants. Mujuru said that 'Another troubling issue had to do with [the] Ms. Zimbabwe [pageant]. The likes of Shelly Nyanyiwa [first Ms Zimbabwe] who were still wearing their bikinis, and we said aaaah aaaah aaaah; we were still within the spirit of the war [and] said we don't want to see such foolish things … this is what came from the party [ZANU-PF]'.[5]

The ban intended to proscribe the activities of urban youths and

5 Joyce Mujuru Interview https://www.youtube.com/watch?v=XW61Kxnz0dl
'Mugabe exploited illiteracy ministers from 1980 to country's doom'.

to channel their energies towards what the ruling-party felt were the productive use of time and acceptable leisure events. These efforts were extended to public media as well. Mataz, a former disc jockey with a local radio station, Radio 3, affirmed that the directors at the Zimbabwe Broadcasting Corporation 'decided…to start to educate guys who had started…to urbanise coming out from Chiweshe, Murambinda coming to town. Radio demystified urbanisation'.[6]

Operation 'Clean-up' and Youth Brigades

The government extended its efforts by attempting to rid the city of delinquent youths during October and November in 1983 when it launched Operation 'Clean-Up' and rounded up suspected sex workers, vagrants, and squatters using the police, army, and Youth Brigade members.[7] The clean-up was informed by facile interpretations of urban areas as places of sexual freedom, while rural areas, supposedly, exerted greater social control over traditional norms about sexuality (Sambisa and Stoke 2006: 187). For instance, one parent from Mabvuku stressed the need to guard against the 'consequences of too much freedom' especially for female youths who could most likely end up in sex work, among other perceived anti-social behaviours.[8]

The clean-up was conducted so indiscriminately that in Gwanda, girls below the age of 15 were only spared because some prison officials refused to admit them into prison.[9] Those who were rounded up in Harare were taken to Goromonzi, a rural area on the outskirts of the city. Another writer to *The Herald*, from Kadoma, celebrated this saying 'Forward, with taking "definitive" prostitutes to the farms [to work]'.[10] Beyond the clean-up exercises, the government resuscitated colonial urban control measures: on 21 November 1983, it modified the Vagrancy Act, empowering Rehabilitation Officers with the authority to bar vagrants from urban areas for three months or to hold them in 'rehabilitation centres'.[11]

The government also introduced the Youth Brigades Movement –

6   TichMataz with So Profound https://www.youtube.com/watch?v=04PnQY_7gB8 99 Lives: The TichMataz Story | Episode 2- Radio 3.

7   'Innocent Blitz Victims Freed', T*he Herald*, 28 November 1983.

8   'Too Much Freedom' [letter to the Editor], *The Sunday Mail*, 8 February 1981.

9   '84 Women Held in Gwanda as Blitz Continues', *The Herald*, 21 November 1983.

10 'Problems in the Clean Up', *The Herald*, 29 November, 1983.

11 'New Law on Vagrants Spelt Out', *The Herald*, 22 November 1983.

which is discussed in more detail in Chapter 6 – to stem unemployment and poverty among the youths. In practice, there was a blurred distinction between the party youth wing and Brigades. Brigades' members were involved in politics, including mobilising meetings for ZANU-PF and in conducting acts of political violence (CCJPZ and LRF 1997). One J.H. May of Shurugwi alleged that during Operation 'Clean-up' in 1983 'ZANU-PF youths swooped on private houses, wielding axes and clubs, hunting and arresting others, no doubt innocent, domestic workers'.[12]

Urban youth activism and self-expression

However, even within ZANU-PF's grand objectives of fostering an authoritarian and repressive one-party state through the use of violence and a hegemonic discourse of unity, urban youths and students still found forms of self-expression in the 1980s. Mataz recalls that in the early 1980s '*Bhoyizi* [i.e. male youths] would gather at Machipisa [shopping centre in Highfield] there for live events by musicians Leonard Dembo, Bundu Boys...James Chimombe and so on'.[13] For 'Christmas and Easter, we would go to Gwanzura Stadium...It was called the 6 [pm] to 6 [am]'.[14] These all-night concerts were also called *pungwes*, an appropriation of a term used to refer to the night rallies in the rural areas during the war. This highlights the urban youths' agency in fashioning the use of their leisure time outside of the state. Moving into the 1990s, urban youths began to insert themselves more onto the urban space as a subculture and expressed their denial of governmental and parental consent through their politics, clothing tastes, social values and leisure activities.

Student activism became more vocal and confrontational in the late 1980s. Young student activists led by Arthur Mutambara took part in anti-corruption demonstrations at the University of Zimbabwe in September 1988 (Zeilig 2006). Hodgkinson (2015) observes that 'these [demonstrations] were the first formal, organised public protests after independence in 1980'.[15] However, Zeilig (2006: 104) is right in

---

12 'Police Image Discredited by Round-Up', *The Sunday Mail*, 27 November 1983.
13 TichMataz with So Profound https://www.youtube.com/watch?v=04PnQY_7gB8
99 Lives: The TichMataz Story | Episode 2- Radio 3.
14 Ibid.
15 'Five lessons from Zimbabwe's game-changing student protests', *The Conversation*, 6 November 2015.

clarifying that the 'demonstrations were only against certain members of the government and regarded by students as supportive of Mugabe's own "anti-corruption drive"'. This notwithstanding, a new critical discourse entered Zimbabwean politics at the time and it became a precursor of the sharp break with the regime that came thereafter.

ESAP and the urban revolt

Zimbabwe's rising debt hastened the nation's plunge into adopting the World Bank/IMF sponsored Economic Structural Adjustment Program (ESAP) in 1991-92. This programme led to massive formal sector retrenchments, an official unemployment rate of 40%, and sudden and frequent increases in the costs of basic foodstuffs and services (Raftopoulos et al. 1998). The prolonged economic downturn starting during ESAP and stretching into the 2000s eroded the emerging African middle class and, in some ways, equalised the experiences of youths in middle-suburbia and the ghettoes.

Another serious outcome was the large number of children who were forced to drop out of school. Mlambo (1997) recorded that secondary school fees increased by 150% in 1992 alone, yet they had been minimal and affordable for most in the 1980s. At the university level, the onset of ESAP rapidly eroded the privileged status of students in higher education as the government moved to introduce fees in 1997 (Zvobgo 1999). The government's economic liberalisation policies caused widespread mobilisation, in which university students played a prominent role.

Zimbabwe's anti-liberalisation protests birthed a new politics. What began as 'protest[s] against corruption, broadened to include two other major issues: opposition to Mugabe's plan for a one-party state…and opposition to his proposed shift to a neoliberal agenda' (Alexander 2000: 386). After 1995, as Zeilig (2008: 215) pointed out, 'student activism converged with the urban revolt that was beginning to shake Zimbabwe'. Building on this, the trade union movement under Morgan Tsvangirai organised a new political party, the Movement for Democratic Change (MDC) in 1999. Several student leaders were incorporated into top party positions, including Learnmore Jongwe, Job Sikhala, Nelson Chamisa, and Tafadzwa Musekiwa.

Precarious survival strategies

Coupled to the striking social and economic upheavals bedevilling Zimbabwean society in the 1990s was the HIV/AIDS pandemic. HIV prevalence rates in Zimbabwe's urban areas affected 'young people... [and caused] deaths in an economically important group (15 to 45 years)' (Bassett and Mhloyi 1991: 143). The socio-demographic effects of the pandemic were devastating and led to a reversal of previous gains in early childhood survival, a rapid decline in population growth, and an inexorable rise in orphanhood (Mugurungi et al. 2007: 195).

The economic downturn and the impacts of AIDS contributed to a breakdown of the nuclear family. This had a particular bearing on the social position of youths in the family and the community at large. A variety of households emerged including the new phenomenon of child-headed households (CHHs) in communities ravaged by AIDS. This indicated the 'saturation of traditional extended-family orphan coping mechanisms' (Foster et al. 1997: 165). However, as one study found, CHHs were 'not always a direct consequence of parental death' (Ciganda et al. 2012). The phenomenon was also an adaptation used by parents who had emigrated to other countries or their rural homes in response to economic pressures. Kufakurinani et al. (2014) have referred to this approach as 'transnational parenting', and the children left behind as 'diaspora orphans'.

An unfortunate consequence of the rise of CHHs in urban areas was the emergence of psychosocial disorders among these children. As a case study of the Mabvuku and Tafara suburbs of Harare revealed, 'psychosocial deficits among children from [CHHs] manifested through poor personal grooming, indecision...avoidance of challenging situations...sexual violence and unplanned teenage pregnancy' (Makuyana et al. 2020). In many cases, these challenges would be reflected through the production of poor results at school and a high rate of school dropouts (Kurebwa and Gatsi Kurebwa 2014: 242). With the rising orphan population, many youths in Mutare began to fend for themselves through various means including cross-border trading and other illegal activities in Mozambique (Gwatirisa and Manderson 2009: 108). Foster et al. (1997: 165), in a survey conducted in the mid-1990s in Mutare, found out that owing to a shortage of accommodation, it was difficult for children to hold on to their homes after the death of their parents since most people resided in rented accommodation. Youths, therefore, had limited access to urban housing because they could not apply for accommodation on their own.

The hopelessness in which these youths found themselves following the deaths of their parents made them resort to precarious forms of urban life. Illegal or adverse coping strategies were increasing. These included commercial sex work, crime (housebreaking, mugging), illicit beer brewing, gambling, and drug dealing. This had the effect of deepening the generation gap between the old and young. Older people reported that they 'live in perpetual fear of the youth' (Bird and Prowse 2009: 21). Likewise, society often associated the so-called 'diaspora orphans' with various negative characteristics. They were 'labelled as delinquent and reckless with life, snobbish and profligate, disrespectful and lacking in good manners, as well as abused, emotionally deprived, and neglected' (Kufakurinani et al. 2014).

Amid all this Zimbabwe continued to experience rapid urbanisation and an accelerating housing crisis. The number of people living in urban areas grew from just under 2 million in 1982 to 3.2 million in 1992 and 4.8 million in 2000 (Murisa 2010: 10). At least 1.5 million people were inadequately housed, many of these in the urban areas (GoZ 1992; Auret 1995). One estimate in 1995 suggested that over 110,000 people were living in squatter settlements in the greater Harare region (Murisa 2010). In the context of both the economic downturn and the AIDS pandemic, aspects of housing vulnerability became even more complex. At the intra-household level, children, youths, and the elderly were at particular risk since they tended to be the most insecure household members. Rwezaura et al. (1995) found that competition for scarce resources was noticeable in the nuclear family itself. The pervasive unemployment levels in the country limited the possibility of financial support from extended family members.

The adoption of ESAP had the effect of reducing the government's role in housing provision. Youths faced issues of 'insecure tenure, overcrowding, lack of privacy, increased personal risk, and lack of opportunities' (Grant 2003: 417). Despite the prevalence of youth in cities and towns, very few programmes or policies were in place for them, and thus much of the burden rested with the family. Furthermore, credit facilities remained inaccessible; it was difficult for youths to access formal finance which often meant that the only recourse was to use community money-lenders who charged usurious interest rates.

Delayed adulthood and the disintegration of the family

Paradoxically, the level of dependence of youths increased despite the attainment of higher levels of education as a result of the contraction of formal sector employment. The realisation of certain milestones and expectations which society often used to define entry into adulthood such as leaving home, marriage, parenthood, and employment were now taking longer than before. This emerging phenomenon, of delayed adulthood, would deepen as the economic crisis worsened in the 2000s (Chirozva et al. 2007; Mate 2014).

As the economic landscape changed radically, parents and guardians wondered how to help launch youths, many of whom had acquired respectable levels of education. This often meant that money had to be re-directed from schooling for one or more younger children. The decision informing this redirection was not without controversy, as male children would often be prioritised. Thus, the re-introduction of school fees, as Makombe and Mhike (2018: 113) correctly point out, reinforced 'culturally institutionalised discrimination at early phases of the life cycle...to deny [girls] the necessary educational qualifications to compete equally in the urban formal economy'.

On the whole, urban youths felt that there was a vacuum when it came to support and guidance. However, some of the alternative avenues for support were found in youth centres. Sports clubs also provided a platform for socialisation; as Godfrey Hove fondly recalls, 'I (actually) did once go and play football with Highlanders Juniors [in Bulawayo] just for the fun of it...It was not (really) structured but that was the dream of every young person when we were teenagers'.16

The older HDAs in Bulawayo such as Luveve and Lobengula still had operational community youth centres, run by the Bulawayo City Council (Grant 2003: 418). The Council's commitment to the training of youths for economic and social roles in the community was exemplary and stood in stark contrast to the relative lack of development in other municipalities (Mapira 2011). However, many youth centres faced difficulties owing to shrinking funding. Unfortunately, money was not available to continue to build youth centres in the newer HDAs such

---

16   WhatsApp Voice Note from Godfrey Hove received on 29 January 2020.

as Nkulumane. This lack of funding and resources fed into low levels of participation in youth centres (Grant 2003: 434), and could, in turn, have contributed to the frustration and despair youths felt, particularly those who had no form of social or emotional support available to them.

Beyond the work of the Council and the churches, a private citizen, Cont Mhlanga, was pivotal in creating a platform for youth socialisation outside the family and school environments. Mhlanga established the Amakhosi Cultural Centre in 1982 (Rubin 1997: 365). Hove recalled his teenage experiences in the late 1990s: 'I grew to love the music of Lovemore Majaivana...Amakhosi [Centre] is just along the way to Mzilikazi High so I used to pass through that place every single day'.17 While many youths and parents agreed on the importance of youth centres, the lack of funding and institutional support from urban councils curtailed their activities and scope.

In-between fading hopes and total despair

By the end of the 1990s, urban youths were experiencing both individual and collective shocks. While the effect of individual shocks, for example parental death, could initially be insured against within the extended family, it became increasingly difficult to recover from shocks that operated at an aggregate level which affected entire communities, and the country at large (Bird and Prowse 2009: 9). By the close of the millennium, many youths had come to view their suffering as a form of injustice. The hopes and aspirations of society embodied in the youth cohort of the 1980s had long since faded. The sense of inclusion in the social contract with the government was also gone when it became apparent that the leaders were only looking out for themselves instead of governing for the majority.

The endemic corruption and cruel underbelly of neoliberalism adopted in the 1990s left many youths feeling hopeless and gravitating towards oppositional politics. Undoubtedly, the factor of age played a part in explaining why many urban youths embraced the MDC as an alternative in 1999. As such, 'Tsvangirai, aged 48, was [presumably] more capable of relating to and articulating the concerns of the younger generations than Mugabe, aged 76' (Zeilig 2006: 103). At the turn of the millennium, the urban youths were delicately poised between fading hopes and total despair.

---

17 ibid.

Into the 2000s: Hyperinflation and economic crises

The next twenty years would witness growing divisions within the urban areas between the 'ghetto youths' from the HDAs, the poor living in peri-urban settlements, the wealthier youths in the 'low-density' suburbs, and the super-rich children of the elite living in gated communities far from the urban poor. For the small group of elite youths, these years would continue as before, as those connected to the ruling party and their access to wealth would insulate their children from the sufferings experienced in other parts of Zimbabwe's cities. Tendai Huchu (2010) nicely captures this contrast in living spaces between former townships, former European suburbs, and the mansions of the new political and economic elite in Harare. For the remainder of this chapter, we will focus on the majority of urban youth, but it is important to note that the children of the wealthy would continue to support the elite institutions and practices established in the pre-independence period.

For the majority of urban youths, the first decade of the 2000s was an extremely challenging period. The fallout of the ruling party's decision to destroy the large commercial farming sector began a real economic crisis that led to the closure of many urban factories and businesses (Raftopoulos et al. 1998). In a short period, Zimbabwe's urban youth, including those with university degrees, could not look to join the formal employment market as their parents' generation had. The alternative was to push larger numbers of working-age youths to leave Zimbabwe, mostly for work in South Africa (Potts 2010; Musoni 2020). For those who remained, the informal sector, and just being able to get by with their wits (i.e. kukiyakiya), became a fact of life (Jones 2010). School fees were difficult to attain, and for the most part only those who had access to foreign exchange from remittances or involvement in cross-border trade were able to continue school during the worst of the economic crisis leading up to 2008.

Overlapping with the economic crisis was a political campaign by the ruling party to remove urban youth and their families from their homes after the 2005 elections. In what seemed to be an act of punishment for urban voters continued support for the opposition. The ruling party began Operation Murambatsvina (remove the filth), in which, by the estimates of the 2005 UN investigation, 750,000 people were removed from urban areas and unceremoniously dumped in satellite areas outside of the city (Tibaijuka 2005; Potts 2006; Musoni 2010).

Many street children were rounded up and transferred to transit camps or overcrowded centres for delinquents. Tibaijuka (2005: 36) noted with concern that 'these youth centres are generally unable to provide adequate care, support and follow-up assistance for street children'. Other 'highly vulnerable children, including orphans as well as children with disabilities or HIV, and those with special needs, were generally disregarded by the authorities during the Operation' (ibid.: 42).

There was a brief reprieve for urban youths during the tenure of the Government of National Unity (GNU) starting in 2009 (Mukuhlani 2014: 172-3). Many youths share fond memories of being able to buy their first cars at this time. Some even paid *lobola* (bride-price) and got married. We must, however, immediately caution that the gains did not trickle down evenly to all youths. The main beneficiaries were those in formal employment who could access salary-based-loans. However, banks were hesitant to extend loans without collateral, so the benefits did not extend to youths in the informal sector. This amounted to a double tragedy. The prolonged economic downturn starting in the late 1980s effectively meant that successive streams of youths had been unable to access new housing stock. This put many young adults at a distinct disadvantage compared to their parents who had been able to advance in life based on owning a house that they could leverage as security to access mortgages.

Regrettably, the growth trends registered from 2009 to 2012 came to a screeching halt in 2013 at the end of the GNU. The economy went into reverse and by the end of the year state revenues were in decline and the banking sector was once again in crisis and unable to pay back its depositors. With this, the hopes and aspirations of many urban youths were also punctured. But that was not the end of it. The new government of Emerson Mnangagwa ushered in by a soft coup that deposed Robert Mugabe in November 2017 inexplicably decided to de-dollarise against expert advice and without satisfying any of the economic fundamentals to reintroduce the Zimbabwean currency.18 Indeed, in no time hyperinflation and a liquidity crunch ensued (Nyamunda 2021).

In the 2010s, 'straddling' strategies re-emerged, when some urban

---

18 'Zim's dollar returns, a decade after it became worthless', Fin 24, 24 June 2019.

families sent younger people to claim land in the Fast Track Land Reform Programme as a way to access additional sources of income (Thebe 2018). These strategies were certainly not new and hark back to colonial times. In the 1980s, most urban families still had strong rural linkages and connections, reinforced through circular migration (Potts 2010). However, over time these linkages began to weaken, such that the wealthier youths had weak or no rural ties as they entrenched themselves in urban options. Nevertheless, as urban poverty intensified, the poorer urbanites reverted to rural affiliations as part of their survival strategies.

Tamba Wakachenjera: Youths and urban violence

Another trend that was heightened in the 2000s was the reliance on ruling party youths to intimidate by violence and threats before, during, and after elections. The so-called 'Green Bombers' became notorious for violence against the opposition, without any recourse for justice by victims of the violence (Kriger 2005; SPT 2003). The ruling party's youth brigades took over houses in HDAs and used them to torture youths suspected of working for, or supporting, the opposition. The MDC youths had their own defence structure, but they were not sufficient to match the combination of ZANU-PF youth operating with the approval of the security forces (Wilkins 2013; Alexander 2010).

Besides violence, ZANU-PF deployed 'political nicknaming' as a strategy to portray the opposition as enemies of the nation, while simultaneously claiming hegemonic control and legitimacy (Nyambi 2018; Nyambi 2017). ZANU-PF party officials began to use the term 'born free' pejoratively to refer to the generation born after independence, accusing them of taking independence for granted while undermining the liberation struggle and its fighters (Mate 2012: 109). Scarnecchia (2012) has also shown that by continuing to label opponents as 'sell-outs' ZANU-PF perpetuated particular styles of political violence. Sadly, this labelling took a xenophobic turn in 2002 when the country's President singled out and castigated the residents of Mbare – which has a large population with Malawian and Mozambican heritage – as comprising 'undisciplined, totem-less elements'.[19]

---

19 'Zanu PF accused of tribalism', *The Daily News*, 14 October 2002. The qualification in the Shona lexicon when one is labelled as 'totemless' is that he is incomplete since he lacks a rural origin. For a fuller discussion of Malawians living in Harare, see Groves (2020).

All of these trends meant that there was a need for the youth to *tamba wakachenjera* (i.e. play it carefully). The political violence of the elections in 2002, 2005 and, especially, 2008 meant that youths in some HDAs were faced with a difficult choice: either work for the ruling party and receive some short-term economic benefits, often access to peri-urban land or housing, or become part of the opposition and face potential beatings and arrest for supporting the MDC. This use of violence led to the realisation among those participating in these brigades that they could continue to use their power to create a mafia-style extortion and protection racket. After the violence of 2008, a new development was the rise of the *Chipangano* in Harare, a youth gang that used violence, and their connections to local ZANU-PF MPs, to build a new economic force.

From Urban Grooves to Zim Dancehall

There was, however, simultaneously a more creative use of youth power in urban music, the 'urban grooves'[20] style of music that began to develop in the 2000s, which helped to not only express an urban counter-culture ethos to a wider audience but also produce a new form of entrepreneurial enterprise that worked against the limits of formal employment. This music also gave Zimbabwean urban youths a way to show pride in their own ability to survive in environments where opportunities are infrequent. Some pioneering urban grooves stars include David Chifunyise, Tererai Mugwadi, Plaxedes Wenyika, Ex Q, and Rocqui (Muzari 2015). The emergence of urban grooves corresponds with the enactment of new media laws such as the Broadcasting Services Act in 2001, which promulgated 75% local content on Zimbabwean radio and TV (Chikowero 2008). Mate (2012: 111) correctly noted that the 'imposition of the local content quota ...gave birth to the urban grooves genre as broadcasters scrambled for local content and talent'. However, there was a 'pre-urban grooves movement' in the early 1990s, which fused western-inspired music with local sounds by artists like Edwin Hama, Prince Tendai, and Fortune Muparutsa (Bere 2008: 109).

Initially, as Manase (2009: 56-57) shows, the emerging Zimbabwean urban grooves artists infused vernacular lyrics in their music as a

---

20 Zimbabwean 'urban grooves' is an umbrella term that refers to Zimbabwean musical outfits that gained prominence during the post-2000 decade. The urban grooves movement drew its musical influences from American hip hop, rhythm and blues, and Jamaican reggae/dancehall beats. See Mateveke (2014).

performance practice that affirmed government expectations that artists sing in local languages. Many of the first artists to embrace the genre were children of senior government bureaucrats and came from well-to-do families. Perhaps inadvertently, these artists advanced the ruling party's 'anti-western cultural imperialism campaign' (Tivenga 2018: 201).

However, around 2010, a cultural turn occurred as a grittier and more organic sub-genre emerged from the urban ghettoes of Mbare, Dzivarasekwa, Budiriro, and elsewhere (Kufakurinani and Mwatwara 2017). Regardless of not getting official airplay this music still found wide circulation as some of the artists distributed their music through their established social networks, on public transport, and through social media. Some of the artists, such as Killer T and Hwindi President, were even public transport conductors. This emerging sub-genre, dubbed Zimdancehall, found wide appeal because it 'expose[d] the bleak lived experiences of the people who live in the "ghetto"' (Tivenga 2018: 157). As in cities all over the world, a much larger audience consumed the music of the 'ghetto', including those in the wealthier suburbs, because it represented youth and a Zimbabwean identity. Perhaps there is nothing particularly new about the consumption of urban music as a source of pride and identity. However, such music also speaks to the limits of mobility and place, in a country where the precariousness of property rights and a lack of viable alternatives continues to recreate the same associations with urban spaces that have been relatively consistent for Zimbabwean youth over the past forty years.

Urban youth activism and social movements

Following the successive electoral losses that the MDC suffered in the 2000s, the participation of youths in traditional political processes began to dwindle. Statistics from the Zimbabwe Electoral Commission in 2018 suggested that out of 5.69 million registered voters, only 44% were between 18 and 34 years.[21] This was even more problematic considering that young people constituted up to 67.7% of the population at this time (ZESN 2018: 1). This reflects the youths' inability to harness their demographic dividend and influence state and community outcomes. A study by the Youth Empowerment and Transformation

---

21   'Low Youth Participation – A Ticking Time Bomb for Zimbabwe's Future', Future Africa Forum, 18 January 2019.

Trust in 2017 revealed that 'youths from the marginalized provinces of Bulawayo, Matabeleland North and South were less enthusiastic about voting in the upcoming 2018 elections' (YETT 2017: 7). Hence, the 'self-exclusion' of youths also had undertones of grievances around long-running regional disparities as well as the unresolved atrocities from the 1980s.

While urban youths disengaged from national politics, they did not disengage from social affairs. Instead, they opted to participate in alternative spaces, including voluntary associations such as social clubs and community associations like sports, drama, and dance clubs, some of which were sponsored by non-governmental organisations. They also socialised in youth clubs in church, where they found fellowship and support.[22] However, just as in the late 1990s, 'many of [the clubs] never grew into something because of corruption … people [used] money [meant] to sponsor clubs for their personal use … and the sponsorship would just stop'.[23]

The advent of social media and ICTs significantly changed the political and socio-economic realities of many urban youths. As such, new urban protest movements that involved large numbers of young people emerged, particularly in the post-2013 elections period. Social media platforms (SMPs) allowed urban youths and activists to sidestep the often restrictive spaces controlled by the state while also engaging in street protests. Some of the most prominent movements included #ThisFlag, #Tajamuka, and #ThisGown (Gukurume 2017). Young people frustrated with the mounting economic crisis, declining employment opportunities, worsening cases of corruption, and growing cases of police brutality against vendors and protestors led and initiated these movements (ibid.).

Urban youths also turned to the arts and cultural expressions using SMPs in multiple and creative ways. Spoken Word poets including Abel Mauchi and 'General Fire Colosso' began to post spoken word videos.[24] These reached a wide audience, and most of them contained messages that resonated clearly with the concerns of the youth. Youth-led YouTube TV channels such as Bustop TV and Magamba TV produced

---

22 WhatsApp Voice note from Melody Moyo, a resident of Mabutweni in Bulawayo (12 February 2021).

23 Ibid.

24 https://www.youtube.com/channel/UCFIIsJg10DtxcrBUEvFGFiQ/

political satire and comedy, which often carried a social justice or public awareness message.[25] Two former University of Zimbabwe students, 'Comrade' Treasure Basopo and 'Brother' Nqobizitha Mlambo, created a YouTube platform where they engaged in passionate and fervent conversations as 'revolutionary intellectuals' on the issues that they felt were affecting the country's youths.[26] Urban youths reclaimed political space on SMPs and any serious engagement of this demographic had to occur on these platforms.

Conclusion

This chapter has focused on the urban experiences of youths in Zimbabwe's first forty years. The emphasis has been on the structural constraints of the urban landscape, and how urban youths managed to operate within these constraints. There is a temptation to talk about resilience here in a somewhat patronising way. However, if we consider resilience to mean the capacity to maintain institutions, or livelihoods, in the face of multiple crises, then it would seem fitting as a description of what Zimbabwe's urban youths have managed after so many crises. While acknowledging the vast racial and wealth differences in urban Zimbabwe, this chapter notes that there were periods of mobility that allowed talented youths to use education and their own creativeness to transform their lives and those of their families. Still, even with these success stories, each new cohort of youths in Zimbabwean cities faced new obstacles, often insurmountable, as poor governance, political violence, and the implosion of the economy, especially after 2000, which blocked the avenues for respectable class mobility. From these waves of crises, however, new generations of youths have at times been on the frontlines of national politics, and at other times have retreated from the violence to express their culture in music and other cultural outlets. The current situation, some 41 years since Independence, seems frustratingly fractured from the standpoint of older models of mass politics and protest. However, if we focus on the cultural output of urban youths in new forms of music and social media, there is some optimism that Zimbabwe's urban youths have found new ways to negotiate the spatial divides that have historically kept them from finding common ground.

---

25 https://www.youtube.com/c/MagambaTV/ ; https://www.youtube.com/c/BUSTOPTV/

26 https://www.youtube.com/channel/UCTgX4irS5bhC372mT6M6F5g/

References

Alexander, J. (2010) 'The political imaginaries and social lives of political prisoners in post-2000 Zimbabwe', *Journal of Southern African Studies*, 36(2), pp. 483-503.

Alexander, P. (2000) 'Zimbabwean Workers, the MDC & the 2000 Election', *Review of African Political Economy*, 27(85), pp. 385-406.

Auret, D. (1995) *Urban Housing: A National Crisis?* Gweru: Mambo Press.

Barnes, T. (1999) *"We Women Worked so Hard": Gender, Urbanisation, and Social Reproduction in Colonial Harare, Zimbabwe, 1930-1956.* Harare: Baobab Books.

Bassett, M.T. and M. Mhloyi (1991) 'Women and Aids in Zimbabwe: The Making of an Epidemic', *International Journal of Health Services*, 21(1), pp. 143-156.

Bere, W.G. (2008) 'Urban Grooves: The Performance of Politics in Zimbabwe's Hip Hop Music'. PhD thesis, New York University.

Bird, K. and M. Prowse (2009) 'Vulnerability, poverty and coping in Zimbabwe'. Working Paper 136. Chronic Poverty Research Centre.

Catholic Commission for Justice and Peace in Zimbabwe (CCJPZ) and Legal Resources Foundation (LRF) (1997) *Breaking the Silence, Building True Peace: A Report on the Disturbances in Matabeleland and the Midlands, 1980 to 1988.* Harare: CCJPZ and LRF.

Chikowero, M. (2008) 'Struggles Over Culture: Zimbabwean Music and Power, 1930s-2007'. PhD thesis, Dalhousie University.

Chirozva, C., C.P. Mubaya and B. Mukamuri (2007) 'The traditional African family in the age of globalization', *Journal of African Studies*, 14(2), pp. 1-16.

Ciganda, D., A. Gagnon and E.Y. Tenkorang (2012) 'Child and young adult-headed households in the context of the AIDS epidemic in Zimbabwe, 1988-2006', *AIDS Care*, 24(10), pp. 1211-1218.

Dambudzo, I. (1979) 'A Social-Economic Survey of Zengeza'. BA dissertation, University of Rhodesia.

Foster, G., C. Makufa, R. Drew and E. Kralovec (1997) 'Factors leading to the establishment of child-headed households: the case of Zimbabwe', *Health Transition Review*, 7(2), pp. 155-168.

Government of Zimbabwe (GoZ) (1992) 'Census 1992: Zimbabwe Preliminary Report'. Harare: Government Printer.

—— (1985) 'Budget Statement'. Harare: Ministry of Finance and Economic Development.

Grant, M. (2003) 'Difficult Debut: Social and Economic Identities of Urban Youth in Bulawayo, Zimbabwe', *Canadian Journal of African Studies*, 37(2-3), pp. 411-439.

Groves, Z.R. (2020) *Malawian Migration to Zimbabwe, 1900-1965: Tracing Machona*. Basingstoke: Palgrave Macmillan.

Gukurume, S. (2017) '#ThisFlag and #ThisGown Cyber Protests in Zimbabwe: Reclaiming Political Space', *African Journalism Studies*, 38(2), pp. 49-70.

Gwatirisa, P. and L. Manderson (2009) 'Food Insecurity and HIV/AIDS in Low-income Households in Urban Zimbabwe', *Human Organization*, 68(1), pp. 103-112.

Huchu, T. (2010) *The Hairdresser of Harare*. Harare: Weaver Press.

Jones, J. (2010) '"Nothing is straight in Zimbabwe": The Rise of *Kukiyakiya* Economy, 2000-2008', *Journal of Southern African Studies*, 36(2), pp. 285-299.

Kay, G. (1971) 'Distribution and Density of African Population in Rhodesia'. Miscellaneous Series No. 12, University of Hull.

Kriger, N. (2005) 'ZANU(PF) Strategies in General Elections, 1980-2000: Discourse and Coercion', *African Affairs*, 104(414), pp. 1-34.

Kufakurinani, U. and W. Mwatwara (2017) 'Zimdancehall and the Peace Crisis in Zimbabwe', *African Conflict and Peace Building Review*, 7(1), pp. 33-50.

Kufakurinani, U., D. Pasura and J. McGregor (2014) 'Transnational Parenting and the Emergence of "Diaspora Orphans" in Zimbabwe', *African Diaspora*, 7(1), pp. 114–138.

Kurebwa, J. and N.Y. Gatsi Kurebwa (2014) 'Coping Strategies of Child-Headed Households in Bindura Urban of Zimbabwe', *International Journal of Innovative Research & Development*, 3(11), pp. 236-249.

Makombe, E.K. and I. Mhike (2018) 'The influence of the State and Patriarchy on Gendered Migration in Zimbabwe', *Zambezia*, 45(i), pp. 100-120.

Makuyana, A., S.P. Mbulayi and S.M. Kangethe (2020) 'Psychosocial deficits underpinning child-headed households (CHHs) in Mabvuku and Tafara suburbs of Harare, Zimbabwe', *Children and Youth Services Review*, 115, pp. 1-6.

Manase, I. (2009) 'Zimbabwean urban grooves and their subversive performance practices', *Social Dynamics*, 35(1), pp. 56-67.

Mapira, J. (2011) 'Urban Governance and Mismanagement: An Environmental Crisis in Zimbabwe', *Journal of Sustainable Development in Africa*, 13(6), pp. 258-267.

Mate, R. (2012) 'Youth Lyrics, Street Language and the Politics of Age: Contextualising the Youth Question in the Third Chimurenga in Zimbabwe', *Journal of Southern African Studies*, 38(1), pp. 107-127.

———— (2014) 'Grappling with Emerging Adulthoods: Youth Narratives of Coming of Age in a Frontier Town, Zimbabwe'. PhD thesis, Erasmus University Rotterdam.

Mateveke, P. (2014) 'Stunning the Nation: Representation of Zimbabwean urban youth identity in some songs by Stunner', *Journal of Hip Hop Studies*, 1(2), pp. 212-225.

Mhike, I., E.K. Makombe and N. Chimhete (2018) 'State Social Engineering, Youth Citizenship, and Social Protection in Zimbabwe, c. 1929-2013', *Zambezia*, 45(ii).

Mlambo, A. (1997) *The Economic Structural Adjustment Programme: The Case of Zimbabwe 1990-1995*. Harare: University of Zimbabwe Publications.

Mugurungi, O., S. Gregson, A.D. McNaghten, S. Dube and N.C. Grassly (2007) 'HIV in Zimbabwe 1985-2003: Measurement, Trends and Impact', in M. Caraël and J.R. Glynn (eds), *HIV, Resurgent Infections and Population Change in Africa*. Dordrecht: Springer.

Mukuhlani, T. (2014) 'Zimbabwe's Government of National Unity: Successes and Challenges in Restoring Peace and Order', *Journal of Power, Politics & Governance*, (2)2, pp. 169-180.

Mungoshi, C. (1980) 'Some Kinds of Wounds', in *Some Kinds of Wounds and Other Short Stories*. Gweru: Mambo Press.

Murisa, T. (2010) 'Social Development in Zimbabwe'. Discussion Paper prepared for the Development Foundation for Zimbabwe.

Musoni, F. (2010) 'Operation Murambatsvina and the Politics of Street

Vendors in Zimbabwe', *Journal of Southern African Studies,* 36(2), pp. 301-317.

———— (2020) *Border Jumping and Migration Control in Southern Africa.* Bloomington: Indiana University Press.

Ncube, W. (1998) *Law, Culture, Tradition and Children's Rights in Eastern and Southern Africa.* Brookfield, VT: Ashgate.

———— J. Stewart, J. Kazembe, B. Donzwa, E. Gwaunza, T. Nzira and K. Dengu-Zvobgo (1997) 'Continuity and Change: The Family in Zimbabwe'. Harare: Women and Law in Southern Africa Research Trust.

Nyambi, O. (2017) '"The Blair that I know is a toilet": political nicknames and hegemonic control in post-2000 Zimbabwe', *African Identities,* 15(2), pp. 143-158.

———— (2018) 'Of Bob, *Madzibaba* Gabriel, and Goblins: The Sociopolitics of Name-Calling and Nicknaming Mugabe in Post-2000 Zimbabwe', *SAGE Open,* 1-11.

Nyamunda, T. (2021) '"Open for Business" but Bankrupt: Currencies, the "New Dispensation" and the Zimbabwean Economy', *Journal of Asian and African Studies,* 56(2), pp. 204-217.

Potts, D. (2006) '"Restoring Order"? Operation Murambatsvina and the Urban Crisis in Zimbabwe', *Journal of Southern African Studies,* 32(2), pp. 273-291.

———— (2010) *Circular Migration in Zimbabwe and Contemporary Sub-Saharan Africa.* Oxford: James Currey.

Raftopoulos, B., T. Hawkins and D. Amanor-Wilks (1998) 'Human Development Report: Zimbabwe'. Harare: UNDP.

Rubin, D. (1997) *The World Encyclopedia of Contemporary Theatre: Africa.* Abingdon: Routledge.

Rwezaura, B., A. Armstrong, W. Ncube, J. Stewart, P. Letuka, P. Musanya, I. Casimiro, and M. Mamashela (1995) 'Parting the Long Grass: Revealing and Reconceptualising the African Family'. Harare: Women and Law in Southern Africa Research Trust,

Sambisa, W. and C.S. Stoke (2006) 'Rural/Urban Residence, Migration, HIV/AIDS, and Safe Sex Practices among Men in Zimbabwe', *Rural Sociology,* 71(2), pp. 183-211.

Scarnecchia, T. (2012) 'The "sellout logic" in the formation of Zimbabwean nationalist politics, 1961-1964', in S. Chiumbu and M. Musemwa (eds) *Crisis! What Crisis? The Multiple Dimensions of the Zimbabwean Crisis*. Cape Town: HSRC Press.

Schlyter, A. (2006) 'Esther's House: One Woman's "Home Economics" in Chitungwiza, Zimbabwe', in D.F. Bryceson and D. Potts (eds), *African Urban Economies*. Basingstoke: Palgrave Macmillan.

Thebe, V. (2018) 'Youth, agriculture and land reform in Zimbabwe: Experiences from a communal area and resettlement scheme in semi-arid Matabeleland, Zimbabwe', *African Studies,* 77(3), pp. 336-353.

Tibaijuka, A.K. (2005) 'Report of the Fact-Finding Mission to Zimbabwe to assess the Scope and Impact of Operation Murambatsvina by the UN Special Envoy on Human Settlements Issues in Zimbabwe'. New York: UNHCS Habitat.

Tivenga, D.R. (2018) 'Zimbabwe Urban Grooves Music and the Interconnections between Youth Identities and Celebrity Culture'. PhD thesis, University of the Free State.

Wild, V. (1992) 'An Outline of African Business History in Colonial Zimbabwe', *Zambezia*, XIX(1), pp. 19-46.

Wilkins, S. (2013) 'Ndira's Wake: Politics, Memory, and Mobility among the Youth of Mabvuku-Tafara, Harare', *Journal of Southern African Studies*, 39(4), pp. 885-901.

Whitsun Foundation (1978) 'Strategy for Rural Development and Whitsun data bank No. 2: The Peasant Sector'. Harare: Whitsun Foundation.

Yoshikuni, T. (2007) *African Urban Experiences in Colonial Zimbabwe: A Social History of Harare before 1925*. Harare: Weaver Press.

Youth Empowerment and Transformation Trust (YETT) (2017) 'Assessment of Issues Influencing Youth Participation in Elections and Decision Making in Zimbabwe'. Harare: YETT.

Zeilig, L. (2006) '"Increasing my value proposition to the struggle": Arthur Mutambara and student politics in Zimbabwe', *African Sociological Review*, 10(2), pp. 94-115.

———— (2008) 'Student Politics and Activism in Zimbabwe: The Frustrated Transition', *Journal of Asian and African Studies*, 43(2), pp. 215-237.

Zimbabwe Election Support Network (ZESN) (2018) 'Position paper: Youth Participation in Governance Process: The Case of Zimbabwe Executive Summary'. Harare: ZESN.

Zvobgo, R.J. (1999) *The Post-Colonial State and Educational Reform: Zimbabwe, Zambia, and Botswana.* Harare: Zimbabwe Publishing House.

8

'Youth Politics'

Marjoke Oosterom and Simbarashe Gukurume

Introduction

This chapter analyses the relationship between Zimbabweans and the
ZANU-PF regime since independence, and the different avenues that
young people have used for political engagement. Many leaders of the
liberation struggle were young themselves at the time and the struggle
was supported by the *vakomana* (Kriger 1992). The chapter explains
how younger generations developed a rather contentious relationship
with the post-independence regime, which largely failed to generate
prosperity and opportunities for the 'born free' generation (Mate 2012).
This tension is not unique to Zimbabwe: other African countries that
have witnessed liberation struggles have also experienced tensions
between the rulers and youth populations (Reuss and Titeca 2017;
Southall 2019).

The question of 'youth politics' is understood as the various ways
in which young people in Zimbabwe have expressed and organised
themselves politically to engage, inform or challenge the ZANU-PF
regime. Rather than focusing on youth active in the youth wings or
assemblies of political parties, or violent youth militias, the chapter
focuses on other forms of political engagement. The ways in which
young people have expressed themselves needs to be understood within

the context of a regime that developed repressive tendencies towards those that oppose it, and clientelist relationships with others. The chapter will argue that, within a de facto context of limited political and civic space, young Zimbabweans have increasingly adopted informal forms of politics, while formal youth civil society is working hard to navigate the closing civic space. The chapter focuses on different arenas of youth politics: one is the arena of formal civil society and student organisations; the other is the informal realm of popular culture and online and street mobilisation. Building on previous chapters, this chapter concentrates on recent history between 2000 and 2020 and ends with youth engagement under the 'new dispensation' after the November 2017 coup that led to the ousting of President Robert Mugabe.

The chapter is structured as follows. The first section discusses the broader relationship between liberation regimes and youth populations, as well as key insights from the debate on civic space. The existing scholarship on civic space is helpful in understanding the dynamics and contestation between the ZANU-PF regime and the country's young population, as young people have been politically active in civil society in ways that have been considered oppositional action by the regime. The next section outlines the shortcomings of Zimbabwe's formal political youth institutions. Subsequent sections analyse the developments in youth civil society, student politics, popular culture and (online) informal urban youth movements.

State-youth relationships in contexts of limited civic space

As in many African countries, the 'youth' now constitute the majority of the population in Zimbabwe, a country that stretched the upper limit of the youth age bracket to 35. Zimbabweans born after 1980 grew up with President Robert Mugabe and 'Mugabeism' until the November 2017 coup. In the early days of independence, they witnessed investments in their education and could identify themselves with government plans (Hodgkinson 2013). Forty years on, this sentiment has changed dramatically. In African countries where governments have emerged as the winning parties in a liberation struggle, such as Mozambique, Uganda, Ethiopia, and also in post-apartheid South Africa, younger generations have grown frustrated with their governments (Mattes 2012; Oyedemi and Mahlatji 2016; Reuss and Titeca 2103; Southall 2019).

They need to cope with poverty and unemployment, they feel frustrated about leaders and political parties, and the length of incumbency of ruling parties has been found as a major deterrent to voting (Resnick and Casale 2014). Aware that large urban youth populations are a potential source of protest, and therefore unrest and potential threat to power, regimes have taken pre-emptive, repressive actions (Nordas and Davenport 2013).

The fact that young Zimbabweans born after 1980 are labelled 'born frees' (those who have not experienced colonialism) is not a mere chronological fact. Being a 'born free' is a deeply political construct: it entwined with the ZANU-PF claim to power based on its liberation victory and its rhetoric that 'born-free' youth no longer respected this claim (Mate 2012; Ndlovu-Gatsheni and Willems 2009; Oosterom and Gukurume 2019). The label 'born-free' became a discursive tactic in the early 2000s when ZANU-PF was first challenged by the Movement for Democratic Change (MDC); a party that attracted many young urban voters. Many young Zimbabweans challenged the liberation narrative of the ZANU-PF government, because they were not living the promise of the liberation due to the successive economic crises (Mate 2012; Oosterom 2019a). In a highly polarised political environment, the concept of 'youth' has become inherently political, with youth often being understood as 'mobilised youth' who are active for the ruling party or the opposition – although this intrinsically assumes *male* youth (Oosterom and Pswarayi 2014; Oosterom 2019a; Wilkins 2013).

The ZANU-PF regime recognises the youth as both a constituency and a potential opposition force. The ways in which youth politics have developed in this context can be understood using insights from wider debates on closing civic space (Carothers and Brechenmacher 2014; Hossain et al. 2018; Van der Borgh and Terwindt 2014). This scholarship has emphasised both the legal restrictions on civic organisations and informal tactics of intimidation and violence, and delegitimation (Brechenmacher 2017; Dupuy and Prakash 2017). Strategies of clientelism and co-optation have been widely recognised in studies of civic space and scholarship on authoritarianism (Goodfellow and Jackson 2020; Carothers and Brechenmacher 2014; Hossain et al. 2018). A combination of these strategies has been deployed in Zimbabwe for civil society and media actors (Dorman 2002, 2003, 2016).

The chapter will discuss how the ZANU-PF regime has indeed

clamped down severely on activist youth and student organisations using formal legislation and violence and intimidation, as part of its wider clampdown on civil society. Reflecting the broader trend of the regime to consolidate its power by using ruling party patronage networks to distribute resources (Alexander and McGregor, 2013; Kriger 2012; McGregor 2013), ZANU-PF is also trying to incorporate the youth into partisan, clientelist relationships by promising them access to resources like youth funds and opportunities in the informal economy (Maringira and Gukurume 2020; Oosterom and Gukurume 2019). The following section will demonstrate how the Zimbabwe Youth Council is a compromised, co-opted institution for youth politics and will reflect on some of the mechanisms for youth participation that were initiated in 2020. The chapter will then continue with an analysis of youth civil society, student politics and informal politics and how this has developed in a context of limited civic space.

The Zimbabwe Youth Council

The Zimbabwe Youth Council (ZYC) was established in 1997 and is a quasi-government body that should function as central communication channel between the government and youth civil society. The ZYC registers all youth organisations, including youth civil society. In the same vein, ministries can also distribute youth-earmarked programme funds to ZYC, which it can allocate to member organisations. ZYC is meant to facilitate the interaction between youth and the ministry responsible for youth affairs and inform youth policy, but it has largely failed to play such a representative role as it is largely dominated by ZANU-PF politics. Such dynamics are not unique to Zimbabwe, as National Youth Councils globally rarely get involved in real decision-making processes by government actors: their recommendations are ignored; they 'lack teeth' (CEPPS 2019; Bangura and Specht 2012; McGee and Greenhalf 2011: 31); and their functioning is often undermined by elite capture, partisan patronage, and political divisions among youth organisations (Cubitt 2012; Oosterom et al. 2019).

The ZYC started out as a desk in the ZANU-PF headquarters and became a separate entity under the GPA, after youth civil society had pressed for it to become more independent.[1] It has elected and

---

1   Interview, former youth civil society activist, 7 October 2020.

appointed members, which paves the way for partisan appointments.[2] Indeed, many critics view the ZYC as an arm and extension of ZANU-PF, functioning and acting to protect the interests of the ruling party. Consequently, many in youth civil society aligned with the opposition hardly participate in, or benefit from, ZYC youth programmes and funding. Youth in civil society have criticised the ZYC for being undemocratic and 'old', and for becoming politicised.[3] In 2015, ZANU-PF was accused of meddling with ZYC elections as all elected ZYC board members were known ZANU-PF activists, a reflection of ZANU-PF reaffirming its grip on all state institutions following the 2013 elections.[4] The ZYC has been accused of allocating youth funds along partisan lines.[5] Critics stated that funds were channelled to ZANU-PF members, who did not pay back revolving funds as they considered it a gift in their client relationship to the party.[6]

As factionalism intensified after 2013, fractures appeared within the ZYC. Accusations of corruption that emerged in late 2016 may have been fuelled by factionalism, as the ZYC stood with Jonathan Moyo, a prominent ZANU-PF politician and leading G40 member.[7] Since 2013, however, funds allocated to the ZYC have been limited, which negatively affected its influence. While it is acknowledged that some ZYC members genuinely aim to be non-partisan and work for all young Zimbabweans, the ZYC is essentially under control of the ZANU-PF government.[8]

In 2020, efforts were underway to formalise more avenues for youth political participation. The ZYC claimed it played a key advocacy role in promoting youth political economic empowerment and the Constitutional Amendment Bill No.2 on youth quotas. However, in civil society, critics centred on this quota system being a top-down and tokenistic approach.[9] In September 2020, the Zimbabwe Youth

2   'Govt announces youth board', *The Herald*, 3 August 2016.

3   'Youths call on leaders to end tyranny', *NewsDay*, 1 March 2019; 'Youth up in arms against ZYC', *NewsDay*, 9 July 2019.

4   'ZANU PF grabs Youth Council seats', *NewsDay*, 31 August 2015.

5   'Parly threatens to charge Youth Council', *NewsDay*, 2 December 2016; 'ZYC boss probed over $17 650 donation', *NewsDay*, 12 May 2016.

6   Interview, former youth civil society activist, 7 October 2020.

7   'ZYC stands by embattled Moyo', *NewsDay*, 13 October 2016.

8   Interview, MDC youth member, 20 March 2020.

9   'Youth say No to Constitution Amendment Number 2 Bill', *Kubatana*, 29 June 2020.

Bill was adopted that provides for youth focal desks in all government ministries and departments.[10] While youth desks have existed in name since 2017, they remained inactive.[11] The youth desk in the Ministry of Agriculture now looks after a number of programmes, but others are largely dormant and underfunded. Some civil society representatives view the youth desks as an extension of ZANU-PF and a way of co-opting youth into ZANU-PF patronage networks, similar to the ZYC; others regard it as a tokenistic measure. Thus, in this given context, the existing formal political institutions for youth engagement are largely dysfunctional. Those who choose not to use ZANU-PF networks need to find alternative means of engagement. The next section discusses formal civil society as an arena of engagement and contestation.

Youth civil society

Apart from student associations, little is documented about the activities of an independent youth civil society during the first two decades of independence. Dorman's work (2002, 2016) on churches and civil society, especially NGOs, has shown how the overall tendency was to collaborate with the ZANU-PF government in the 1980s, sometimes to the extent of being co-opted. Youth mobilising only became visible in large-scale student protests from the late 1980s, which we elaborate in detail in the next section. Also, for the 1990s, literature on youth mobilising is restricted to student activism, with the broader literature on civil society focusing on organised labour movements (Sachikonye 1995; Raftopoulos 1992). Children and youth are mainly portrayed as 'receivers' of aid in the context of, for instance, education, rather than as active citizens, despite the increasing funding for civil society for democratisation that was popular in the 1990s.

As the political crisis deepened in the 2000s, restrictive laws such as the Access to Information and Protection of Privacy Act (AIPPA) and Public Order and Security Act (POSA) restricted the freedom of expression and activities of youth civil society as much as other CSOs. Prominent youth activists in civil society and the MDC were targeted by intimidation. Indeed, the years 2000 and 2008 were particularly hard for civil society and opposition activists. Over the years, both AIPPA

---

10 Principles of the proposed Zimbabwe Youth Bill, *Harare Live*, 2 September 2020.

11 'Government launches youth focal desks in all ministries', *NewsDay*, 2 October 2017.

and POSA have been invoked to clamp down on dissenting voices, including student activists and members of the MDC's youth wing (Dorman 2016); civic space was shrinking, and civil liberties were severely constrained, including for youth organisations that became outspoken about contentious political issues.

Civic space opened up between 2009 and 2013, as civil society was able to engage the Government of National Unity – in particular MDC-controlled ministries – on democratic reforms. The main agenda issues were the participation of young females in politics and reconciliation processes. However, in January 2013, the government tabled a law that required all youth organisations to register with the ZYC, making it compulsory to pay fees, submit annual reports and renew registration annually; this was perceived as a tactic to control youth civil society ahead of the referendum on the new Constitution and the 2013 elections.[12] Several youth organisations started a court case to challenge this move, and the bill was not passed into law.[13] Yet, thanks to the relative openness of civic space at the time, youth civil society actors were able to go into urban *and* rural areas for the 'First Time Voters' Campaign to persuade young people to vote in 2013.

After ZANU-PF had won the 2013 elections, many youth organisations were disillusioned: 'We had to go back to the drawing board', said one former activist.[14] Eventually they came to terms with having to work with the new reality and started engaging the ZANU-PF government. It was possible to engage on 'soft issues' (e.g. sanitary products) while 'hard governance issues' received no traction with the Parliamentary Portfolio Committee on Youth. Civic space was again closing, but through administrative hurdles rather than overt coercion. At district level, civil society organisations were facing bureaucratic barriers to implement their programmes in rural areas, with police and district offices scrutinising activity plans (Oosterom 2019b). Factionalism in ZANU-PF was shaping operations on the ground. One respondent narrated how her organisation planned to start working in a certain district, but because this was a stronghold of a G40 member they had to relocate elsewhere to avoid being seen

---

12 'Zimbabwe Introduces Tough Regulations Targeting Youth Groups', *VOA*, 5 February 2013.

13 'Youth groups slam statutory instrument', *Daily News*, 1 May 2013.

14 Interview, former youth activist, 15 October 2020.

as supporting this faction.[15]

Initial hopes about prospects of political change faded soon after the 2018 elections, especially because of the post-election violence on 1 August 2018 and the even more severe violent crackdown on protestors in January 2019 (Beardsworth et al. 2019; Helliker and Murisa 2020). It was a clear sign that the Mnangagwa government would not tolerate protest as an avenue for voicing discontent, and targeted violent has since increased (UNOCHR 2020). In spite of promises to repeal them, AIPPA and POSA have not been amended to align with the 2013 Constitution, thus limiting the political freedoms of youth CSOs. Nonetheless, youth-led civil society organisations have been outspoken about their grievances against the state. For instance, the National Association of Youth Organisations bemoaned the dwindling civic space in the 'new dispensation',[16] expressing concern about the concerted crackdown on youth-led CSOs perceived to be critical to the state. The lockdown that was enforced in response to the covid-19 pandemic in 2020 was soon used to quell political organising. Three prominent young MDC-A activists, among them MP Joana Mamombe, were allegedly abducted and tortured when they had called for a protest, and a list of activists, many of them youth, was leaked by state security.[17]

Student organisations

Many young people have launched their political careers through student organisations and student unions. Indeed, many youthful politicians from the MDC had been active members of the Zimbabwe National Students Union (ZINASU): the current MDC president Nelson Chamisa was once the its secretary general, and former MDC Member of Parliament Learnmore Judah Jongwe was its president. This section explains how student organising became increasingly linked to anti-corruption and pro-democracy struggles.

In the early 1980s, students had a cordial relationship with the government and were supportive of the government's socialist-welfarist approach. From 1980, the government heavily subsidised tertiary education and paid stipends to all tertiary university students. It initiated student grants, and tuition fee waivers for many students . The

---

15 Interview, civil society activist, 28 October 2020.

16 'Youth Worry over Shrinking Civic Society Space', *NewsDay*, 17 April 2019.

17 Interview, female youth activist, 28 October 2020.

campus of the University of Zimbabwe, then the only university, offered housing facilities that were in good condition. Thus in the early years of independence, the life of Zimbabwean students at tertiary institutions was supported by many state privileges, leading what Zeilig (2006: 108) referred to as a 'rarefied and privileged existence'. Consequently, in the 1980s students marched in solidarity with the government. For instance, around 1983 students marched in the streets in support of Mugabe's call for a 'leadership code' that would, they hoped, stop corruption before it started (Moore 2006).

Yet the tide turned from the mid-1980s. In 1986, a student march to mourn the death of the Mozambican President Samora Machel turned violent, and students castigated growing levels of government corruption and mismanagement. The student union's relationship with the government shifted significantly to one of contention. Students viewed themselves as the vanguards of democratic principles, and had openly criticised Mugabe's plans to make Zimbabwe a one-party state (Mlambo 2013). After the Machel march and anti-corruption protests, the government arrested student leaders, including Arthur Mutambara, a future opposition leader. The student movement increasingly engaged in pro-democracy and anti-corruption activities. The Willowgate scandal in 1988 triggered large-scale student protests, and Mutambara and the University of Zimbabwe Student Representative Council organised a mass demonstration against corruption. The government's response was again heavy-handed, leading to the arrest of student leaders and the then Zimbabwe Congress of Trade Union (ZCTU) secretary general Morgan Tsvangirai for his solidarity with the students. These events further strained the relations between student organisations and the government. Not deterred by state repression, students continued their actions. The SRC released an 'anti-corruption document', in which they expressed misgivings over what they called betrayal by an 'ideologically bankrupt leadership'. This infuriated Mugabe and his allies, who castigated the students, as well as academics allegedly collaborating with them. Professor Shadreck Gutto was expelled, accused of helping students to write the anti-corruption document, and Professor Kempton Makamure was detained for supporting the student protests and criticising the government during a radio interview. In September 1989, the SRC organised a commemorative gala, which had a corruption theme, but the government banned students from attending and used presidential 'emergency powers' to deploy state security agents on campus. In response, the Mutambara-led SRC released an open letter condemning the brutality with which the police had blocked the seminar, insinuating that the Mugabe regime was becoming more repressive and brutal than that of his predecessor Ian Smith. In 1989, Mutambara sided with the Zimbabwe Unity Movement, an opposition party, against the government's decision to forbid a demonstration. He asserted that the SRC did not support any political party, but was strongly committed to the upholding of democratic rights. According to Zeilig (2006) the Mutambara era, popularly labelled the 'AGO years',[18] are regarded by many as the first urban opposition movement to the government, and in some accounts as the force that stalled the regime's plans for a one-party state (Saunders 2000). Students had turned into a 'revolutionary intelligentsia' (Hodgkinson 2013: 869).

As corruption and economic challenges deepened in the early 1990s, the government reduced and withdrew students' benefits. Students increasingly questioned the regime, leading to protests in the 1990s (Dorman 2016), and by the mid-1990s, ZINASU and the student population had grown into a formidable political force. As their concerns were not limited to students' welfare but included broader national challenges, student organisations cemented their working relationship with other civil society organisations to force the government to be accountable and transparent. In 1999, at the height of the economic and political crisis, student organisations were among the civic organisations that joined ZCTU to form the National Constitutional Assembly (NCA), which later established the Movement for Democratic Change (ibid.). The MDC handed ZANU-PF its first electoral defeat since independence. Following this, the government began to treat ZINASU and the civil society as a more serious political threat. Student organisations deepened their relationships with the MDC between 2000 and 2008, and were often at the receiving end of state violence (Hodgkinson 2013). To counter the growing influence of ZINASU, the government started funding a new student union, the Zimbabwe Congress of Student Union (ZICOSU), at tertiary institutions. Student leaders were arrested and imprisoned for organising protests. After the adoption of POSA, students were required to get police clearance before organising any form of protests, on or off campus; they often

---

18 Derived from Mutambara's full name: Arthur Guseni Oliver.

refused to apply for clearance, leading to frequent clashes with security forces (Hodgkinson 2013).

During the Government of National Unity, new students bodies emerged. Associations such as YARD (Youth Advocacy for Reform and Democracy) felt that the two main unions were concentrating on party politics rather than student concerns.[19] However, ZINASU continued to play a key role in fighting for students' rights and democratic principles. The relationship between the students and the government became less confrontational. In fact, during the 2009-2013 unity government, students from across the political divide were invited to parliament by the portfolio committee on higher education to discuss challenges that they faced on campus (Moyo 2020). Consequently, the committee ordered the two rival unions to hold meetings and discuss students' grievances before coming to present them to the parliament. Moyo (ibid.), noted that ZICOSU and ZINASU met frequently to craft a common position before meeting the committee. This reduced tensions between the two rival unions. In fact, in an interview with one former ZICOSU president it emerged that students were beginning to work together in addressing students' grievances and championing campus-based struggles.[20]

Post-2013, ZICOSU got embroiled in factionalist battles within the party. One of its leaders was allegedly aligned with Mnangagwa's faction in 2016, and it denounced G40 leaders Jonathan Moyo and Kasukuwere in 2017, accusing the latter of meddling with tertiary institutions.[21] Factionalism also affected the financial support ZANU-PF offered to ZICOSU. In fact, Jonathan Moyo, the former minister of higher and tertiary education complained that ZICOSU was getting of a lot of money.[22] Backed by ZINASU, UZ students refused to write their end of semester/year examinations when Mugabe initially refused to resign after 17 November 2017. They protested on campus, demanding that Mugabe resign.[23]

---

19 'Desperate students look to campus politics for solutions', *University World News*, 19 May 2017.

20 Interview, former ZICOSU leader, 24 October 2020.

21 'Zanu-PF factionalism seeps down to tertiary students', *NewsDay*, 16 April 2016; 'Moyo, a half war veteran: ZICOSU', *NewsDay*, 15 July 2017; 'ZICOSU aim guns at Kasukwere', *Sunday Mail*, 16 April 2017.

22 'ZICOSU milks government', *The Independent*, 5 February 2016.

23 'University of Zimbabwe students refuse to take exams until Robert Mugabe steps down - while demanding Grace Mugabe be stripped of her PhD', *Evening Standard*, 20 November 2017.

Repression against civil society in general and ZINASU in particular has intensified since the 2018 elections, reflecting the regressive trend of shrinking civic space. Under the Mnangagwa government, students and ZINASU have protested against the economic situation and education fees, and surveillance of universities. The crackdowns on civil society in 2019 and 2020 saw some ZINASU leaders arrested.[24] ZINASU President Takudzwa Ngadziore was arrested in 2020 for protesting against the abduction and torture of a journalism student and other youth civil society leaders.[25] While surveillance on campus has a long history – dating back to the colonial era – it intensified after independence and again after Mugabe. Focusing on state surveillance on campus, Gukurume (2019) asserted that a large network of secret agents was deployed on campus by the Central Intelligence Organisation (CIO). ZICOSU students were allegedly co-opted into these network as campus- and classroom-based informants. As before, the regime viewed student activists as powerful critics *and* a political threat, in particular those aligned with ZINASU. The arrests of ZINASU activists, for instance, echoed the practices of the Mugabe regime.[26]

Popular culture

Art, literature and popular culture can be channels of subversion as well as being used to legitimise the most powerful actors. Both have happened in Zimbabwe (Ndlovu-Ghatsheni and Willems, 2009; Ravengai 2010; Vambe 2010), and music in particular became a major avenue of subversive practice amongst the (mainly urban) youth. Throughout the 1980s and 1990s, literature and theatre were monitored for presenting a version of history that emphasised the victimisation of black people at the hands of colonisers and glorified the liberators (Ravengai 2010; Vambe 2010; Veit-Wild 1992). This did not force all artists to self-censor their work, with the Over the Edge theatre company creating comic political satire. When challenged by the MDC in 2000, ZANU-PF started promoting a cultural nationalism as part of

24 'Pressure grows on Zimbabwe to free detained student leader', *The Guardian*, 16 October 2020; 'ZINASU Leader Abducted During MSU Graduation Ceremony', *Zim Eye*, 22 November 2019; 'ZINASU threatens to protest over "students' arrest"', *Zim Morning Post*, 6 March 2019.

25 'Pressure grows on Zimbabwe to free detained student leader', *The Guardian*, 16 October 2020.

26 'Zinasu president gets $2000 bail, 9 students arrested for protest', *NewsDay*, 15 September 2020.

the *Third Chimurenga*, encompassing a revival of anti-colonial rhetoric and Chimurenga songs, music galas and commemorations of national heroes and holidays (Ndlovu-Ghatsheni and Willems, 2009). The Broadcasting Services Act (April 2001) stipulated that 75% of radio and television content should consist of local and African material, later increased to 100% (Manase 2009, 2011; Gukurume 2017a). This led to a flourishing of 'urban grooves' or dancehall music (Ndlovu-Gatsheni and Willems, 2009; Manase 2011). The government appropriated urban grooves to promote its version of nationalism, central to which were the liberation war and President Mugabe, organising music galas and involving government officials in writing songs (ibid.; Manase 2011, p.57). These cultural events were a deliberate attempt to reach a young audience that lacked direct experience with the liberation war, to inculcate them with ZANU-PF's version of nationalism and against Western imperialism represented by the MDC (Ndlovu-Gatsheni and Willems, 2009).

Repressive laws, surveillance and intimidation restricted artists and playwrights (Ravengai 2008). However, urban youth found alternatives and illegal ways to access other music and they attended 'underground theatre' (Ndlela, 2006; Zenenga 2008). Urban grooves artists emerged, using their music to critique the regime. Musicians who became part of ZANU-PF events made 'subtle subversions' by creatively using certain language, rhythms, tunes and themes from outside the country, influences the regime intended to resist (Manase 2009:60). Urban grooves artists remain hugely popular with youth, though the genre is controversial in terms the gendered 'microviolence' some songs are said to promote (Kufakurinani and Mwatwara 2017). Songs by the artist Winky D, who entered the scene in 2002, are about the struggles of the 'ghetto masses', critiquing the economic crisis that resulted from bad governance (ibid.; Manase 2011). His 2019 album 'Njema' (Shona for 'chains' or 'handcuffs') was considered a direct challenge to Mnangagwa and an attempt to mobilise the population to protest.[27] Artists such as Platinum Prince and Junior Maskiri have used their music to challenge both former President Mugabe and Mnangagwa, and have been targeted with violence as a result.[28] The spread of

---

27 'Time to leave Pharaoh and Egypt' – Winky D gets Zanu PF cracking', *Zimbabwe Mail*, 31 December 2019.

28 'ZimDancehall artist, Platinum Prince abducted and assaulted by suspected govt agents', *ZimNews Online*, 28 October 2019.

subversive music and the fame of its artists have been enabled by the growth of social media, [29] which we turn to next. This tends to reach urban rather than rural youth, as access to internet and also local radio and TV networks is still limited in some rural areas.

Online mobilisation and the streets

After 2013, a vacuum emerged in political mobilisation with the weakening of two actors who had historically been crucial for opposition politics: the MDC was internally divided and the ZCTU lost members due to the economic downturn. Several movements emerged that combined online action with street protests. While not all were youth-driven, they attracted a large youth following. Mobile internet facilitated this newer form of youth politics. Access to mobile phones increased from about 250,000 active subscribers in 2000 to 12.8 million in 2015; 25% of the population had access to mobile broadband (Leijendekker and Mutsvairo 2014: 1036; Otieno 2020: 9; Gukurume and Mahiya 2020). Zimbabweans used the online space and social media in particular to comment on everyday hardship and the governance failures that had caused it. Some of these developed into street protests that became major disruptions.

The #ThisFlag movement emerged spontaneously in May 2016, when Pastor Evan Mawarire posted a video about living conditions in Zimbabwe. He called for a national stayaway, dubbed 'Shutdown Zimbabwe', on 6 July 2016. Although state media reported that it was business as usual, pictures circulated through WhatsApp and other social media. Several newspaper reports noted that business came to a total halt across the country (Gukurume 2017b). The arrest of Pastor Mawarire, under the POSA, only strengthened the support of the movement. Thousands of supporters came to the provincial magistrate's court in solidarity with Pastor Mawarire during his trial on 12 July 2016 (ibid.). Initially the response from the government was ambivalent, but it tried to crush the protests through the intimidation and arrest of protest organisers, construing them as 'dissidents' and enemies of the state. State actors involved in intimidation included the CIO, the Zimbabwe National Army and the Zimbabwe Republic Police. Oosterom (2019b: 18) found an initial lack of synergy between many conventional NGOs and these new movements, citing a member

---

29 'Chin'ono's "Dem Loot" song goes viral', *New Zimbabwe*, 10 February 2021.

of #ThisFlag who said NGOs had been reluctant to take the movement seriously. Later on, cross-fertilisation occurred as formal civil society challenged human rights violations of the activists involved and took court action, whereas the #activists supported the ZCTU when it called for a stayaway in January 2019. Mawarire was arrested when protests turned violent in Harare and other cities.[30] These developments suggest a potential divide between the younger and older generation activists and how they organise.

Following #ThisFlag, the movement #ThisGown was initiated by unemployed graduates, some of whom worked as informal vendors on the streets wearing their graduation gowns (Gukurume, 2017). These movements came up in direct response to increasing hardship that was believed to be caused by corruption and bad governance (Gukurume 2017b). Another movement, Tajamuka, was formed in 2014 by a group of independent civil society and independent youth activists linked to organisations like ZINASU, Youth Alliance for Democracy, the Youth Forum and the Youth Agenda Trust. The various #movements were in solidarity with one another, as when Tajamuka followers joined the protests concerning Mawarire's 2016 arrest, but they did not necessarily coordinate their strategies. Whereas #ThisFlag had emerged more spontaneously, Tajamuka's formation and actions were planned, aimed to put pressure on the government to implement democratic reforms. It explicitly wanted to use non-violent means of action, but not necessarily using the rule book as it felt that some laws were undemocratic, such as those requiring police clearance to stage a protest.[31] Tajamuka reached out to 'ghetto youth', attracted many informal workers and street vendors, and tried to spread into rural areas viewed as ZANU-PF strongholds. Whereas Tajamuka reached relatively disadvantaged youth, #ThisFlag reached all ages and also youth from relatively better-off neighbourhoods.[32] From 2016, the government started to crackdown heavily on Tajamuka protests and gatherings, using police violence to disperse gatherings. The movement then decided to shift its actions to doing more online and to conduct smaller activities in other cities. By late 2017, the strength of the Tajamuka movement had waned and one of

---

30 'Zimbabwe pastor Evan Mawarire leaves prison on bail', *Deutsche Welle*, 30 January 2019.
31 Interview, founding member, 15 October 2020.
32 Interview with youth activist, 15 October 2020.

its leaders, Promise Mkwananzi, was forced to resign after allegations of corruption.

For Ndebele youth in Matabeleland, social media has been an outlet to speak out against marginalisation of the region and in particular against the silencing of mass killings in the 1980s (Mpofu 2019).[33] After Mnangagwa said 'let bygones be bygones' in his inauguration speech, online comments from Ndebele youth centred on ZANU-PF dominance (ibid. 2019). For Ndebele youth involved or sympathising with the Mthwakazi movement, the Mthwakazi Republic Party and its youth league has been an important channel of expression.[34]

The internet and social media continue to be a source of oppositional activity, to air grievances and organise protests. In the wake of the global #BlackLivesMatter movement, a #ZimbabweLivesMatter campaign began trending in mid-2020 in response to an increase in the brutal political repression of journalists, activists and opposition leaders. The state responded heavily when a mass demonstration was planned for 31 July 2020, brining together members of other #movements, activists, the journalist Hopewell Chin'Ono, MDC-A youth and the expelled ZANU-PF Youth League leader, Godfrey Tsenengamu, and his followers.[35]

In the months following the January 2019 protests, the government cracked down on civil society and some prominent youth activists were arrested.[36] This trend continued in 2020, when one young MDC-A parliamentarian and two other female MDC-A youth leaders were allegedly abducted and tortured by state agents (UNOCHR, 2020).[37] Aware of the potential of online mobilisation, the government sought to curtail online spaces and digital political agency. It has developed legislation and ordered temporary internet shutdowns when protests are planned, as happened in January 2019 (HRForum 2019; Otiono 2020: 90). In August 2016, the government drafted a bill that criminalised cyber activism, and a Cyber Security and Data Protection Bill was

33 Referred to as 'Gukurahundi', this violent campaign of mass killings was orchestrated by ZANU-PF in the Matabeleland region in the early 1980s to quell resistance from the rival revolutionary group and its supporters.

34 The MRP Youth League has a twitter account with over 1,300 followers [accessed 15.10.2020].

35 'Ngarivhume's Arrest Will Not Stop 31 July Protests', *AllAfrica*, 23 July 2020.

36 'CIZC youth chairperson Pride Mnkono remanded in custody', *Kubatana*, 17 August 2019.

37 'Zimbabwe activists jailed, awaiting charges', *The Guardian*, 15 June 2020.

gazetted in May 2020. The legislation makes it easy for the government to target activists and mobilisers, and activists have been arrested for online posts that were interpreted as anti-government. The government accuses social media activists of fabricating fake news and undermining the Constitution. Newspapers also reported that the government is concerned about G40 members who use social media to critique the Mnangagwa government.[38]

The government is also learning how to mobilise internet for its own interests. Karekwaivanane and Msonza (2021) write about the *varakashi* phenomenon, which refers to the use of online mobs of individual trolls deployed by the government, and sock-puppet accounts that harass opposition voices and coordinate dis-information campaigns. They were actively used in the 2010 election period. *Varakashi* engaged in cyber warfare with critics of the government and sought to discredit any reports that exposed ZANU-PF and its officials. Indeed, *varakashi* became a ZANU-PF propaganda mouthpiece. Activists experienced online surveillance as well as threats in their offline lives (ibid.). Activists reported that ZANU-PF networks, including the youth league and ZICOSU, were used to mobilise youth to engage government critics as *varakashi*.

Conclusion

This chapter has illustrated the various forms of youth politics that have existed and grown in Zimbabwe since 1980. While it is often assumed that young Africans are indifferent to politics, the chapter supports existing scholarship arguing that that young people are politically engaged in a variety of ways. This is despite the repression of civil society and activists that has been sustained over time, and repressive strategies against youth voices and parallel developments in civil society. The formal political institutional set-up is failing genuine democratic participation, and alternative channels for youth politics have been significant for the born-free generation. The dynamics of closing civic space and youth politics occur in dialectic: where action emerges, state responses follow. While it remains to be seen whether the hashtag-movements will have any effects, it is clear they are now part and parcel of political dynamics in the country. It is also clear that

---

38 'Zimbabwe: G40 gives Mnangagwa sleepless nights over insurgency fears', *All Africa*, 22 October 2020.

young people play a significant part in these movements, including when they spill over to the streets.

Acknowledgements

Interviews used for this chapter have been conducted as part of the project 'Youth employment and political representation in Africa', which is funded by NorGlobal in Norway (grant number 288489, Principal Investigator Dr Lovise Aalen, Chr. Michelsen Institute, Bergen). We thank the participants for their generous time offered to the project.

References

Alexander, J. and J. McGregor (2013) 'Introduction: Politics, Patronage and Violence in Zimbabwe', *Journal of Southern African Studies*, 39(4), pp. 749-763.

Bangura, I. and Specht, I. (2012) 'Work not War: Youth Transformation in Liberia and Sierra Leone', in Accord, *Consolidating Peace: Liberia and Sierra Leone*, Issue 23.

Beardsworth, N., N. Cheeseman and S. Tinhu (2019) 'Zimbabwe: The coup that never was, and the election that could have been', *African Affairs*, 118(472), pp. 580-596.

Brechenmacher, S. (2017) *Civil Society under Assault. Repression and responses in Russia, Egypt and Ethiopia*. Washington, DC: Carnegie Endowment for International Peace.

CEPPS (2019) 'Raising Their Voices: How effective are pro-youth laws and policies?' Washington, DC: Consortium for Elections and Political Process Strengthening.

Carothers, T. and S. Brechenmacher (2014) *Closing Space: Democracy and Human Rights Support under Fire*. Washington, DC: Carnegie Endowment for International Peace.

Cubitt, C. (2012) 'Political youth: Finding alternatives to violence in Sierra Leone', in G. Maina (ed.), *Opportunity or Threat: The Engagement of Youth in African Societies*. Africa Dialogue Monologue Series No. 1/2012. Umhlanga Rocks: ACCORD.

Dorman, S.R. (2002) 'Rocking the boat? Church NGOs and democratization in Zimbabwe', *African Affairs*, 101, pp. 75-92.

————(2003) 'NGOs and the Constitutional Debate in Zimbabwe: from Inclusion to Exclusion', *Journal of Southern African Studies*, 29(4), pp. 845-863.

———— (2016) *Understanding Zimbabwe. From liberation to authoritarianism*. London: Hurst and Co.

Dupuy, K. and A. Prakash (2017) 'Do Donors Reduce Bilateral Aid to Countries with Restrictive NGO Laws? A Panel Study, 1993-2012', *Non-Profit and Voluntary Sector Quarterly*.

Goodfellow, T. and D. Jackman (2020) 'Control the capital: cities and political dominance'. ESID Working Paper No. 135.

Gukurume, S. (2017) '#ThisFlag and #ThisGown Cyber Protests in Zimbabwe: Reclaiming Political Space', *African Journalism Studies*, 38(2), pp. 49-70.

———— (2017) 'Singing Positivity: Prosperity Gospel in the Musical Discourse of Popular Youth Hip-Hop', *Muziki*, 14(1), pp. 36-54.

———— (2019) 'Surveillance, Spying and Disciplining the University: Deployment of State Security Agents on Campus in Zimbabwe,' *Journal of Asian and African Studies*, 54(5), pp. 763-779.

———— and I.T. Mahiya (2020) 'Mobile Money and the (Un)Making of Social Relations in Chivi, Zimbabwe', *Journal of Southern African Studies*, 46(6), pp. 1203-1217.

Helliker, K. and T. Murisa (2020) 'Zimbabwe: continuities and changes', *Journal of Contemporary African Studies*, 38(1), pp. 5-17.

Hodgkinson, D. (2013) 'The "Hardcore" Student Activist: The Zimbabwe National Students Union (ZINASU), State Violence, and Frustrated Masculinity, 2000–2008', *Journal of Southern African Studies,* 39(4), pp. 863-883.

Hossain, N., N. Khurana, S.K. Mohmand, S. Nazneen, M. Oosterom, T. Roberts, R. Santos, A. Shankland and P. Schröder (2018) 'What Does Closing Civic Space Mean for Development? A Literature Review and Proposed Conceptual Framework'. Working paper 515. Brighton: Institute of Development Studies.

HRForum (2019) '#ZimShutdown Update for 21 January 2019'. Harare: Zimbabwe Human Rights NGO Forum.

Karekwaivanane, G. and N. Msonza (2021) African digital rights. Country landscape report Zimbabwe. In: T. Roberts (ed.), *Digital*

Rights in Closing Civic Space: Lessons from Ten African Countries. Brighton: Institute of Development Studies.

Kriger, N. (1992) *Zimbabwe's Guerrilla War: Peasant voices.* Cambridge: Cambridge University Press.

———— (2012) 'ZANU PF politics under Zimbabwe's "Power-Sharing" Government', *Journal of Contemporary African Studies*, 30(1), pp. 11-26.

Kufakurinani, U. and W. Mwatwara (2017) 'Zimdancehall and the Peace crisis in Zimbabwe', *African Conflict & Peacebuilding Review*, 7(1), pp. 33-50.

Leijendekker, I. and B. Mutsvairo (2014) 'On digitally networked technologies, hegemony and regime durability in authoritarian regimes: a Zimbabwean case study', *Information, Communication & Society*, 17(8), pp. 1034-1047.

Manase, I. (2009) 'Zimbabwean urban grooves and their subversive performance practices', *Social Dynamics*, 35(1), pp. 56-67.

———— (2011) 'The aesthetics of Winky D's Zimbabwe urban grooves music and an overview of his social commentary on the post-2000 experiences in Harare and other urban centres', *Muziki*, 8(2), pp. 81-95.

Maringira, G. and S. Gukurume, (2020) 'Youth patronage: Violence, intimidation and political mobilization in Zimbabwe'. African Peacebuilding Network Working Paper No. 28.

Mate, R. (2012) 'Youth Lyrics, Street Language and the Politics of Age: Contextualising the Youth Question in the Third Chimurenga in Zimbabwe', *Journal of Southern African Studies*, 38(1), pp. 107-127.

Mattes, R. (2012) 'The "Born Frees": The Prospects for Generational Change in Post-*apartheid* South Africa', *Australian Journal of Political Science*, 47(1), pp. 133-153.

McGee, R. and J. Greenhalf (2011) 'Introduction: Seeing Like a Young Citizen: Youth and Participatory Governance in Africa', in R. McGee and J. Greenhalf (eds), *Young Citizens: Youth and Participatory Governance in Africa,* Participatory Learning and Action 64. London: International Institute for Environment and Development

McGregor, J. (2013) 'Surveillance and the City: Patronage, Power-Sharing and the Politics of Urban Control in Zimbabwe', *Journal of*

Southern African Studies, 39(4), pp. 783-805.

Mlambo, A. (2013) 'Student Activism in a time of Crisis – Zimbabwe 2000-2010: A tentative exploration', *Journal for Contemporary History*, 31(1), pp. 184-204.

Moyo, Z. (2020) 'Opposition Politics and the culture of polarisation in Zimbabwe, 1980-2018', in S.J. Ndlovu-Gatsheni and P. Ruhanya (eds), *The History and Political Transition of Zimbabwe*. London: Palgrave Macmillan.

Mpofu, S. (2019) 'For a nation to progress victims must "move on": a case of Zimbabwe's social media discourses of Gukurahundi genocide silencing and resistance', *African Identities*, 17(2), pp. 108-129.

Ndlela, N., (2006) 'Alternative media and the global popular: Youth and popular culture in Zimbabwe', *Glocal Times* [online], 5.

Ndlovu-Gatsheni, S.J. and W. Willems (2009) 'Making Sense of Cultural Nationalism and the Politics of Commemoration under the Third Chimurenga in Zimbabwe', *Journal of Southern African Studies*, 35(4), pp. 945-965.

Nordas, R. and C. Davenport (2013) 'Fight the Youth: Youth Bulges and State Repression', *American Journal of Political Science*, 57(4), pp. 926–940.

Oosterom, M. (2019a) 'Youth and Social Navigation in Zimbabwe's Informal Economy: "Don't end up on the wrong side"', *African Affairs* 118(472), pp. 485–508.

———— (2019b) ' The Implications of Closing Civic Space for Sustainable Development in Zimbabwe'. Research report for Act Alliance. Brighton: Institute of Development Studies.

—— — and S. Gukurume (2019) 'Managing the Born-free Generation: Zimbabwe's Strategies for Dealing with the Youth'. CMI Working Paper No. 2. Bergen: Chr. Michelsen Institute.

———— and L. Pswarayi (2014) 'Being a Born Free: Violence, Youth and Agency in Zimbabwe'. Research Report 79. Brighton: Institute of Development Studies.

———— R. Wignall and S. Wilson (2019) *Youth Action in Fragile Settings*. London: Plan International UK and Institute of Development Studies.

Otiono, N. (2020) 'Dream delayed or dream betrayed: politics, youth agency and the mobile revolution in Africa', *Canadian Journal of African Studies*, 55(1), pp. 121-140.

Oyedemi, T. and D. Mahlatji (2016) 'The 'Born-free' Non-voting Youth: A Study of Voter Apathy Among a Selected Cohort of South African Youth', *Politikon*, 43(3), pp. 311-323.

Raftopoulos, B. (1992) 'Beyond the house of hunger: democratic struggle in Zimbabwe', *Review of African Political Economy*, 19(54), pp.59-74.

Ravengai, S. (2008) 'Political theatre under threat: the impact of POSA, AIPPA and censorship on theatre-making in Zimbabwe'. Harare: Savannah Trust.

————— (2010) Political theatre, national identity and political control: the case of Zimbabwe, *African Identities*, 8(2), pp. 163-173

Resnick, D. and D. Casale (2014) 'Young populations in young democracies: generational voting behaviour in sub-Saharan Africa', *Democratization*, 21(6), pp.1172-1194.

Reuss, A. and K. Titeca (2017) 'When revolutionaries grow old: the Museveni babies and the slow death of the liberation', *Third World Quarterly*, 38(10), pp. 2347-2366.

Sachikonye, L. (1995) 'Civil society, social movements and Democracy in Southern Africa', *Innovation*, 8(4), pp. 399-411.

Saunders, R. (2000) *Never the Same Again: Zimbabwe's Growth Towards Democracy, 1980-2000*. Harare: Edwina Spicer Productions.

Southall, R. (2019) 'Presidential transitions and generational change in Southern African liberation movements', *Review of African Political Economy*, 46(159), pp. 143-156.

UNOCHR (2020) 'Zimbabwe: UN experts demand an immediate end to abductions and torture'. Geneva: UN Office of the High Commissioner for Human Rights.

Vambe, M.T. (2010) 'Zimbabwe's creative literatures in the interregnum: 1980–2009', *African Identities*, 8(2), pp. 93-116.

Van der Borgh, C. and C. Terwindt (2014) *NGOs Under Pressure in Partial Democracies*. London: Palgrave Macmillan.

Veit-Wild, F. (1992) *Teachers, Preachers, Non-Believers: A Social History of Zimbabwean Literature*. London: Hans Zell Publishers.

Wilkins, S. (2013) 'Ndira's Wake: Politics, Memory and Mobility among theYouth of Mabvuku-Tafara, Harare', *Journal of Southern African Studies*, 39(4), pp. 885-901.

Zeilig, L. (2006) 'Increasing my value proposition to the struggle: Arthur Mutambara and student politics in Zimbabwe', *African Sociological Review*, 10(2), pp. 94-115.

Zenenga, P. (2008) 'Censorship, surveillance, and protest theatre in Zimbabwe', *Theater*, 38(3), pp. 63–79.

9

'Subverting Controls': Historicising the Multi-dimensions of Female Youth Sexuality in Post-colonial Zimbabwe

Ngonidzashe Muwonwa

Introduction and background

The chapter looks into the development of discourses around young people's sexuality in Zimbabwe from 1980 to 2020. It analyses the post-colonial condition of young people regarding their sexual expressions and activities and how laws and policies have sought to control and curtail the sexual enterprises of young people. Furthermore, the chapter investigates how young people have continued to respond to challenges of control and censure, subverting policies and laws within the state. This study seeks to engage with the moral discourses that emerge, or are centred, in urban set-ups in Zimbabwe.

There exists a conceptual oversight whereby notions of African youth sexuality are a mere duplication of experiences of youth in other parts of the world, particularly those in the West. This chapter gives prominence to the study of youth sexuality in Zimbabwe, while connecting it to important concepts such as gender, sexual subjectivity, sexual decision-making, and body politics, to highlight its changing dynamics. Sexuality is broadly defined as personal feelings, desires, beliefs and socially accepted attitudes, norms, and meanings which determine interactions with members of the same or opposite sex (Dixon-Mueller 1993). Gupta (2000) defines sexuality as the social construction of a biological drive which includes whom to have sex with, in what ways, why, under what circumstances, and with what outcomes. Sexuality is influenced by rules, both explicit and implicit, imposed by the social definitions of gender, age, economic status, and ethnicity (Dixon-Mueller 1993; Zeidenstein and Moore 1995).

Since independence in 1980, the government of Zimbabwe has been under pressure on various socio-economic and political fronts and the issue of sexual and reproductive rights has also been imbricated in the discourses of nation-building and national identity. According to Franke (2004), contemporary Zimbabwe gained an 'official sexuality' as state power was being solidified in new forms. Franke argued that the management of sex has become a tool of governance that produces individual 'unfreedom' in the name of expanding national freedom or independence in an effort to deliberately erase colonial pasts and call forth a more authentic indigenous present. Furthermore, Zimbabwe was one of the countries hardest hit by the HIV/AIDS crisis (UNAIDS 2016), which presented an opportunity for the government to police sexual and reproductive issues within a framework of heterosexual nationalism. For example, the government has opposed the legalisation of same–sex marriages and relationships in the country, resulting in the criminalisation and harassment of any individuals contravening the law (Dunton and Palmberg 1996; Epprecht 1998)

The chapter juxtaposes a review of literature with research findings. The research findings are based on ethnographic fieldwork with young people which utilised participatory artistic productions, such as stage plays, radio drama, forum theatre presentations, and short films, to reconstruct the lived experiences of young people. The youth have often been considered an 'invisible' category with neither voice nor agency (Mlingo 2008). The lived experiences and reflections of young people as they encounter post-colonialism associated with socio-economic decay in Zimbabwe provide an alternative interpretation of how young people imagine and experience their sexual lives. Against such definitions, the chapter highlights young people's socio-sexual beliefs and desires as knowledge in circulation within their community. Such a perspective dismantles traditionally held perspectives which deny sexual agency and power in young people, especially while positioning sexuality as an exclusive realm of adults who do it and experts who understand and talk about it. Therefore, conceptualising young people as active and critical co-generators of knowledge is aimed at unblocking knowledge systems in existence within the universe of young people's sexuality.

Traditionally, young people in both rural and urban Zimbabwe have lived under social, cultural, political and religious frames which extensively affect, influence and control their sexuality. For example, sexual and reproductive health policies appear to be in a mutually reinforcing relationship with adult hegemonic conceptualisations of youth, constricting and governing the expression and articulation by young people of their own interests. In this regard, the sexuality terrain in Zimbabwe has many intersecting policies that regulate sexual and reproductive issues with serious implications for young people's sexuality. Zimbabwe is still operating within a culturally relative constitution which undermines the effectiveness of international law, particularly in raising the status of sexual and reproductive rights of girls and women. However, as shall be explored later in the chapter, the bounded, bordered and embodied terrain of youth sexuality is slowly moving towards an eclipse of tradition through modernity.

Sexuality in post-colonial Zimbabwe seems to have undergone major shifts which are however very difficult to pin down. Emerging out of the liberation war, which saw the opening up of movement between towns and cities, women's presence in urban spaces connected with the changes in sexual controls. More 'unbridled' relationships between men and women began to flourish in urban centres (Kambarami 2004). However, the laxity that might have become the order of the day before the early 1990s changed drastically with the increase in HIV infections. The laws and policies surrounding access to sexual and reproductive health for young people have, however, changed little over the course of the years (Matswetu and Bhana 2018). Stringent conditions towards access have remained, strongly affecting young women, as evidenced by the high HIV infection rates among this group, and the increase in early marriages and childbirth among young women.

De-institutionalising normative discourses of womanhood

Despite the limitations, young people, and especially young women, have continued to be sexually active outside these restricted parameters, albeit with consequences to their health and future developmental prospects. Zimbabwe has since 1980 recorded high rates of early childbearing, which impacts negatively on adolescent women through the impairment of their health and that of their offspring. The use of modern contraceptives has thus been identified as one of the main interventions to reduce the negative effects of early childbearing.

However, there are diverging movements towards the cultural valorisation of virginity, especially among young women. Historically, male and female virginity have been an important cultural ideal through which adolescents anchored their sexuality, while adults used the concept of virginity to monitor and control young people's sexual enterprises. While trying to understand the cultural notions of virginity among young people in rural areas, Matswetu and Bhana (2018) note that they have continued to reproduce patriarchal interests, as the necessity of virginity is reinforced by its connection to bride price paid by the prospective husband to the woman's family (Museka and Machingura 2014). Similarly, in Shona culture, from the pre-colonial era to the present, the husband pays *mombeye chimanda* as part of the bride price (Vengeyi 2016), which is a cow that is yet to give birth as a symbol and token of appreciation for the bride's purity. Matswetu and Bhana (2018) highlight how rural young women are made to value their virginity. One interviewee they spoke to recalled:

> It is important to remain a virgin because you might sleep with a boy then he does not marry you. The one who eventually wants to marry you will say he wants a virgin. Then you may not find someone to marry you at all (Ruth, girl).

However, such notions are slowly changing, especially within urban settings. Such a scenario is exemplified by young students at the University of Zimbabwe who organised a discussion around the topic in 2014 after the then First Lady, Grace Mugabe, publicly declared that her soon-to-be-married daughter was a virgin. A public discussion ensued, which was designed within a theatre play as a direct response to the perceived importance of purity and chastity through virginity.

Young women at the University sought to understand and challenge the symbolic significance of virginity as a marker of prestige and personal achievement.

The performance-cum-discussion, *My Body – My Business,* reveals young women's attempts at deinstitutionalising womanhood by interrogating the normative discourses of virginity in circulation:

> As young women we don't want the pressure of being asked if you are a virgin or not. It's a baggage. If it was so important, everyone must be asked to be a virgin, not only women.[1]

From the above response, it seems that some young women viewed discourses of virginity as 'technology of self', defined by Foucault (1998: 18) as:

> behaviours of self-maintained well-being or as practices that permit individuals to effect by their own means or with the help of others a certain number of operations on their own bodies and souls, thoughts and conduct.

Therefore, the focus on virginity was viewed by some young women in the workshop as disruptive to a woman's psychosocial development. In challenging the worth and importance of virginity as an important aspect of one's womanhood, young women seem to be 'undoing' 'technologies of self' while positioning new ways of valuing and controlling their bodies. For example, one young woman from the focus group claimed:

> Virgins are dying of HIV because, you think just because you are a virgin, your husband is also a virgin and you don't go for HIV testing before your honeymoon.

In underemphasising virginity as a key marker of good womanhood, while amplifying issues around HIV testing before marriage, young women were responding to the lived challenges which place surveillance mechanisms on women while allowing men to sexually experiment freely before marriage. Such a critical consciousness in young women exposes possible vulnerabilities associated with passivity and innocence as markers of good womanhood.

At the same time, some young women pointed towards attempts at breaking away from traditional patterns, transforming virginity into a

---

1   Response from a young girl during a workshop.

responsibility rather than an obligation:

> If some men live with the experience of premarital sex why should the same girl whom he had sex with not also live through it. If he is not going to be asked if he is a virgin or not, then let's also do the same to the girl.[2]

In rejecting virginity as an acceptable public narrative, it seems as if the young woman is agreeing that virginity is important but she must not be the only one obligated to maintain her virginity as a required attribute of her gender. The awareness of the duality of responsibility and obligation fostered on young women is very telling against those who deny young women space to openly talk about sexuality issues. Instead of encouraging sex, this is evidence that young women can talk about issues of their sexuality and still reproduce progressive ideas that support gender equality:

> I am not defined by my virginity. Just because I am no longer a virgin doesn't mean I am no longer a respectable person. I am not damaged goods…I am a person who made the decision to lose it. The moment you see yourself as damaged goods, then you will be abused…this is why Joe must find his virgin.[3]

The above response coincides with the framework of objectification that places female bodies in a socio-cultural context with the aim of illuminating the lived experiences and mental health risks of girls and women who encounter sexual objectification. The young woman's response was able to conceptualise the focalisation on virginity as an ideology on one hand and a form of gender oppression on the other that enables the perpetuation of other oppressions on women. In refusing to be 'defined' by virginity, the young woman revealed that she was aware of how sexual objectification occurred whenever a woman's body, body parts or sexual functions were separated out from her person and reduced to the status of mere instruments, or regarded as if they were capable of representing her (Bartky 1990). Furthermore, it is important to highlight that the issue of the young woman's choice to lose her virginity suggests a strong sense of agency, and control of her sexuality,

---

2   To access information from young women, the researcher used focus groups and semi-formal interviews. Other such responses were recorded during workshops and public discussions.

3   Response from one young woman in the forum discussion.

which helps to disempower any possibilities of sexual objectification and abuse.

These responses can be read as an attempt at breaking down hegemonic discourses of virginity. Such an analysis points to a need to acknowledge some of the complexities and ambiguities associated with attempts to challenge and reposition oneself within frameworks of normative institutional cultures as such cultures were embedded within and shape the structure of young women's responses and the performance of their femininities (Epstein 2007; Muwonwa 2014). The status of virginity is at odds with the new definitions of femininity aligned with the values of sexual modernity. It also seems as if young women have begun to position premarital sex as a means of expressing modern liberated sexuality while pushing for the acceptance of premarital sex as a new social norm. The responses introduced a vocabulary of gender equality and power central to the development of positive sexuality in young women. This confirms Bay-Cheng's (2003) articulation that neoliberalism has infiltrated the sexual lives of young women, especially after the 1990s as modernity settled in within the Zimbabwe socio-political landscape. As neoliberal conceptions, power and equality are predicated on virginity being a personal choice rather than a necessity, evolving from a marker of conformity to become a marker of power and subjectivity.

The forum theatre presentation and discussions shed light on the effect and meanings associated with young women's challenges to the dominant norm of virginity. Most young women who participated in the discussion seemed to be challenging the importance of virginity which reveals a latent capacity to destabilise the resilient societal classification on the basis of their sexual experiences. The narratives collected in the workshop reveal a convergence on the view that societal insistence on female virginity is a mark of patriarchal traditionalism, strongly rejecting the idealisation of female chastity and the symbolic value of virginity, and its equation with honour and female respectability. Such a positioning, according to Ozyegin (2009), reveals how the intact hymen is no longer seen as the property of 'others', the family, parents or the nation.

It seems that some young women in Zimbabwe are now subscribing to the principle that losing or preserving one's virginity should be a personal choice. The concept of personal responsibility and ownership of the hymen shifts external authority to internal authority, as 'power located externally to the individual (tradition) is rejected but restraint from within is emphasized (modernity)' (Adam 1996: 138). In probing the significance of virginity as a charged site of control over their sexuality, the young women illuminated the violations and conundrums of the preservation of virginity norms within a context of multi-layered societal and sexual transformations. At the same time, there was evidence that discourses of virginity figure centrally in the ways young women enter, negotiate or exit romantic and sexual relationships. It is important to note that the shifting notions of sexuality were couched in the dichotomy of tradition and modernity. This opposition exercises a special potency in organising experience and consciousness in young women as they continuously assess their feelings and conduct for their modernity or tradition (Ozyegin, 2009). To an extent, this highlights how class and status may be affording new freedoms to young women.

Ultimately, the forum theatre contributed to the dismantling of virginity as a hegemonic discourse, as the young women discursively challenged and attempted to reconceptualise normative discourses of womanhood beyond their body parts. Their attempts at challenging and reconceptualising such discourses were based on ideological foundations of new definitions of femininity aligned with the values of sexual modernity which position premarital sex as a means of expressing modern liberated sexuality and premarital sex as a new social norm. Within this framework, a vocabulary of gender equality and power exists, which is central in the development of positive sexuality in young women.

Access to and use of contraceptives as border crossing

Zimbabwe is recognised as one of the first countries in sub-Saharan Africa to make contraceptives widely available. The use of modern methods of family planning has gradually expanded since 1980, in both rural and urban areas. Between 1980 and 1990, the percentage of women who were using modern contraceptives rose by more than 58%, and after 1990, condom use began to be more common among sexually active men against the background of the emergence of HIV and AIDS (Marindo et al. 2003). However, against this successful usage of contraceptives, there is an untold story of the exclusion of young women and men in accessing contraceptives to curtail unwanted pregnancies and to prevent sexually transmitted diseases. Results from the 1984 Zimbabwe Demographic and Health Survey indicated that one-third of Zimbabwean women had their first child before the age of 18. Numerous cases of 'baby dumping', or abandoning new-born babies and infants, became prevalent, highlighting the problem of unintended pregnancy (CSO 1995).

Sexual and reproductive laws in Zimbabwe have continued to exclude young people from accessing the necessary services such as contraceptives. As in many other nations, contraception use among young people in Zimbabwe has remained a highly emotive subject. Access to and use of contraceptives by young people is officially and unofficially sanctioned despite the country having one of the highest HIV infection rates in sub-Saharan Africa. However, despite the escalating problems of HIV/AIDS, a multi-sector approach to combat the pandemic has failed to develop comprehensive strategies that address its gender dynamics (Muwonwa 2004). Despite being one of the first countries in sub-Saharan Africa to recognise the HIV/AIDS problem, Zimbabwe has failed to implement organised action at national level to ameliorate its spread, as programmes continue to deal with effects rather than preventive strategies to empower the most vulnerable groups: women and youths (Marindo et al. 2003).

It is against this background that a performance workshop, *The Power of Choice*,[4] was undertaken as an attempt to institute reforms in the arena of young women's reproductive and sexual rights, particularly in relation to accessing contraception and making decisions about their own fertility. In the performance workshop, young people are shown struggling to access contraceptives or information relating to their use, which later leads to them having unprotected intercourse. Most young women agreed that accessing contraceptives, especially from the clinic, was a 'non-starter' as the sister in charge was 'intimidating'. One young woman opened up and said:

---

4   *The Power of Choice* was a play with six scenes. The play opens up with three friends, Precious, Bee and Gee discussing the death of their friend, Tee, who died in an attempted abortion. Precious blames Tee for falling pregnant as she had always warned Tee against using the 'withdrawal method'. She explains that the withdrawal method is not 100% safe. Bee defends Tee, pointing out that Tee's boyfriend, Q, refused to use a condom as he said it defeated the purpose of pleasure. Precious still blames Tee, pointing out that they could have used the rhythm method.

The sister in charge at the clinic looks like my mother. You know, when you are there, you are not free. Even when she doesn't ask you any personal questions, I was not free around her.

An invited representative from the Student Health Services department agreed that they had received numerous complaints from female students who were not comfortable with the elderly staff at the clinic. She acknowledged that the university administration was in a difficult situation as they could not terminate their employment before their retirement age. However, she pointed out that they had begun training their elderly staff to be 'youth friendly' and to accommodative to young people's needs.

The drama performance strategically exposed the critical crossroads that Zimbabwe has reached in terms of sexual identity and permissiveness. This crossroads is marked by generational differentiation which the young women seem to emphasise during the workshop, positioning themselves in opposition to youths from earlier generations as they are 'objects' of modernist projects (Neyzi 2001). One young woman during the workshop discussion pointed out that:

These days there are no longer life-time partners. So one way or the other you are likely going to be intimate with more than one man in your lifetime, unlike long back, during the times of our parents. Therefore, the earlier we know and access contraceptives, the better we are to face the realities and protect ourselves.

What the above response reflects is an emerging discourse that positions young women at a cultural crossroad. Furthermore, it reflects a transitional young woman who has a greater consciousness towards the need and ability to act as a subject of her generational identity, renouncing her parents' gender ideals, to express a desire for an individualised and autonomous self. Ozyegin (2009) argues that the ideology of individualism is pivotal in fashioning new gender and sexual identities. Therefore, as 'tradition-free' agents, the new values subscribed to by some young women mark an important transition to what may be considered 'sexual modernity'.

However, some young women seemed to be aware that the escape from traditional views on femininity and respectability to individual selfhood is likely to be fraught with tensions and contradictions, because it occurs amid a continued societal emphasis of normative socio-sexual indices such as chastity and abstinence (Alemdaroglu 2007). For example, a young woman, in her second year, shared her anxieties about contraception use during an informal interview after the workshop:

> I have been tested for HIV and AIDS twice, but I will never ever consider putting Jadelle or using pills. What would my parents think if they found out...or even my boyfriend or husband, if he knows that I was using pills or had injections before getting married? It would send the wrong message. I don't want people to think I was like a prostitute when I was younger.

It is important to note how young women are reflexively aware of future tensions that may arise in being sexually agentive while they are still single. In her journal, Nyarie (not her real name), who was leading the development of the forum theatre production, wrote:

> The problem has always been that analysis and focus on young women's behaviours begins and ends with their behaviours, just looking at consequences of their behaviours. Its time people looked at issues from the point of view of a young woman to fully appreciate and understand her plight

If the above may be taken as the underlying motivation of the forum theatre presentation it shows that the project was aimed at 'reversing the gaze' (Bachechi 2009:11) and to understand the lived experiences of young women from their perspectives while critically exposing the dominant prohibitive and risk fermenting social norms. From the onset, it was evident that the young women attempted to position the intervention as a response to their lived realities and experiences. Of importance, from the conceptualisation of the project, was the shifting of focus and blame of unhealthy sexual consequences from individual decisions of young women to socio-cultural barriers which hinder their access to sexual health services.

The deaths of the young women in the play was constructed as a direct consequence of barriers faced by young women to access their sexual and reproductive rights, which include the right to access health care services, and seek, receive and impart information in relation to sexuality. Through such a positioning, the play attempted to expose and structure a social model of youth sexuality which views society as the major disempowering element to youth sexual health, as it imposes disability, and infantilises and denies youth sexual agency (Chivandikwa and Muwonwa 2013). The project seems to have been conceived as a political struggle directed at challenging society's perspectives on youth sexuality as deviance, which denies, controls and superintends youth sexuality, while also attempting to empower young women to challenge, resist and demand space as legitimate sexual citizens. Such a positioning articulates a challenge to a depoliticised and individualised ideology of youth sexuality which attributes blame and responsibility only to, and for young women, obfuscating systems of oppression that impinge upon or deny access to their own sexuality.

The forum theatre workshop attempted to create space for young women to cross normative youth sexuality boundaries imposed by adults through challenging the discourse of youth sexuality that denounces it as abnormal, unhealthy, illegal or criminal, and that is reinforced by intimidation about the dangers of sex. The theatre project acknowledged the inevitability of youth sex, revealing how young women subscribe to an emerging code of sexual ethics that allows premarital sex. Within the safe space created for discussion, young women admitted that they were sexually active. This is an act which resists prohibition on the one hand while on the other hand exposing the need for a new and valued discourse of youth sexuality. The acknowledgement of youth sex challenges the legal and moral denial of the existence and acceptance of sexual activity in non-married youth as it 'poses a threat to the norms which the state and religion feel responsible for' (Holzner and Oetomo 2004: 40).

The number of young women who had accessed or attempted to access sexual health services, or were tested for sexually transmitted infections, brings to the foreground evidence of early sexual activity as a reality among young people which is prevalent well before the age of adulthood or marriage. There is evidence from other research that the manner in which sexual initiation and conduct occur is still relatively uninformed and unprotected. Explicit in the notion of inevitability of youth sex is the debunking of notions of sexual purity and innocence that challenges the desexualisation of unmarried women, and the normative expectation that the transition from girlhood (non-sexual) to womanhood (sexual) should occur within the institution of marriage (Ozyegin 2009).

Testimonies of young women who had visited the clinic to

access contraception or information regarding protecting unwanted pregnancies or infections helped to engage a different discourse about youth sexuality which includes notions of competence to make decisions about sex in a mature way. The notion of competent citizenship includes participation, access, and equal and just treatment. Instead of prohibitive and regulatory frameworks, discourses of competence build on information and education which help to inform rational choices and self-control. It seems, within this discourse of self-regulation, that a new moral principle is asserted – responsible abstinence. Providing information and the means to sexual health develops street-wise youth who know when and when not to engage in sex, and know how to protect themselves from unwanted outcomes, whether pregnancy, STIs or HIV (Holzner and Oetomo, 2004).

Conclusion

The chapter has highlighted the lived sexual experiences of young people who have been undergoing a reframing process to help them make sense of the complex interrelationships between tradition and modernity. It is evident that young people have been struggling with attempts to live up to traditional expectations and codes of young adulthood, while identifying their sexuality as a charged site of control, and slowly reconstructing traditional concepts of purity, abstinence and the centrality of marriage. What is evident from this chapter is that young women are developing a political agenda that seeks to turn the discourse of prohibition into one that should respect young women's needs and rights, and by so doing crossing boundaries of social expectations regarding their sexuality. Discussions in this chapter provided a solid articulation of how neoliberalism has infiltrated the sexual lives of many young Zimbabwean women and sought to promote a non-prohibitive sexuality discourse for them built on their ability to balance needs and rights.

References

Adam, B. (1996) 'Detraditionalisation and the Certainty of Uncertain Futures', in P. Healas, S. Lash and P. Morris (eds), *Detraditionalisation: Critical Reflections on Authority and Identity*. Oxford: Blackwell.

Alemdaroglu, A. (2007) 'Formations of Femininity at the Intersection of

Class, Gender and Age: Young Women in Turkey'. Paper presented at the 2007 American Sociological Association Meetings, New York.

Bachechi, K.N. (2009) 'The Pure, the Pious and the Preyed Upon: A Celebration of Celibacy and the Erasure of Young Women's Sexual Agency'. PhD thesis, Boston College.

Bartky, S.L. (1990) *Femininity and Domination: Studies in Phenomenology of Oppression.* New York: Routledge.

Bay-Cheng, Y.L. (2003) 'The Trouble of Teen Sex: The Construction of Adolescent Sexuality through School-Based Sexuality Education', *Sexuality, Society and Learning*, 3(1), pp. 61-74.

Chivandikwa, N. and N. Muwonwa (2013) 'Forum Theatre, Disability and Corporeality: A Project on Sexuality in Zimbabwe', *Platform Journal of Theatre and Performance*, 7(1), pp. 55-66.

Central Statistical Office (CSO) (1995) 'Zimbabwe Demographic and Health Survey 1994'. Harare: Central Statistical Office.

Dixon-Mueller, R. (1993) 'The Sexuality Connection in Reproductive Health', *Studies in Family Planning*, 24(5), pp. 269-282.

Dunton, C. and M. Palmberg (1996) 'Human Rights and Homosexuality in Southern Africa'. Uppsala: Nordiska Afrikainstitutet.

Epprecht, M. (1998) 'The "Unsaying" of Indigenous Homosexualities in Zimbabwe: Mapping a Blind Spot in an African Masculinity', *Journal of Southern African Studies*, 24(4), pp. 631-651.

Epstein, R.M. (2007) 'Assessment in Medical Education', *New England Journal of Medicine,* 356(4), pp. 387-96.

Foucault, M. (1998) *Discipline and Punish: The Birth of the Prison.* London: Vintage Books.

Franke, K. (2004) *Sexual Tensions of Post-empire'*, in A. Sarat (ed.), *Studies In Law, Politics and Society.* Bingley, UK: Emerald Publishing.

Gupta, G.R. (2000) 'Gender, Sexuality, and HIV/AIDS: The What, the Why, and the How'. Washington, DC: International Center for Research on Women.

Holzner, B.M. and D. Oetomo (2004) 'Youth, Sexuality and Sex Education Messages in Indonesia: Issues of Desire and Control', *Reproductive Health Matters*, 12(23), pp. 40-49.

Kambarami, M. (2004) 'Femininity, Sexuality and Culture: Patriarchy and Female Subordination in Zimbabwe'. Lagos: Africa Regional Sexuality Resource Centre.

Marindo, R., S. Pearson and J.B. Casterline (2003) 'Condom Use and Abstinence Among Unmarried Young People in Zimbabwe: Which strategy, whose agenda?' New York: Population Council.

Matswetu, V.S. and D. Bhana (2018) '*Humhandara and hujaya*: Virginity, Culture and Gender Inequalities Among Adolescents in Zimbabwe, *Sage Open,* 8(2), pp. 1-11.

Mlingo, M. (2008) 'HIV/AIDS Knowledge and Sexual Behaviour and School Learners in Harare, Zimbabwe'. Master's thesis, University of South Africa.

Museka, G. and F. Machingura (2014) 'Interaction of Old Testament with the Shona traditions on children', in L. Togarasei and J. Kügler (eds), *The Bible and Children in Africa.* Bamberg: University of Bamberg Press.

Muwonwa, N. (2004) 'Theatre as Alternative Media: The Case of Patsime Edutainment Trust'. BA Honours dissertation, University of Zimbabwe.

―――― (2014) 'Entering the Liminal: Campus Culture, Retreating Femininities and Sexual Disempowerment at the University of Zimbabwe', *Pax Academica*, 3, pp. 184-202.

Neyzi, L. (2001) 'Object or Subject? The Paradox of "Youth" in Turkey', *International Journal of Middle East Studies*, 33(3), pp. 411-432.

Ozyegin, G. (2009) 'Virginal Facades: Sexual Freedom and Guilt among Young Turkish Women', *European Journal of Women's Studies*, 16(1), pp. 103-123.

UNAIDS (2016) 'Global AIDS Response Progress Report 2016: Zimbabwe Country Report'. Harare: UNAIDS.

Vengeyi, E. (2016) 'The Bible, violence, women and African initiated churches in Zimbabwe', in L. Togarasei and J. Kügler (eds), *The Bible and Children in Africa.* Bamberg: University of Bamberg Press.

Zeidenstein, S. and K. Moore (eds) (1995) *Learning about Sexuality: A Practical Beginning.* New York: The Population Council.

10

Youth in Artisanal Gold Mining

Eve Musvosvi Chandaengerwa and Michael Bourdillon

This chapter illustrates the involvement of young people in artisanal mining, where dangerous and exploitative working conditions provide an available option for survival. Such activity is an indicator of how, in the years since the independence of Zimbabwe, many young people have suffered from collapsing social structures combined with repeated droughts, a deteriorating national economy, and the HIV and AIDS epidemic. The involvement of young people in artisanal mining also illustrates how they overcame some of the obstacles they faced and improved their lives, creatively utilising whatever means became available to them. Opportunities in artisanal mining provided some with wealth that they could never have aspired to from small-scale rain-fed agriculture or even from employment available in rural areas. That youth, and even children under the age of majority, found they could improve their lives through strenuous and dangerous labour in artisanal mines is evidence both of how the state and their communities have failed to provide them with adequate safe livelihoods, and of their brave resilience to make something of their lives with whatever has been made available to them.

Mining in Zimbabwe

The Shona-speaking agricultural people settling on the Zimbabwean plateau around the sixth century already had pre-industrial technology for mining and smelting copper and iron, which continued until goods made from cheaper and better quality industrial process became readily available from the turn of the twentieth century (Prendergast 2019; Solberg 2019). Trade with the coast in ivory and gold from what is now Botswana and Zimbabwe goes back to the beginning of the second millennium, and the trade in gold through Mozambique rose and fell through the centuries with the value of gold in the wider world, and as political centres waxed and waned. In the fourteenth and fifteenth centuries, the capital at Great Zimbabwe was a major centre for trade in gold. Turmoil and the exhaustion of easily accessible gold resulted in a falling off in the production of gold early in the nineteenth century (Viewing 2019).

When colonialists entered the country around the turn of the twentieth century looking for gold and diamonds, as had been found in South Africa, they were disappointed to find little that was readily available. But the search resulted in the discovery of other useful minerals and mining of over 40 minerals became a major feature of the colonial economy. The trend to extend mining to smelting and refining was accelerated in the period after the Unilateral Declaration of Independence in 1965, which resulted in the UN imposing economic sanctions on the country. By the time of independence in 1980, there was a well-developed industrialised mining sector, accounting for 9.3% of GDP (Hawkins 2019).

Immediately after independence, industrial mining received a boost from increased exploration that had been hindered by the war; subsequently, industrial mining suffered from increasing input costs and low metal prices in the 1980s, before reviving in the 1990s with increasing foreign investment and improved international metal prices. The mining industry was boosted by increased production of platinum-group metals after the turn of the twenty-first century. The collapse of the Zimbabwean dollar, together with controls on the use of foreign currency and a policy of resource nationalisation, hindered the exploitation of rising gold prices in first decade, but this was partly rectified in the second decade after the return to the use of the US dollar. The sector had increased to around 17% of GDP by 2014. Nevertheless, formal employment in mining had dropped from 66,200 (6.5% of formal employment) to 36,800 in 2016 (3.1% of formal employment) (Hawkins 2019: 587, 581).

Alongside the industrial mining was a thriving semi-formalised small-scale sector owned by local entrepreneurs, utilising the country's pre-independence laws that allowed anyone to prospect for minerals and stake mining claims, and employing many thousands of workers. By 2019, over 200,000 people – around 7% of the total labour force (including over 75,000 youth – nearly 10% of those employed) – were in mining and quarrying, up from 92 000 in 2014 (Zimstat 2020, p.60 table 4.6b, p.89 table 5.5aii; 2015, p. 71 table 4.7(b))

Dominant in this surge was mining for gold. In addition to digging for gold, economic hardships encouraged thousands of people to pan for gold in dried river beds, which became legal only in 1991 (although it was again declared illegal in 2006, partly due to fears of uncontrolled mining damaging the environment). Parallel markets developed in trading gold, some of which was refined illegally (Chachage et al. 1993). Artisanal gold mining received a boost at the turn of the twenty-first century. The occupation of farms from 1998 was formalised as Zimbabwe's Fast Track Land Reform Programme by the Land Acquisition Act of 2002. On the one hand, this programme changed the structure of agricultural production in the country and created particular problems for certain categories of person, such as farm workers and widowed women. On the other hand it made available quality agricultural land to many small-scale farmers and to increased mobility across formerly inaccessible large-scale commercial farms (Mkodzongi 2013). Apart from making available agricultural land, this mobility enabled prospecting for gold in these previously inaccessible lands and the opening up of numerous artisanal mines, which provided increased income for many under increasing financial hardship. Small-scale entrepreneurs often mined gold in conjunction with other activities, especially to supplement farmers' incomes from agriculture (Mkodzongi and Spiegel 2019); sometimes it was controlled by powerful elites (Mawowa 2013). In 2018 and 2019, over 60% of the country's gold was produced in artisanal mining, much controlled by powerful persons not directly involved in the mining (ICG 2020). There is evidence that as a result of economic hardships and loss of income relating to the Covid-19 pandemic, ever more people, including children and youth who are no longer able to attend school, are turning in desperation to informal mining.[1]

---

1 '"I need money for school": the children forced to pan for gold in Zimbabwe', *The*

As in other informal sectors, the economic effectiveness of informal mining often relies on the exploitation of one's own and family labour, and the employment of people desperate for meagre incomes. A lack of control meant low standards of safety and little regulation of employment: many miners died as result of unsecured tunnels caving in.[2] It has been argued that contemporary small-scale miners are still using pre-colonial methods (only minor technological improvements), with poor working conditions, lack of capital, and environmental problems largely related to their small-scale nature and lack of government support or legal control (Masiya et al. 2012).

Not all benefited equally from the surge in informal mining. While Zimbabwe had legislation to encourage local initiatives in mining, it addressed communities as whole, which are dominated by male authority, and failed to address the needs of specific groups of people such as women (see Zamasiya and Dhlakama 2019) and young people. Although the Mines and Minerals Act (1996) legitimises the operations of small-scale miners, its formalities and fees could exclude small-scale artisanal miners working on their own. Policies towards artisanal gold miners have been inconsistent, with encouragement interspersed by heavy police crackdowns (Spiegel 2015). The apparently informal nature of artisanal mining often conceals the influence of economically and politically powerful people, who use violence to maintain their control over the resources and capture large profits for themselves through their exploitation of workers and sometimes defrauding the state by evading laws controlling trade in mined minerals; this became evident in the battles over diamonds discovered in the eastern districts of Zimbabwe (Saunders and Nyamunda 2016), and appears in a recent report on gold mining (ICG 2020). Such operations exploit many people desperate for a little income, and young people are easily drawn into such activities.

Nevertheless, with the deterioration of the formal economy, especially in the 1990s, informal gold mining has provided improved livelihoods for many, including youth and even children.[3]

Guardian, 13 November 2020.

2   In November 1992, the Minister of Home Affairs stated that at least three miners were dying in this way each week (Chachage et al. 1993: 18).

3   There have been some studies on children in mining (McIvor 2000; Save the Children UK 2000; Bourdillon and Musvosvi 2014; Chandaengerwa 2014), but we have found none specifically on youth who have reached the age of majority.

The involvement of children in dangerous underground mining rouses international outrage as one of the worst forms of child labour, which it undoubtedly is. Nevertheless, as this chapter shows, it has provided some young people with a short-term solution to problems caused by disease, poverty and neglect. It also provided an entry for some into an entrepreneurial livelihood as they matured.

Young people take up mining

Save the Children conducted a study in 1999 of teenagers involved in informal chrome mining and gold panning in two districts in Zimbabwe (McIver 2000). Many of these were helping parents in the work. The chrome mines had links to the formal sector, which requires attention to laws prohibiting those under the age of 15 from going underground, but children of all ages could help their parents in surface tasks. Much of the gold panning was illegal, and the children involved risked accidents and other health hazards as did the adults involved. The young people and their families were aware of the dangers of their work and the unhealthy conditions in which they had to live; in many cases, the work kept them from school but they pointed out that they had no money for schooling and needed to work in order to survive. While involvement in this work was clearly an indicator that the children were not receiving all that they should have by right, the study concluded that interventions to defend their rights needed to address the poverty that lay behind their work; simply to prohibit the work would not improve the situation. Indeed, at a workshop for working children, representatives of these child miners asked to be allowed to work in large formal mines, where working conditions and pay are better, in order to enable them to avoid working in informal mines (Bourdillon 2000: 15).

It is possible for children to help their families in informal mining outside school hours and during school holidays. When they do this, they are exposed to dangers to health and the possibility of accidents that adults also face. However, when families move to areas where mining is profitable, the children in such remote places may lose access to schooling, and lack the incentive to attend school when profits from mining are good; in practice, involvement in mining often kept children from school (Kori 2006). We have pointed to reports on how the hardships of the Covid-19 pandemic have recently driven more children into gold panning. While such activity comprises a clear indication of the failure of the state and of local communities to provide for the needs of these young people, it remains possible for them to use this work to overcome the difficulties they face.

The Chiweshe case study

In what follows, we draw from a detailed ethnographic study (Chandaengerwa 2014; Bourdillon and Musvosvi 2014) to show how careful attention to the contexts of children's lives reveals a variety of failures of the societies in which they live. The case illustrates how young people can constructively use the hazardous work of mining not only to provide essential food and medicines for themselves and their families, but also to contribute towards their schooling and broader education.

The study was conducted by Eve Chandaengerwa in Chiweshe communal lands, about 100 km north-east of Harare, from January 2007 to March 2008. At the time, the communities and the children there were suffering from several crises, some of which affected the country as a whole. Zimbabwe was suffering from unsurpassed hyperinflation that rendered its currency barely usable. While the HIV infection rate was dropping, AIDS-related deaths were just below their peak of over 100,000 per year in 2003. The land reform of the early 2000s meant that many lost jobs and homes on neighbouring farms that had previously been owned by white farmers, adding to the numbers of unemployed in the communities. For their livelihood, they used a variety of informal legal and illegal self-employment tactics, referred to generically as '*kukorokoza*' or 'doing business', and including mining and trading gold. The communities in the study were living on thin granitic soils not well suited to agriculture; the harvest of 2007 had been badly affected by rains that were well below average and interspersed with long dry spells, and after previous poor harvests in 2002 and 2004 agriculture was no longer a reliable source of livelihood for many people (Chiweshe 2011). Although the area was rich in resources, a complex web of political, gendered and generational inequalities combined with a collapsing economy and the ravages of the HIV and AIDS epidemic to make the lives of many children and youth extremely precarious. Poverty was and remains widespread, leaving many children without adequate adult support.

The ward in which the research took place had two under-resourced primary schools and a secondary school. It had no medical facilities, although there was a clinic staffed by nurses a few kilometres away. The nearest full medical facility was the Salvation Army's Howard Hospital some 20 kilometres away. The work of the clinic was hampered by the inadequacy of its government grants and by erratic supplies of drugs, which also affected the hospital. These problems, together with difficulties of transport, resulted in children frequently resorting to traditional sources of treatment.

The ethnographic study explored how children were growing up in a context of multiple crises. It focussed on 50 children aged 4-16 years: 12 were orphaned; 19 were staying with grandparents; and 9 were heads of their households. Thirty-seven indicated that they had to supplement inadequate food in their homes through foraging, and only three reported regularly having three meals a day. More than half the children's recollections of dreams were about hunger and lack of food.

The study was based on over a year of anthropological participant observation, and used a variety of techniques to ensure that the children's perspectives received due prominence. This child-centred approach exposed the agency of children in dealing with the problems they faced. Far from passively submitting to difficulties, some showed enterprise and resilience in looking after themselves and their families. Involvement in mining was part of this response and provided for some a means of livelihood extending into young adulthood.

Survival bands

One strategy employed by the children in the study was for friends to group together to work for survival, forming loose bands,[4] which adopted some kind of descriptive name. About two-thirds of the children were regular members of such groups or bands, with others joining occasionally. Participation in the bands' activities was flexible, based on ability to contribute, to take on a variety of tasks, and learn a variety of skills: the more roles one could take on, the more work one could do, and the more one could earn. The main activities of the bands were income-generating – '*kukorokoza*': members spent upwards of two hours a day on these activities, but children also foraged for consumption in their bands. Income and food earned and collected was

---

4 Similar to the 'survival bands' in response to extreme hunger described by Colin Turnbull (1972).

shared between those who actively took part. The children talked about *kudya tese* (to eat together), a phrase that normally applies to close family relations and now referred to sharing the resources of the band.

The bands included children who had been orphaned, as well as children whose parents had migrated out of the district for work; also children from large polygamous families and some whose parents had divorced. Some band members were staying with kin who had fostered them but made heavy demands on them to work.

The main reasons that children gave for participating in the bands were hunger, and the need to survive in a harsh economic climate. Others included the payment of school expenses, and travel for medical treatment. One girl had parents with poorly paying jobs in the city, who could rarely afford to visit home and often could not pay her school fees on time; her work in the band ensured that she could meet school and examination expenses.

Some boys joined to establish their status. Dependent on the kin with whom they were living, they undertook domestic work to negotiate relations, which they regarded as girl's work. Boys said that going back home carrying a live chicken made them feel like 'real men'; their material contributions to the households in which they lived made them feel they had retained their manhood.

There could be strategic reasons for joining a band. One girl was invited to join a band because her father's shop was sometimes used for gold exchanges with strangers whom the villagers did not want to take into their homes. The shop also served as the storage place for the substantial monthly rations of groceries that the band acquired in payment for regular work. Due to food shortages and high inflation, children generally preferred to be paid in kind.

Leadership of the bands arose from the personal charisma of older members, who combined interpersonal skills, mastery of survival-enhancing knowledge, and social connections. Control of money and food distribution could give the leader a small manipulative advantage, but the leader had to maintain the support and respect of the group as a whole.

Mining

The most lucrative work was the extraction of gold. A clampdown on illegal mining after 2006 primarily targeted stereotypical adult males.

By 2008, adult miners were employing children, who were less likely to be suspected by the police. Girls were preferred, since gangs of boys were more likely to attract the attention of the authorities; nevertheless, the children risked trouble with authorities. Extracting and trading in gold required dealing with adults: children could not acquire mining rights, and outside traders did not deal with children. Although groups of child miners were initially established under the partial supervision of adults, the children considered themselves as self-employed *makorokoza*, rather than employees. Subsequently, girls established groups comprising only girls, and working with elderly women, who offered a higher price for gold than did adult males; this was partly because some women were involved in cross-border trading and could sell gold where the price was higher.

Those involved in extracting gold were characterised as 'owls' or 'chameleons'. The owls worked at night, usually from 7 p.m. to 10 p.m. They worked underground, digging shafts to find the 'gold belt', and hauling and transporting rubble and gold on their own. They earned more, partly because their work was more dangerous as there was no system of inspection to ensure the safety of the shafts.

The chameleons panned gold during the day. Girls in this group often aspired to become owls for greater income and expanded options for survival, notwithstanding the greater danger in underground mining. As their name suggests, chameleons were able to blend into the forest and not be seen, even during the day. The invisibility of the chameleons was aided by close networks with 'connectors', who always made them aware of the activities of the police.

The bands pooled their labour to roast and crush gold-bearing stones, using mortar and pestle or conventional grindstones – tools used every day by women to process grains for food. These activities took place at the homesteads of women who were referred to as 'mothers'; they supervised the activities, bought the gold, and allowed flexible working hours.

The children were well aware of the risks of mining, particularly of underground mining, and of their exploitation by adults. They did not, however, want the protection of being prevented from earning money in this way; rather they wanted to be independent of exploiting adults. They complained that they were not allowed to stake their own mining claims, forcing them to work for low wages. They sometimes attempted to break the exclusion of children from trading the gold by making their own contacts with buyers and thus retaining a larger share of income; by the time they reached early adulthood, some had become competent traders. They saw no reason why they should be excluded from new forms of entrepreneurial development that seemed, more than schooling, to have attainable goals in a context of high unemployment and uncertainty.

Associated with the mining bands were the *makonekts* – those who connect between children's bands, between children and adults, between producers and the market, and between the police and child workers. Some of these roles were taken up by members of the band in turn, such as staying on guard at strategic points on the road to watch for police while others were working. Sometimes the *makonekts* were more specialised, setting up market stalls as a front for their main activity in connection with the miners. They often worked in pairs, and learnt their roles from each other together with their own improvisations.

Foraging

Apart from gold, the bands obtained food, medication, and raw materials from their environment, though some children also grew vegetables in home gardens. Very young children learn the skills of foraging by accompanying adults. In the bands, members shared their knowledge and experiences, and pooled labour. Gender roles were flexible and could be interchanged provided they enhanced survival chances, although all the girls still had to perform their gendered tasks when they returned home.

On their daily commute to and from school, children often contributed to the requirements of their households by collecting vegetables, fruit, edible insects, herbs for infusions, and firewood. In the bands, these activities became more intensive, and what children learnt in the bands contributed to their daily activities. The children ate more fruit and knew more varieties than most adults, who sometimes learnt from the survival-enhancing knowledge of the children.

For example, eleven-year-old Mutsa[5] proudly displayed her knowledge of four types of mushroom that come out at different seasons, and continued:

> The mushrooms can be eaten fresh, boiled or dried and are a good

---

5   All personal names in this chapter are pseudonyms.

substitute for meat. At times we sell them to raise income, but because our 'zim-kwacha'[6] is now useless, we prefer to exchange our mushrooms for food, chickens or anything else of value.

Children below the age of ten mainly participated in foraging, a widespread activity that took place at any time from five in the morning to midnight; working hours of individual children or groups depended on their needs and their other activities, including school. Girls and boys as young as four years old could join a band, in which they could be tasked with gathering edible insects like chafer beetles, grasshoppers, and termites; termites in particular are plentiful in the rainy season, and could be shared by the group, or dried and later exchanged for vegetables. Although these comprise low status food, the issue for the children was finding the only food available for the next meal, or the only available option to raise school fees for the next term.

One group made artefacts for sale and foraged for materials. The members belonged to a church that had a reputation for producing and trading in crafts, and called themselves 'Young Fathers'. Their crafts used natural products – reeds, grass, sisal, cattle and goat hides, rabbit skin, and natural dyes derived from indigenous trees – to make wall hangings, baskets, mats, shoe straps, shawls, blankets, and various wooden utensils and musical instruments. The leader of another group confided that when things are tough economically, certain fruits could be fermented quickly with the aid of yeast and heat, to produce a popular, cheap, but illegal alcoholic brew for sale.

So we see that the involvement of children in mining was only one activity among several that were adopted by young people to provide sustenance and to improve their lives. Their problems were neglected by those in authority at the local and national levels, and their solutions were based on effectiveness rather than legality.

Matriq's story

Matriq was aged 15 at the time of the study, and was the leader of one of the bands. Her story illustrates how her involvement in mining can be understood only in the context of the privations in her life, coming from natural adversities and political neglect at a variety of levels – national, local, and familial.

---

6   A derogatory term dating from the time of the collapse of the Zambian *kwacha*, long before the much more dramatic collapse of the Zimbabwean dollar.

Both Matriq's parents died of AIDS some years before our study. She lived with her twin sisters (seven years old) and four male cousins, aged nine, seven, six, and four, all under the care of their elderly grandmother until her death in 2007. Two of the boys were also AIDS orphans, and the youngest was the child of a young unmarried mother who subsequently left the home to marry. The grandmother had been using her assets on food, health care, and burials in the family, and had few resources. She was in poor health and had no stable income. Matriq, the eldest child, became responsible for the provision, production, and consumption of food; organising work within the household; and the health needs of all, including her grandmother until she died. She was the de facto head of household even before her grandmother died.

The grandmother had been a well-known herbalist in the area, often receiving from satisfied patients gifts of groceries, which helped her to care for her grandchildren. When gathering herbs, she often took Matriq as an apprentice, who thus acquired knowledge which she shared with others in the bands and acquired status. Before the grandmother's death, however, she had lost clients to a young spiritual cleanser who accused her of being a witch, an accusation that appeared to be supported by the multiple deaths in her family and deaths of her patients by AIDS. Even her only remaining child, a son, shunned her.

When Matriq's father died, her father's brother took over the property, cattle and land his late brother had left. He should have taken over the care of the children as well, but they were left largely on their own in their grandmother's home, her supposed witchcraft being an excuse to mistrust and shun them. Matriq wrote in her diary:

> It was a terrible time for us, my sisters and I had just lost our parents, but people turned us away, nobody wanted us to visit their houses or even help us with clothing or food. They said they were afraid that we would bewitch them and eat them. We almost starved to death while our relatives watched. What was surprising was that my father's brother was not afraid of utilising the land that belonged to witches.

He refused her request for help with examination fees, accusing her of using mining as a cover for prostitution. So she resolved to work hard and succeed on her own.

Matriq ensured that her siblings had food to eat at school, and invented recipes for tasty treats from what she learnt from her grandmother. She stated that since she joined the gold diggers, there was always bus fare to take her sisters to the HIV and AIDS programme at Howard Mission hospital where they get free cotrimoxazole. She complained that since Howard was one of the few hospitals with such a programme, it was always crowded. Children without connections were at a disadvantage in such crowds, and sometimes Matriq had to go home without any medication for her sisters.

From this story we see how national economic problems are compounded by problems of climate and health, and by actions of the local community, including political and religious elders as well as senior kin. The work of mining contributed significantly to enabling Matriq to care for her family – young and old – and to continue her own development, providing entrepreneurial and other livelihood skills that remained important to her as she entered adulthood.

Youth in mining 2020

A visit to the field in November 2020 showed that Chiweshe had experienced the recent national surge in artisanal mining mentioned in the introduction to this chapter. Mining had become more extensive and formalised, with digging areas being fenced off and entry restricted by security personnel to genuine and suitably attired miners. The mines were largely sponsored by older patrons, who for a share of the profits provided work clothes and mining equipment that the youths could not initially afford. Youths did the dangerous underground work. The patrons were also often the buyers of the gold, but did not live in the area, a fact which enabled some of the gold to remain undeclared and sold elsewhere, improving the profits for the youth working the mines. The soil brought up from the shafts by the youths is deemed to belong to the older owners of the land, who were able to extract more gold from it with appropriate machinery and chemicals; although initially the youths were happy with the wealth they could achieve from underground mining, they later perceived the elders as unjustly extracting with little work a greater amount from the soil so perilously brought to the surface.

Many young people see the hope of disposable income through mining, which offers more promise than erratic rain-fed agriculture or the scarcity of formal employment. Indeed, some gold miners prospered: two are known to have bought peri-urban houses in Harare. One young man commented:

> The pressure of being a young male are no joke... At least if you die underground, you die with dignity rather than being alive and not being able to help your family or achieve anything... For some of us who were not brilliant in school this may be our only way out. I have built a seven-roomed house for my parents and am planning to buy a Honda Fit, something even educated teachers and nurses in this village have failed to do their whole working lives.

Others were now excluded. Girls like Matriq were kept out of mining on the grounds of protecting their morality. Even girls involved in surface work considered appropriate to females, such as cooking, were stigmatised as looking for opportunities to earn by prostitution (cooking was usually undertaken by boys who were afraid to go underground and were regarded as effeminate). Younger children were also now excluded; the age of those working the mines ranging from 15 upwards.

Some who had worked in the mines as children were later able to avoid underground work by acting as intermediaries between miners and patrons, or between miners and investors to bring in more expensive equipment, or by employing younger boys to do the dangerous work. While these sometimes earned significant spending money, the big incomes that allowed capital investment went to those doing or controlling the dangerous underground work. The growing inequality was reflected in a number of incidents of violent robbery of miners' wealth.

In the absence of industrial investment, the work remained heavy and hazardous. Youths were aware of the recent accident in Bindura (some 100 kilometres away), in which around 40 miners were trapped and died underground when the shaft of the long disused mine they were informally opening collapsed.[7] Several youths confessed to smoking marijuana to overcome their fear of going underground. Some have indeed been banned from their churches for taking such drugs, but this did not stop church leaders from acceding to requests for prayers for safety and good luck charms, which were frequently requested by youths before going underground.

In such a desperate environment, the earnings from mining become

---

7   'Zimbabwe mine shaft collapse leaves about 40 people trapped', *eNCA*, 28 November 2020.

essential, and override other considerations. As one youth said,

> When you are poor and have nothing in this world, that's when you realise that even with relatives around you, you are all alone in this world. Nobody will rescue you so you have no choice but to go underground – because even to be able to farm next season, you still have to go underground and earn US$.

Hazardous mining, and taking drugs to make it bearable, are on the one hand indicators of the desperate situations in which youth find themselves, and on the other a constructive attempt to overcome the problems in the absence of institutional support.

Conclusion

Youth have not been the focus of attention of formal policy on mining. Indeed, young children are excluded from involvement in industrial mining, and opportunities for future work and a career in this sector have diminished. However, opportunities in informal mining have opened up, exposing young people to exploitation and abuse as well as new possibilities for earning.

This chapter illustrates the devastation to the lives of many young caused by poverty, disease and neglect, combined with social injustice at the local, national and international levels. The involvement of children and youth in dangerous underground mining is a clear indicator that the country and its communities have not provided adequately for them.

This involvement also shows how some young people could improve their own lives and those of their families through new opportunities in artisanal mining, both in the short term as part of their broader survival tactics, and in providing an entry into longer term entrepreneurial activity. This does not necessarily result in the use of resources to develop the communities and reduce inequalities. Some young people in mining have followed the example of many political leaders in using a community resource, in this case gold, to acquire for themselves an improved life outside the community and at the expense of some people in the community, a far cry from an idealised *ubuntu* that promotes social responsibility and co-operation.

Investment in mining from outside might mitigate the hazards of this work and make it more profitable. Appropriate control, and addressing the social inequalities and injustices that lie behind the desperate situation of many, could assist in spreading the benefits from the resource to others in the community and ensure that all have a chance to benefit; however, controls that simply remove or restrict opportunities without offering anything in their place do not help. Any attempt to help these young people to improve their lives needs to start by understanding their needs and aspirations: if we cannot adequately provide for them, we should at least listen to them and respect their efforts to provide for themselves.

References

Bourdillon, M. (2000) 'Introduction', in M. Bourdillon (ed.), *Earning a Life: Working Children in Zimbabwe*. Harare: Weaver Press.

———— and E. Musvosvi (2014) 'What can children's rights mean when children are struggling to survive? The Case of Chiweshe, Zimbabwe', in N. Ansell and A. Twum-Danso Imoh (eds), *Children's Lives in an Era of Childrens' Rights: The Progress of the Convention on the Rights of the Child in Africa*. London: Routledge.

Chachage, S.L., M. Ericsson, and P. Gibbon (1993) *Mining and Structural Adjustment: Studies on Zimbabwe and Tanzania*. Uppsala: Nordic Africa Institute.

Chandaengerwa, E.A. (2014) 'Growing up in the era of AIDS: Childhood experiences in rural Zimbabwe'. D.Phil thesis, University of Pretoria.

Chiweshe, M.K. (2011) 'Farm Level Institutions in Emergent Communities in Post Fast Track Zimbabwe: Case of Mazowe District'. PhD thesis, Rhodes University.

Hawkins, A.M. (2019) 'Zimbabwe's Mining Economy', in M. Prendergast and J. Hollaway (eds), *Mining in Zimbabwe from the 6th to the 21st Centuries*. Harare: Chamber of Mines of Zimbabwe.

International Crisis Group (ICG) (2020) 'All That Glitters is Not Gold: Turmoil in Zimbabwe's Mining Sector'. Report No. 294. Brussels: International Crisis Group.

Kori, A. (2006) *Makorokoza: Small scale gold mining in the Midlands Province of Zimbabwe*. Silveira House Social Series no. 18. Gweru: Mambo Press.

Masiya, T., L. Mlambo and M. Motive (2012) 'Small-Scale Mining in Zimbabwe: Historical Perspective', Global Conference on Business and Finance, 7(2), pp. 286-295.

Mawowa, S. (2013) 'The political economy of artisanal small-scale gold mining in Central Zimbabwe', *Journal of Southern African Studies*, 39(4), pp. 921-936.

McIver, C. (2000) 'Child labour in informal mines in Zimbvabwe', in M. Bourdillon (ed.), *Earning a Life: Working Children in Zimbabwe*. Harare: Weaver Press.

Mkodzongi, G. (2013) 'New people, new land and new livelihoods: A micro-study of Zimbabwe's fast-track land reform', *Agrarian South: Journal of Political Economy,* 2(3), pp. 345-366.

Mkodzongi, G., and S. Spiegel (2019) 'Artisanal Gold Mining and Farming: Livelihood Linkages and Labour Dynamics after Land Reforms in Zimbabwe', *The Journal of Development Studies*, 55(10), pp. 2145–2161.

Prendergast, M. (2019) 'Pre-colonial iron', in M. Prendergast and J. Hollaway (eds), *Mining in Zimbabwe from the 6th to the 21st Centuries*. Harare: Chamber of Mines of Zimbabwe.

Saunders, R., and T. Nyamunda (eds) (2016) *Facets of Power: Politics, Profits and People in the Making of Zimbabwe's Blood Diamonds*. Harare: Weaver Press.

Save the Children UK (2000) *A Situational Analysis of Children in the Informal Mining Sector in Mutorashanga and Shamva*. Harare: Save the Children UK.

Solberg, H.F. (2019) 'Pre-colonial copper', in M. Prendergast and J. Hollaway (eds), *Mining in Zimbabwe from the 6th to the 21st Centuries*. Harare: Chamber of Mines of Zimbabwe.

Spiegel, S. (2015) 'Shifting Formalization Policies and Recentralizing Power: The Case of Zimbabwe's Artisanal Gold Mining Sector', *Society & Natural Resources*, 28(5), pp. 543–548.

Turnbull, C.M. (1972) *The Mountain People*. New York: Simon and Schuster.

Viewing, K.A. (2019) 'Pre-colonial gold', in M. Prendergast and J. Hollaway (eds), *Mining in Zimbabwe from the 6th to the 21st Centuries*. Harare: Chamber of Mines of Zimbabwe.

Zamasiya, B., and T. Dhlakama (2019) 'An Analysis of the Legal, Institutional and Policy Constraints affecting the Participation of

Men and Women in Local Content Development Outcomes in the Mining Sector in Zimbabwe', in *Putting Women at the Centre of Extractivism: A Compendium on Gender and Extractives*. Harare: Women and Law in Southern Africa.

Zimbabwe National Statistics Agency (Zimstat) (2015) *2014 Labour Force Survey*. Harare: Zimstat.

Zimbabwe National Statistics Agency (Zimstat) (2020) *2019 Labour Force and Child Labour Survey*. Harare: Zimstat.

11

Stranded and Straddling? The Youth in Zimbabwe's Agricultural Sector, 1980-2020

Toendepi Shonhe and

Rangarirai Gavin Muchetu

Introduction

The youth land question remains unresolved in Zimbabwe (Moyo 2004; Murisa 2016), and has taken a peculiar trajectory characterised by a general youth disenfranchisement since independence. The priority has predominantly been on war veterans and war collaborators who seem to wield never-ending political clout. The youth continue to access land through customary and inheritance laws in the communal areas, and to some extent, in the resettled farming areas (Chipenda 2020). However, these channels are unreliable because they are affected by improving life-expectancy, possible disputes over inheritance among family members, and potential land appropriation through land-grabs (Chipato et al. 2020; de Janvry et al. 1991). Additionally, inheritance and customary law usually exclude young women from accessing land. Due to failing economic fortunes and increasing unemployment, the youth also face difficulties in buying land (Bryceson 2002). Zimbabwean youth are thus caught up in the 'missing jobs' crisis emanating from structural shocks and constraints affecting sub-Saharan African economies (Fox et al. 2020: 1).

Thus, although the youths played a vital role in the jambanja (the violent and so-called chaotic land grabbing) of commercial farming land after 2000, replacing designated state institutions and processes (Chipenda 2020), they were not the primary targets for land allocation.1 As a result, no quota was assigned for the youth, compared to women (20%) and war veterans (15%) (Moyo 2004: 24; Thebe 2018).

No universal definition of youth exists. The youth can be viewed as a class, and hence its internal and external contradictions (with the older generation) are a class struggle (Sargeson 2016 cited in Chipato et al. 2020: 62). In some parts of rural Africa, youth are simply those incapable of sustaining 'legal' marriage (Abdullah 1998). In other traditions, it is associated with undergoing certain rituals (Thorsen 2007 as cited by Thebe 2018) or may be defined by way of age. Irrespective of the definition, the underlying principle is the transition from childhood to adulthood. This transition is everchanging and involves a combination of sexual maturation, securing socio-economic autonomy from parents and guardians (Bennell 2007), or the gaining of responsibility (Leavy and Smith 2010). The United Nations identifies youth as 15–24 year-olds, while the Commonwealth uses 15-29. Zimbabwe identifies youth as those between 15 and 35 years, as applied in this chapter.

Debates on the youth problem have mostly been framed around the need to secure sustainable employment and agriculture opportunities, lest they indulge in 'crime and juvenile delinquency; rebelliousness and conflict; apathy; antisocial behaviour' (Biriwasha 2012: 4). There are nonetheless suggestions that despite the centrality of agriculture as a source of food, employment, and industrial raw materials, youth are losing interest in the sector (Biriwasha, 2012). It is thought that the general trends towards de-agrarianisation associated with increasing environmental damage, landlessness, and economic distress linked to low agricultural funding contribute to de-peasantisation and changing aspirations on farming by the youth (Habtu et al. 1997). In this sense, the youth perceive agriculture as primitive and requiring hard labour, especially in the absence of adequate infrastructure and modern technology (ibid.). However, Moyo and Yeros (2005) have argued for the existence of semi-proletarianisation tendencies, where peasants straddle

---

1 The characterisation of the FTLRP as chaotic remains highly debated; see Chaumba et al. (2003) for instance.

urban and rural areas, working in urban areas and support agricultural activities in rural areas. The semi-proletarianisation thesis explains how the peasantry did not disappear, but rather evolved to lead the militant land movement, forcing land reform from 2000 (Moyo 2001; Sadomba 2008). In this sense, while Moyo and Yeros (2005) observed the coexistence of semi-proletarianisation and re-peasantisation associated with the fast track land reform programme (FTLRP), the economy-wide crisis (Muchetu 2019; Scoones et al. 2010) might have reconfigured the rural-urban linkages in ways that may have diminished options for the youth two decades after the reform.

How, then, have the youth been involved in agriculture since 1980? In the context of a reconfigured agrarian structure, deindustrialisation, and the informalisation of the economy in a long-standing crisis, how have the youth worked their way around the challenges? As noted by Chipenda (2020: 500), while there are several studies on youth participation in agriculture and land reform in Zimbabwe, the empirical examination of the extent to which the local and national level are involved remains weak. This chapter constitutes a qualitative and quantitative examination to fill in this gap. The chapter concludes that youth participation in agriculture is comparable to other generations, and the production and accumulation patterns indicate differentiated outcomes not easily delineable to age differences. Zimbabwe's exhausting economic crisis is all-engulfing, and only the politically connected thrive, particularly in the agricultural sector.

The chapter is based on a tracking study of 20 households and intersectional household surveys administered in communal areas and A1 farms in the Hwedza and Goromonzi districts (Mashonaland East province), and the Mvurwi farming area in Mazowe District (Mashonaland Central province) for triangulations and trend analysis.[2]

---

2   The tracker study of 20 household members linked to an earlier (1988/9) survey administered in Chiweshe by Ministry of Agriculture and another carried out by Ruzivo Trust in the A1 farm in 2007, provided qualitative life histories to augment survey data and document analysis, relying on documents collected from the Zimbabwe Central Statistics Office between 2016 and 2020. Using multi-cluster random sampling, the surveys selected 53 and 46 communal and A1 farmers in Hwedza district, compared to 100 CA and 100 A1 farmers in Goromonzi as well as 519 and 310 in Mvurwi area, respectively. The three districts experienced extensive land redistribution, mainly from 2000 when 2,861, 1,673 and 4,994 A1 farmers were settled in Hwedza, Goromonzi and Mazowe districts, respectfully. Hwedza has 12,491 households compared to 17,090 and 2,709 CA farming households for Goromonzi and Mvurwi farming areas, respectively.

Archive data from the ZimStat collections are also analysed. Following this introduction, section two discusses youth, agriculture, and the land question in Zimbabwe after 1980. In section three, emerging evidence on youth participation after 2000 is presented while section four contextualises the youth problem within the economy-wide crisis. Section five discusses the 'old' and new youth in agriculture before a conclusion is made in section six.

The youth continue to straddle the urban and rural areas for livelihoods with precarious land ownership statuses; however, their engagement in agriculture differed over the period under review. High youth unemployment is undoubtedly a problem in 'low-paying economic activities, especially in informal settings' for Africa's youth (Mabiso and Benfica 2019: 11). Arguably, agriculture remains a crucial employer in developing countries (see Proctor and Lucchesi 2012), as the Zimbabwean case attests. A key enabler for youth participation is institutional frameworks that ensure youth access to resources with an impact on agricultural production and accumulation by differentiated farming classes. At a total population of 3.6 million or 44.2% of adults (those above 15 years) (ZimStat 2019), the youth constitute the majority of those in the job market in Zimbabwe (Table 11.1). From 63% in 2004, the youth involved in family labour and agriculture waged labour increased to 84.4% by 2019. Those employed gainfully in agriculture rose from 32.4% in 1980 to 37% in 2019, even though a drop to 24.4% was experienced in 1990. Mkodzongi and Spiegel (2020) observed that the land reform opened up access channels to natural resources previously closed under the colonial dual economy.

There has been an increase in youth involvement in mining and quarrying, from 2% in 2004 to 9% in 2019 (ZimStat 2019). Access to these previously enclosed farming lands has enabled a wide range of social groups to engage in diversified livelihoods activities, including artisanal mining, known as chikorokoza (Chipangura 2019; Mawowa 2013; Mkodzongi and Spiegel 2020). However, the local commodity circuits are inherently informal (see Chapter 10), with politics playing a crucial role in moderating access. The youth are found at the very bottom of the production chain receiving exploitative labour wages. In postcolonial Zimbabwe, the struggle for access to land and mining opportunities on the land has been daunting for youth, as discussed henceforth.

Table 11.1: Distribution of employed youth by occupation and industry, Zimbabwe 2011 - 2019

	Managers, Professionals, Technicians, and associate professionals			Services, Sales and Support workers			Skilled agricultural, forestry and fishery workers			Craft, plant, and Machinery assemblers			Elementary occupations			Totals in Percentages			
	2011	2014	2019	2011	2014	2019	2011	2014	2019	2011	2014	2019	2011	2014	2019	1980	1990	2000	2019
Agriculture, forestry, and fishing	7,188	7,777	4,815	16792	9436	16276.95	1,951,125	2,164,239	263,788	15,770	30,015	17,228	117,582	193,436	243,117	32.4	24.4	26.3	37
Mining and quarrying	2,608	3,927	2,452	1569	1032	536	0	0	0	33,787	49,734	1,835	22,614	11,619	14,766	6.6	4.3	3.6	9
Manufacturing	11,537	11,103	7,187	14661	11554	4219	322	813	537	88,000	87,733	37,922	29,097	14,541	33,752	15.8	16.5	14.7	6
Other industries & the public sector	154,080	134,181	116,002	373045	431717	271758	5,748	6,420	3,757	106,889	130,712	45,160	239,180	265,444	237,316	45.2	54.8	55.4	50
Total	175,413	156,988	130,456	33022	22022	21031	1,951,447	2,165,052	264,325	137,557	167,482	56,985	169,293	219,596	291,635	100	100	100	100
Percentage of agriculture per skills sector	4.1	5.0	3.7	50.9	42.8	77.4	99.7	99.7	99.8	11.5	17.9	30.2	69.5	88.1	83.4				

Source: Authors, Compiled from Zimstats, 2019

Youth participation from 1980-1999

The initial land reform plans after 1980 were optimistic, as they sought to redefine how agriculture operated in the country. The objectives included correcting the legacies of colonialism (Moyo 1995), to satisfy social and productivity goals (Nkomo 1984), decongest communal areas and give land to restless war veterans and refugees (Thebe 2018), and propel land utilisation and national development (Geza 1986). A modern technocratic approach sustained by bureaucrats (Cliff 1988) was used in allocating land in the early phases of the land reform programme. Various studies have shown land reform in this period was limited and highly constrained, but did produce positive results. While the successes of many land reform beneficiaries was down to their own hard work and enterprise there were still indications of improving livelihoods (Kinsey 2004; Zamchiya 2012). To the extent that they constituted part of the land-short population in Zimbabwe, these objectives, to some extent, included the youth at that time.

However, from 1980-1996, the land reform missed many of its targets, including 'to provide, at the lower end of the scale, opportunities for people who have no land, and are without employment and may therefore be classified as destitute' (Chitsike 2003: 3). In 1980, only 32.4% of the economically active population were employed in agriculture (MLSS and MYDIE 2009: 11). Soon after the war, the biggest issue was how to provide jobs for the returning war veterans and youth, and agriculture had the potential to soak up many of them; thus, land reform became a priority. In the first phase carried out from 1980 to 1985, the government managed to settle 35,000 families on vacant commercial farm land. By 1990 this number increased to 54,000 households (Alexander 1994: 335) against a target of 162,000 families on nine million hectares (Selby 2006: 131). In the 1990s, land reform took on an even slower pace, with less than 20,000 households resettled by 1996. The government had hoped to resettled over 1.6 million people by this time (Chaumba et al. 2003b: 3). The early land reform carried out in the 1980s mainly targeted the poor communal area people and those returning from the war (ibid.: 4). The aim of the land reform was to 'improve the agricultural capacity of peasant households' (Moyo 1995: 64). Women were a key part of both policy and study at this point (Gaidzanwa 2011; Mutopo 2011).

The Zimbabwean youth, on the other hand, continuously got caught in the 'missing jobs' crisis emanating from structural shocks and constraints that were affecting sub-Saharan African economies (Fox et al. 2020: 1). These shocks were exacerbated by issues of landlessness. The youth as a social class had not become part of policy discourse even though they were active as agricultural labour. Thebe (2018) observed that the 18-35 year-olds were more prepared to resettle and abandon existing communal land rights. It is argued that the youths were theoretically an ideal population to resettle but were mainly excluded because they lacked farming competencies, agricultural resources, or formal jobs. The fear of disconnecting with the broader extended families also affected youth participation during the early resettlement programmes (Potts and Mutambirwa 1990).

Despite the established view that land utilisation was low on the large-scale commercial farms (LSCFs) in the 1990s (Weiner et al, 1985) and there was an increasing demand for land by the black population, the transfer of land from the minority white farmers remained low (Moyo 1995). The limited land redistribution persisted despite the expiry of the restrictive provision of the Lancaster House constitution in 1990 and the passing of the 1992 Land Acquisition Act which enabled the compulsory acquisition of land by the government (Shonhe 2017). The shift towards the production of cash crops and eco-tourism by the LSCF farmers resulted in the peasant farmers carrying the burden of producing food crops (Moyo 2000). The newly resettled farmers were also doing well, mostly on account of their own investment (Gunning et al. 2000; Kinsey 1999). The 1997 resettlement programme, however, sought to expand the targeted population to include the poor landless communal villagers and capitalist oriented farmers with agricultural training (Chaumba et al 2003, p. 538). The lack of progress in resettlement, as epitomised by the lack of movement after the 1998 Donor Conference also affected access to land by the youth, women and the liberation war veterans (Moyo 2000), resulting in increasing pressure for land in the late 1990s.

Youth participations after the 2000-FTLRP

The dramatic nature of the FTLRP elicited changes in land administration structures and processes at the local and national level. As Matondi (2012: 3) argued, the FTLRP was 'a theatre of contests' that included policy interests, shifting relationships, changing production patterns, new farming systems, evolving commodity circuits in the input and output markets, and constraining social and cultural practices. These contestations impacted land access and local politics and played an important role in controlling and managing access to land (Chaumba et al. 2003b). The government largely bypassed the legal constraints to land reform as well as state structures involved in land administration under the FTLRP (Chaumba et al. 2003b; Sadomba 2011; Zamchiya 2012; Matondi 2012). War veterans were often the most influential and powerful actors on the ground and dictated much of how land was parcelled out and distributed. Even though, in some cases, traditional leaders and youths were co-opted, the war veterans chaired the committees that oversaw land redistribution. These were called the Committees of Seven (Co7).[3]

The Co7 had influence in the land allocation and state subsidy distribution, and had power over farm infrastructure left by the former white farmers (Chiweshe 2011: 11). The operation of the Co7 was often at loggerheads with the law; thus, the government created and superimposed the Provincial Land Committees (PLCs) and the District Land Committees (DLCs) to oversee Co7's farm-level operations. They preferred 'action-oriented ad-hoc arrangements', which often generated power struggles at all levels, such that many potential beneficiaries could not know who was in charge and how the land allocation was proceeding, leading to their exclusion (Matondi 2012: 39).

Youth participation in the FTLRP was multifaceted, yet remained low in terms of the overall numbers who benefited. War veterans were estimated to be between 2% and 22% of the beneficiaries of the FTLRP. Women in their own right received 15-25% of the land allocations and former farmworkers approximately 5% (Moyo 2004: 24). There have been a few studies that quantify the actual amount of land that accrued to those aged 15-35 years (Chaumba 2003a: 591). In some cases, the youth and the older generation fought together to access land, as shown in Chipato et al. (2020: 65). As a result, some youths have accessed land through political party affiliation (Zamchiya 2011). However, young men were mostly used as foot soldiers during the occupations because 'young men were deployed as sentries to guard against "infiltrators",

---

3   The Co7 were local level authorities that reported to the District Lands Committees (and other state land agents) in the initial stages of the FTLRP. They were composed of representatives from war veterans, village heads, youth and women (Chiweshe 2011: 11).

morning and evening roll calls were held, and men and women were segregated at night' (Chaumba et al. 2003b: 9). Chipato et al. (2020: 70) even point out that some youths were paid to represent older men during the farm occupations. Notably, the emergent agrarian structures after 2000 illustrate how the youth have struggled to access and use the land (Moyo 2011).

Overall, the village heads controlled access to land (Chimhowu and Woodhouse 2006; Chipato et al. 2020) while political connections played a critical role in land allocations (Chaumba et al. 2003b; Chiweshe 2011; Marongwe 2011; Moyo 2003). In the post-settlement era, as Shonhe (2019: 24) observed, participation by the youth in tractor cooperatives in Mvurwi was low, with the highest being 13.3% at Hariana farm. In this sense, post-resettlement support for the youth has also been low.

The youth were used as tools by a variety of actors. However, in some cases, they managed to buy land and have become successful farmers. Some took advantage of the land reform process to gain positions within the village committees responsible for giving land to gain land access (Chaumba et al. 2003b: 8). Youths must also be understood within the context of capital flight inspired by sanctions and the nature of the resettlement programme, which contributed to a decline in production during the first five years of the FTLRP (Shonhe and Mtapuri 2020). The re-insertion of finance capital through contract farming has increased youth participation in tobacco production, enabling some to access new ways to accumulate capital. Contract farming and politically moderated access to state finance programmes shape agricultural production (Shonhe et al.2020).

Who is on the land, two decades after the fast track?

The survey results show that the older population – over 52 years of age – held more land than those younger. This was observed among communal area farmers in Goromonzi district (55%), where it was the highest (Table 11.2). The old youth (those who were 15-35 years old at the time of land occupation) have higher access to land than the new youth (those currently between 15 and 35 years old), but less than those over 52 years of age. A lower proportion of the new youth accessed land in the communal areas and A1 farming areas across the three study sites, ranging from 5% in Goromonzi communal areas to 20%

in Mvurwi communal areas. In comparison, the older (over 52 years of age) population's land ownership ranged from 37% to 55%.

Table11. 2: Land access by age and gender

			Male %	Female %	Total %
Mvurwi	A1	New youth	16	11	14
		Old youth	46	38	42
		> 52 years	39	51	45
	CA	New youth	29	10	20
		Old youth	43	30	37
		> 52 years	28	61	45
Hwedza	A1	New youth	25	10	18
		Old youth	42	50	46
		> 52 years	33	40	37
	CA	New youth	8	18	13
		Old youth	52	25	39
		> 52 years	40	57	49
Goromonzi	A1	New youth	9	3	6
		Old youth	38	26	32
		> 52 years	54	37	45
	CA	New youth	6	3	5
		Old youth	35	46	41
		> 52 years	59	51	55

Source: Own Study. Sample: Mvurwi NA1=310; NCA=520; Hwedza: NA1=46; NCA=53: Goromonzi: NA1=92; NCA=100

These findings contrast with other studies where youth were generally observed to have been excluded from the land reform process (see Chipato et al. 2020; Chipenda 2020; Scoones et al. 2019). While today's youth struggle for more land, those who constituted the youth at the time of the land reform had access. For example, landlessness among today's youth was explained by Tawanda Fireshu in the Hwedza old resettlement area, who observed that:

> My father got settled here in the early 1980s and had three wives and 16 sons. All of us had to share his six hectare farm allocation. My father allocated the first five sons, one hectare each for farming activities. But soon, there was not enough for the rest of

us. When the fast track land reform programme came, five of my brothers were part of those who occupied land in neighbouring farms. Three were lucky to be allocated land and have since moved to their new land. Five of my brothers went to Harare and other towns where they were working, but after 2004, three got retrenched, and two are now in South Africa. One went back to Mukamba in Hwedza communal area, and occupied my father's land (personal Interview, TF ORA, Hwedza, 12 March 2016).

How then are the youth accessing the land? While this differs across sites, Table 11.3 shows that the old youth and the older beneficiaries mostly got land allocated by the district lands officer during the *jambanja* period. In comparison, only a few new youths across the sites secured land through this means, with 6%, 23% and 8.6% in Mvurwi, Hwedza and Goromonzi districts, respectively. In Mvurwi, the new youth either formally inherited the plot (67%), got an informally subdivided plot, or rented the plot.

For both the new and old youth, buying a plot from somewhere else is very common, ranging from 25% to 100% in the different sites. Even though the older population mostly benefitted from the land reform, they are also more involved in illegal settlement in all the sites, seen through 26%, 23.5% and 57.7% of Mvurwi, Hwedza and Goromonzi, respectively. The new and old youth have also settled illegally or through village head allocations in the grazing lands.

Educational and gender dynamics

The level of education attained determined the extent to which youth straddle or remain stranded. Zimstat (2020) shows that in 2004, approximately 69% of the youth had achieved some secondary education, and 6% had acquired a diploma or certificate after secondary education (Table 11.4). Only a few, 1%, had attained a graduate or postgraduate qualification. By 2019, the situation had improved significantly. Approximately 76.5% of the youth had completed secondary education, and 6.5% had diplomas and certificates. Those who had attained graduate or postgraduate degrees had increased to 4.2%. A minute proportion of 0.4% had not attained any education. This shows a total increase of 8.2%, across the education levels, over the 15-year period, from 2004 to 2019.

A study by Scoones et al. (2019: 121) observed that education was

Table 11 3: Methods of accessing land (%)

Channel/Source of land access	Mvurwi (%)			Hwedza (%)			Goromonzi (%)		
	New youth	Old youth	> 52 years	New youth	Old youth	> 52 years	New youth	Old youth	> 52 years
District lands officer soon after *jambanja*	6	46	48	23	40	38	8.6	27.6	62.8
Village chairman/headman/chief	29	36	36	0	0	0	21.1	28.3	50.6
Inherited the plot	67	33	0	0	100	0	17.8	31.6	50.5
Informal subdivision from relative	100	0	0	0	0	0	34	5	61.0
Rented the plot	100	0	0	0	0	0	0	0	0
Bought the plot from someone else	0	100	0	25	75	0	66.7	33.3	0
Illegal settlement	33	41	26	0	0	23.5	12.8	29.4	57.7

Source: Zimstats, 2020, Sample: Mvurwi NA1=310; NCA=520; Hwedza: NA1=46;
NCA=53: Goromonzi: NA1=92; NCA=100

Table 11.4: Youth educational levels by gender for 2004 and 2019

Highest level of education achieved	Male (N)	%	Female (N)	%	Total (N)	% in 2004	% in 2019
None	10,868	1	26,154	2	37,022	1	0.4
Primary	437,902	27	494,164	34	932,066	30	23.1
Secondary	1,048,394	64	824,827	57	1,873,221	61	60.4
Diploma/Cert. After Primary	4,423	0	5,198	0	9,621	0	0
Diploma/Cert. After Secondary	110,954	7	80,146	6	191,100	6	6.5
Graduate/ Postgraduate	1,4561	1	7,256	1	21,817	1	4.2
Not Stated	0	0	774	0	774	0	0
Total	1,627,103	100%	1,438,517	100	3,065,620	100	100
Percentages	53%		47%		100		

Source: Zimstats, 2020, Sample: Mvurwi NA1=310; NCA=520; Hwedza: NA1=46; NCA=53: Goromonzi: NA1=92; NCA=100

considered a critical 'route to a better life'. Thomas Chikuze in Hwedza old resettlement area, at Sengezi farm, noted that:

> My parents had always wanted me to get educated and become a prominent person in Harare. I passed my Form 4 with four subjects and could not proceed further as planned. In the end, just like my two sisters, who both failed to achieve five O' level passes, I ended up joining our parents at the farm where we grow tobacco and maize. Eventually, my two sisters got married, and I was left behind to continue farming on a section allocated to me by my father. We all wanted quality life in urban areas, but things turned out as they are today. We are stuck on the farm. There are no jobs in town, but also, having failed to attain five O' Level passes, farming is the most likely option (interview with TC, Hwedza, 25 July 2020)

The use of youth family labour in the absence of proletarianised male urban workers continues to illuminate debates (Thebe 2018). It is suggested that the use of youth labour disrupts their schooling (Chinyemba et al. 2006; Kawewe 2007; Thebe 2018) as parents often end up sending their children to nearby less endowed schools so that they can support agricultural activities before and after school hours. This has an adverse effect on success at school and exam pass rates. In addition, some parents end up withdrawing their children from school either due to the inability to pay school fees or during periods of labour-intensive agricultural activities (weeding/harvesting) (Grier 1994; see also Chapters 4 and 5). Perhaps indicative of how access to education is differentiated between urban and rural areas, the levels of education for the youth in or study areas are lower than the national figures. Table 11.5 shows a pattern that is the reverse of national educational levels. For instance, a greater percentage of the old youth had attained ordinary level education across the three study sites, even though Hwedza district lagged, at 25% compared to 70% for Mvurwi, and 52.5% for Goromonzi districts. The new youth generally lag behind in terms of education, with a few having attained Form 4, as survey results reveal. Without comparative figures, this study was unable to carry out a trend analysis over time. As Thomas (2003) asserted, those who fail to attain Form 4 are currently more involved in agriculture, possibly due to limited options outside agriculture. This was also the case for the youth working in commercial farms before the FTLRP. Shortage of schools, limited capacity, and absence of zeal to send children to school were limiting factors.

From an early age, the youth's fate is decided by the quality of education received or the extent to which agriculture tends to disrupt this pathway. Once the former is interrupted, the latter assumes priority and access to land becomes pivotal, with minor variations, as we discuss in the section to follow. Even though the level of education attained does not correlate with the participation rate in agriculture, people tend to try their other options, especially those promised by excelling in education. Thus, the youth might not be interested in farming and hope to find work and livelihoods in the urban areas or outside the country. Some scholars argue that one reason for this is that the school curriculum adopted in many post-colonial African countries sometimes ridicules manual work and teaches children at a young age to dislike agricultural production (Biriwasha 2012). White (2012: 12) described this as the 'general downgrading of rural life and an assault on the rural culture'. However, this was not a sentiment shared by all in our study areas. In Mvurwi area, 32-year-old Takudzwa Chitauro informed us in an interview that:

> I prefer farming as I report to nobody and with inputs I can produce and go to Harare, Mvurwi or Concession towns for marketing of my produce and to buy my needs only. Otherwise, my life is simple and easy. I do not want a job in town.

Youth participation in agricultural production and commodity value chains is thus ultimately a matter of how access to finance and commodity markets are articulated. Participation in is moderated by how the youth interface with these financing options. For instance, the *pfumvudza* programme, previously known as the Presidential Input Scheme, was welfarist and targeted the low rural households, and not necessarily the youth. Command agriculture targets A2 farmers endowed with irrigation infrastructure, and thus unless the youth occupy such farms, they would automatically be excluded. However, as Table 11.6 shows, even though the older populations tend to have greater access to state input support, no particular patterns are observed for command agriculture and contract farming.

Political structures and their connectedness to governmental service

Table11.5: The highest level of education for farmers' age, 2016-18 (percentage)

	Mvurwi			Hwedza			Goromonzi		
	New youth	Old youth	> 52 years	New youth	Old youth	> 52 years	New youth	Old youth	> 52 years
no schooling	0	0	100	0	33	67	0.	14.3	85.7
up to grade 7	8	16	77	0	75	25	4.35	31	65
up to form 2	12	44	44	25	75	0	5.7	40	54.3
up to form 4	26	70	21	25	25	50	20	52.5	27.5
college diploma and above	4	52	44	0	0	0	0	0	35.7

Source: Zimstats, 2020, Sample: Mvurwi NA1=310; NCA=520; Hwedza: NA1=46;
NCA=53: Goromonzi: NA1=92; NCA=100

delivery infrastructure is also critical. It is not only the older population that has secured roots in the patronage networks. The two identified youth groups in our study sites have demonstrated how participation through the security services and other traditional and government operations directly impacts access to land, finance and output markets. Access to contract farming, which is less politicised, shows greater participation by all age groups, indicating that individual effort and creditworthiness do not observe age differences.

Production and accumulation post-FTLRP

Indeed, a number of youths, both rural and urban, benefitted from the FTLRP (see Table 11.3) and opened up livelihood spaces and access to natural resources (Chipenda 2020: 508-511). On average, the new youth struggled to increase the total area under production while the old (and those over 52 years of age) dedicated more land to crops than the new youth in both the resettled areas and the communal areas as well as across the three research areas (Table 11.7). As Table 11.7 shows, across all settlements and research sites, the youth seemed to dedicate a more significant portion of their cropped land to cereals (maize) than to cash crops (tobacco), indicating a desire to put food security before cash income. This data supports the fact that age is not the main driver for the resettled areas and communal areas rural farmer contradictions.

The amount of income received from agricultural activities, on the other hand, differed according to the study area. These differences can be explained more by the level of access to variegated markets for each of the three research sites than by age-class dynamics. The youths in Goromonzi seemed to be doing better in terms of the proportion who owned infrastructure and assets (but not statistically significant), followed by youth in Hwedza. For example, higher proportions of the new youth owned deep wells, poultry runs, tobacco barns, grading shade, brick/iron/zinc houses, and Blair toilets in Goromonzi (Table 11.8). The Hwedza new youth dominated ownership of fixed assets such as cattle handling facilities, pig sties, tobacco barns and brick/iron/zinc housing infrastructure. In Mvurwi, however, the infrastructure ownership patterns were dominated by the old youth (Table 11.8). This information suggests that the new youth in Goromonzi were investing more in fixed assets than in Mvurwi. Our data supports the fact that

Table 11.6: Financing options for 2016/17 for Mvurwi, Hwedza and Goromonzi areas

A1		Contract farming		Command agriculture		Government input scheme	
		CA	A1	CA	A1	CA	A1
Mvurwi (2016/17 season)	New youth	23	19	16	5	0	15
	Old youth	20	13	5	3	1	27
	> 52 years	25	10	9	4	2	43
	Average	22.7	14.0	10.0	4.0	1.0	28.3
Hwedza (2015/16 season)	New youth	20	0	0	0	10	29
	Old youth	15	5	0	0	15	21
	> 52 years	25	0	0	0	6	50
	Average	20.0	1.7	0.0	0.0	10.3	33.3
Goromonzi (2016/17 season)	New youth	0	0	0	0	16.7	0
	Old youth	38	8	46	0	0	22.7
	> 52 years	51	29	52	0	0	17.9
	Average	29.7	12.3	32.7	0.0	5.6	13.5

Source: Own Study; Sample: Mvurwi N_{A1}=310; N_{CA}=520; Hwedza: N_{A1}=46; N_{CA}=53: Goromonzi: N_{A1}=92; N_{CA}=100

Table 11.7: Land utilisation and income from agricultural production (2014-2017 averages)

Variable	Age	Hwedza		Mvurwi		Goromonzi		Overall	
		A1	CA	A1	CA	A1	CA	A1	CA
Average cropped area (ha)	0-35	2	1	3.3	1.8	1.14	0.39	2.15	1.06
	36-51	2	2	5.1	2.2	2.15	0.39	3.08	1.53
	>52	2	1	5.5	2.3	2.47	0.38	3.32	1.23
	Average	2.0	1.3	4.6	2.1	1.9	0.4	2.9	1.3
% owned area under Maize	0-35	60	60	27	27.6	70.6	70.32	52.5	52.6
	36-51	55	90	27	26.7	58.28	72.17	46.8	63.0
	>52	80	100	28	24.8	64.18	68.16	57.4	64.3
	Average	65.0	83.3	27.3	26.4	64.4	70.2	52.2	60.0
% of owned area under Tobacco	0-35	40	0	19.1	26.5	29.4	29.68	29.5	18.7
	36-51	25	10	20.8	25.1	22.56	15.18	22.8	16.8
	>52	20	0	20.9	18.1	26.28	13.15	22.4	10.4
	Average	28.3	3.3	20.3	23.2	26.1	19.3	24.9	15.3
Income from agriculture (US$)	0-35	414	0	2627.9	946.7	2292.43	149.2	1778	365
	36-51	21	1	4548.9	821.4	2206.72	786.85	2259	536
	>52	634	50	3908.7	746.8	3615.57	695.84	2719	498
	Average	356	17	3695	838	2705	544	2252	466

Source: Own Study: Sample: Mvurwi NA1=310; NCA=520; Hwedza: NA1=46; NCA=53; Goromonzi: NA1=92; NCA=100

Table 11.8: Ownership of Housing and farm infrastructure (% of people)

	Hwedza			Mvurwi			Goromonzi		
	New Youth	Old youth	> 52 years	New Youth	Old youth	> 52 years	New Youth	Old youth	> 52 years
Deep well	29.6	43.2	44.3	26.7	58.3	61.7	83.3	74.6	80.7
Cattle handling facilities	67.6	60.8	73	-	-	-	8.3	9.9	25.7
Pigsty	8.8	2.7	4.1	-	-	-	0	2.8	6.4
Poultry runs	47.1	59.5	63	-	-	-	83.3	60.6	68.8
Dip tanks	2.9	1.4	2.5	-	-	-	0	0	4.6
Brick/asbestos house	47.1	54.1	65.6	40	51.5	62.5	25	36.6	46.8
Tobacco barns	5.9	0	1.3	40	59.6	58.6	8.3	7	4.6
Grading shade	8.8	4.1	2.5	-	-	-	33.3	11.3	13.8
Brick/iron/Zinc	14.7	9.5	10.7	44.4	63.6	60.9	83.3	31	27.5
Blair toilets	55.9	64.9	64.8	-	-	-	83.3	74.6	83.5
Granary	0	0	0.4	-	-	-	16.7	9.9	4.6
Storage house	0	0	0.4	2.2	7.6	14.8	33.3	11.3	11.9

Notes: Some of the variables in this table were not captured in the Mvurwi survey

Source: Own study: Sample: Mvurwi NA1=310; NCA=520; Hwedza: NA1=46; NCA=53: Goromonzi: NA1=92; NCA=100

being a youth was not a significant factor in the farmers' production and accumulation trajectory.

Youth and livelihoods options in an economy in crisis

Zimbabwe's political and economic crises have meant that while many of the youth are employed or work in agriculture, the precarious nature of farming leads them to often straddle agriculture and the informal sector. In this sense, despite their significant participation in agriculture, as revealed in this chapter, also contrary to an analysis by other scholars (Chipenda 2020; Scoones et al. 2019), youth have diversified into other sectors in response to an emerging agrarian structure and a new economy in which no single activity can be relied on. It is a *feja faja* (lottery) economy in which one leg has to be in one area while the other is elsewhere. This diversification enables the youth to invest off-farm income into agriculture, improving their yield potential. Through land rentals, it is common for urban youth to participate in agricultural activities, mainly in tobacco, following the boom in that sector.

The youth's participation in artisanal mining, informal trading, cross-border trading, and employment, including joining the diaspora and other off-farm income-earning activities, is a natural response to complex problems bedevilling the Zimbabwean economy more generally (see Chapters 10 and 13). Be that as it may, this diversification by the youth and older population is tied to agricultural activities, either as offshoots, broadening of income-earning activities, or re-investment of earning from off-farm activities into agricultural production. This was mainly observed to be the case for the youth involved in artisanal mining and tobacco production, and those involved in cross-border trade during the dry season (interview, FH, Hwedza 23 February 2020). Simply put, our evidence shows that the youth are participating in a wide array of activities, not necessarily to indicate that they are disdainful or do not find space in agriculture. It is a form of securing more comprehensive survival options. We argue that our evidence shows that the youth are located within the broad categories of labour that are negatively affected by globalisation and its effect on accumulation for the working people (Shivji 2017). This observation is line with what Bernstein's (2006: 455) 'fragmented classes of labour' associated with petty commodity trading among the peasantry. This fragmentation:

encapsulates the effects of how classes of labour in global

capitalism, and especially in the 'South', pursue their reproduction, that is, through insecure and oppressive – and in many places increasingly scarce – wage employment, often *combined with* a range of likewise precarious small-scale farming and insecure 'informal sector' ('survival') activity, subject to its own forms of differentiation and oppression along intersecting lines of class, gender, generation, caste, and ethnicity. In short, most have to pursue their means of livelihood/reproduction across different sites of the social division of labour: urban and rural, agricultural and non-agricultural, wage employment and self-employment (ibid.: 455)

Discussion: The 'old youth', the 'new youth' and class politics

Analysis of youth participation in the changing agrarian economy after the land reform of 2000 has to date been guided by a misidentification of the youth. Many analysts have confined themselves to the 'new' youth aged between 15 and 35 years, thus missing the group of 'old' youth who occupied this category when the FTLRP was carried out. This error leads to the erroneous conclusion that the youth were not included in the agrarian economy. Our findings show that the youth constitute a large proportion of the population involved in agriculture in Zimbabwe and secure access to agricultural land in various ways. Access to land and access methods can be differentiated across generations, for the new youth are entirely different from the old youth and the older populations. The new youth mostly access land through subdivision of lands belonging to their parents and village heads' allocations or purchases. This quest for land by the new youth demonstrates a high appetite for participation in agriculture. Some get allocated land due to limited options outside agriculture, yet others buy land using earnings from other activities (Jayne et al. 2016) and thus invest in agriculture out of choice. Arguably, even though in 1980s and 1990s opportunities were constrained compared to the period after 2000, many barriers and constraints still affected youth participation, much as they do with other generations.

The future land struggles ought to link those who demand land to political elites and the government to be successful. The advent of the second republic might have muted the youth land struggles compared to the youth's momentum during the Mugabe era, as observed in Chipato et al. (2020). This means the land question, especially for the youth, remains unresolved and shelved indefinitely – creating a time bomb. This is made worse by the increasing role of politics and patronage in moderating access to land and agricultural support, as cartels connected to the ruling elites consolidate their hold on various economic sectors, agriculture included. The new youth who have the least of connection will potentially face greater disadvantage. Those who want to take part in agricultural production must navigate the harsh terrain of the gerontocracy, imperfect commodity markets, and degenerating political and socio-economic situations. The corona pandemic will add to the problem, with youth having wait out the pandemic by enrolling in educational courses which they will seldom use upon graduation.

The future of youths in agriculture can indeed be linked to the future of world agriculture in general. Thus, in the light of limited land, intergenerational land transfers will remain the most critical access mechanism. Simultaneously, land grabbing of small-scale land for large-scale land projects will remain the greatest threat to youth participation, as land sold cannot be bequeathed, as White (2012) also concluded. As the state de-radicalises, it remains to be seen if the resulting state of government will create more youth access opportunities than when it was highly radicalised. However, based on the state's recent announcement to repay the white-settler farmers for the lost land, the chances of improved youth access to land remain low.

Conclusion

This chapter has shown that youth participation in agriculture is comparable to that of other generations. Even though the youth did not get a quota similar to women and the war veterans, their involvement in the land reform programme was relatively high. Today, the old youth are visible in the agricultural value chains where they compete favourably with other generations. Equally, the new youth are also visible, albeit in lower proportions than the older population, as land tenure systems tend to exclude them or require a longer wait. However, they compete favourably in productivity, accumulation, and social mobility. Therefore, assessing participation from a generational perspective misses the point by a wide margin.

In the three sites of our study, all the farmers struggle to access financing and commodity markets due to the economy-wide challenges that Zimbabwe is going through. Thus, farmers across generations are stranded and straddling and often diversifying into petty commodity production, including in the informal sector where cross-border trading and artisanal mining predominate. Overall, political connectedness varies across classes of farmers, with mainly the larger farmers able to access patronage mediated input support and thus accumulate from above. The youth struggle to carry out agricultural production as a working people, in similar fashion as with other generations. Bernstein's (2006) 'fragmented classes of labour' underpins ongoing struggles of access and accumulation as well as class formation among the youth. To this end, participation is more accurately assessed from a political economy perspective, whereby politics, gender, generations, education and the broader economic performance in contemporary as well as the future Zimbabwe will shape how the youth will perform. However, some youth can compete equally in these spaces. This notwithstanding, most of the masses across ages are struggling under the weight of a failing economy.

References

Abdullah, I. (1998) 'Bush Path to Destruction: The Origin and Character of the Revolutionary United Front/Sierra Leone', *The Journal of Modern African Studies*, 36(2), pp. 203-235.

Alexander, J. (1994) 'State, peasantry and resettlement in Zimbabwe', *Review of African Political Economy*, 21(61), pp. 325-345.

Bennell, P. (2007) 'Promoting Livelihood Opportunities For Rural Youth'. Rome; IFAD.

Bernstein, H. (2006) 'Is there an Agrarian Question in the 21st Century?', *Canadian Journal of Development Studies*, 27(4), pp. 449-460.

Biriwasha, L. (2012) 'Agriculture and the school curriculum in Zimbabwe'. International Conference on Young People, Farming and Food: The Future of the Agrifood Sector in Africa, Accra, March 19-21.

Bryceson, D.F. (2002) 'The scramble in Africa: Reorienting rural livelihoods', *World Development*, 30(5), pp., 725-739.

Chaumba, J., I. Scoones and W. Wolmer (2003a) 'New politics, new livelihoods: Agrarian change in Zimbabwe', *Review of African Political Economy*, 30(98), pp. 585-608.

Chaumba, J., I. Scoones, and W. Wolmer (2003b) 'From *jambanja* to planning: The reassertion of technocracy in land reform in south-eastern Zimbabwe?', *Journal of Modern African Studies*, 41(4), pp. 533-554.

Chimhowu, A. and P. Woodhouse (2006) 'Customary vs private property rights? Dynamics and trajectories of vernacular land markets in Sub-Saharan Africa', *Journal of Agrarian Change*, 6(3), pp. 346-371.

Chinyemba, M.J., O.N. Muchena and M.B.K. Hakutangwi (2006) 'Women And Agriculture', in M. Rukuni, C.K. Eicher, P. Tawonezvi, P.B. Matondi and M. Munyuki-Hungwe (eds), *Zimbabwe's agricultural revolution revisited*. Harare: University of Zimbabwe Publications.

Chipangura, N. (2019) '"We are one big happy family": The social organisation of artisanal and small scale gold mining in Eastern Zimbabwe', *Extractive Industries and Society*, 6(4), pp. 1265-1273.

Chipato, F., L. Wang, T. Zuo and G.T. Mudimu (2020) 'The politics of youth struggles for land in post-land reform Zimbabwe', *Review of African Political Economy*, 47(163), pp. 59-77.

Chipenda, C. (2020) 'The youth after land reform in Zimbabwe: exploring the redistributive and social protection outcomes from a transformative social policy perspective', *Canadian Journal of African Studies*, 54(3), pp. 497-518.

Chitsike, F. (2003) 'A Critical Analysis of the Land Reform Programme in Zimbabwe'. Paper presented to the 2nd FIG Regional Conference, Marrakech, Morocco, December 2-5.

Chiweshe, M. K. (2011) 'Farm Level Institutions in Emergent Communities in Post Fast Track Zimbabwe: Case of Mazowe District'. PhD thesis, Rhodes University.

de Janvry, A., M. Fafchamps and E. Sadoulet (1991) 'Peasant Household Behaviour with Missing Markets: Some Paradoxes Explained', *The Economic Journal*, 101(409), pp. 1400-1417.

Gaidzanwa, R.B. (2011) 'Women and Land in Zimbabwe'. Paper presented to the conference 'Why Women Matter in Agriculture', Sweden, April 4-8.

Geza, S. (1986) 'The Role of Resettlement in Social Development in Zimbabwe', *Journal of Social Development in Africa*, 1(1), pp. 35-42.

Grier, B. (1994) 'Invisible Hands: The Political Economy of Child Labour in Colonial Zimbabwe, 1890-1930', *Journal of Southern African Studies*, 20(1), pp. 27-52.

Gunning, J.W., J. Hoddinott, B. Kinsey and T. Owens (2000) 'Revisiting forever gained: Income dynamics in the resettlement areas of Zimbabwe, 1983-96', *The Journal of Development Studies*, 36(6), pp. 131-154.

Fox, L., P. Mader, J. Sumberg, J. Flynn and M. Oosterom (2020) 'Africa's "youth employment" crisis is actually a "missing jobs" crisis'. Brooke Shearer Series No. 9. Washington, DC: Brookings Institution.

Habtu, Y., D.F. Bryceson and V. Jamal (1997) 'Farmers without land: The return of landlessness to rural Ethiopia', in D.F. Bryceson and V. Jamal (eds), *Farewell to Farms: De-agrarianisation and employment in Africa*. Aldershot: Ashgate.

Kawewe, S.M. (2007) 'Disenfranchisement of Zimbabwean women in public policy and national machinery undermines human rights, social development, peace and social justice', in F. Columbus and J.H. Owusu (eds), *Politics and Economics of Africa*. Huntington, NY: Nova Science Publishers.

Kinsey, B. (1999) 'Land Reform, Growth and Equity: Emerging Evidence from Zimbabwe's Resettlement Programme', *Journal of Southern African Studies*, 25(2), pp. 173-196.

———— (2004) 'Zimbabwe's Land Reform Program: Underinvestment in Post-Conflict Transformation', *World Development*, 32(10), pp. 1669-1696.

Leavy, J. and S. Smith (2010) 'Future Farmers: Youth Aspirations, Expectations and Life Choices'. Discussion Paper 013. Future Agricultures Consortium, University of Sussex.

Mabiso, A. and R. Benfica (2019 'The narrative on rural youth and economic opportunities in Africa: facts, myths and gaps'. IFAD Research Series Issue 61.

Marongwe, N. (2011) 'Who was allocated Fast Track land, and what did they do with it? Selection of A2 farmers in Goromonzi District, Zimbabwe and its impacts on agricultural production', *The Journal of Peasant Studies*, 38(5), pp. 1069-1092.

Matondi, P. (2012) *Zimbabwe's Fast Track Land Reform*. London: Zed Books.

Mawowa, S. (2013) 'The Political Economy of Artisanal and Small-Scale Gold Mining in Central Zimbabwe', *Journal of Southern African Studies*, 39(4), pp. 921-936.

Mkodzongi, G. and S.J. Spiegel (2020) 'Mobility, temporary migration and changing livelihoods in Zimbabwe's artisanal mining sector', *Extractive Industries and Society*, 7(3), pp. 994-1001.

Ministry of Labour and Social Services (MLSS) and Ministry of Youth Development, Indigenisation and Empowerment (MYDIE) (2009) 'Zimbabwe National Employment Policy Framework'. Harare: Government of Zimbabwe.

Moyo, S. (1995) *The Land Question in Zimbabwe*. Harare: SAPES Books.

───── (2000) 'The political economy of land acquisition and redistribution in Zimbabwe, 1990-1999', *Journal of Southern African Studies* 26(1), pp. 5-28.

───── (2001) The Land Occupation Movement and Democratisation in Zimbabwe: Contradictions of Neoliberalism', *Millenium*, 30(2), pp. 311-330.

───── (2003) 'The Land Question in Africa: Research Perspectives and Questions'. Dakar: Codesria.

───── (2004) 'The Land and Agrarian Question in Zimbabwe'. Paper presented to the conference on 'The Agrarian Constraint and Poverty Reduction: Macroeconomic Lessons for Africa', Addis Ababa , 17-18 December.

───── (2011) 'Three decades of agrarian reform in Zimbabwe', *The Journal of Peasant Studies*, 38(3), pp. 493-531.

───── and P. Yeros (2005) 'Land occupations and land reform in Zimbabwe: Towards the national democratic revolution', in S. Moyo and P. Yeros (eds), *Reclaiming the Land: The Resurgence of Rural Movements in Africa, Asia and Latin America*. London: Zed Books.

Muchetu, R.G. (2019) 'Understanding Human Security in African

Agrarian Societies: The Case for a Cooperative Model', *Journal of Human Security*, 8(1), pp. 20-44.

Murisa, T. (2016) 'Prospects for Equitable Land Reform in Zimbabwe: Revisiting Sam Moyo's Work on the Land Question', *Agrarian South: Journal of Political Economy*, 5(2-3), pp. 240-264.

Mutopo, P. (2011) 'Women's struggles to access and control land and livelihoods after fast track land reform in Mwenezi District, Zimbabwe', *The Journal of Peasant Studies*, 38(5), pp. 1021-1046.

Nkomo, J.N. (1984) *Nkomo, The Story Of My Life*. London: Methuen.

Potts, D. and C. Mutambirwa (1990) 'Rural-urban linkages in contemporary Harare: Why migrants need their land', *Journal of Southern African Studies*, 16(4), pp. 677-698.

Proctor, F.J. and V. Lucchesi (2012) 'Small-scale farming and youth in an era of rapid rural change'. London/The Hague: IIED/HIVOS.

Sadomba, Z.W. (2008) 'War Veterans in Zimbabwe's Land Occupations: Complexities of a Liberation Movement in an African Post-Colonial Settler Society'. PhD thesis, Wageningen University.

———(2011) *War Veterans in Zimbabwe's Revolution: Challenging Neo-colonialism & Settler & International Capital*. Woodbridge: James Currey.

Scoones, I., N. Marongwe, B. Mavedzenge, J. Mahenehene, F. Murimbarimba and C. Sukume (2010) *Zimbabwe's Land Reform: Myths & Realities*. Woodbridge: James Currey.

Scoones, I., B. Mavedzenge, and F. Murimbarimba (2019) 'Young people and land in Zimbabwe: Livelihood challenges after land reform', *Review of African Political Economy*, 46(159), pp. 117-134.

Selby, A. (2006) 'Commercial Farmers and the State: Interest Group Politics and Land Reform in Zimbabwe.' PhD thesis, University of Oxford.

Shivji, I.G. (2017) 'The concept of "working people"', *Agrarian South: Journal of Political Economy*, 6(1), pp.1-13.

Shonhe, T. (2019) 'Tractors and Agrarian Transformation in Zimbabwe : Insights From Mvurwi'. APRA working paper 21, Future Agricultures Consortium.

——— (2017) *Reconfigured agrarian relations in Zimbabwe*. Bamenda,

Cameroon: Langaa RPCIG.

———— and O. Mtapuri (2020) 'Zimbabwe's Emerging Farmer Classification model: a 'new'countryside', *Review of African Political Economy*, 47(165), pp. 363-381.

————, I. Scoones and F. Murimbarimba (2020) 'Medium-scale commercial agriculture in Zimbabwe: The experience of A2 resettlement farms', *The Journal of Modern African Studies*, 58(4), 601-626.

Thebe, V. (2018) 'Youth, agriculture and land reform in Zimbabwe: Experiences from a communal area and resettlement scheme in semi-arid Matabeleland, Zimbabwe', *African Studies*, 77(3), pp. 336-353.

Thomas, N.H. (2003) 'Land reform in Zimbabwe', *Third World Quarterly*, 24(4), pp. 691-712.

White, B. (2012) 'Agriculture and the Generation Problem: Rural Youth, Employment and the Future of Farming', *IDS Bulletin*, 43(6), pp. 9-19.

Zamchiya, P. (2011) 'A synopsis of land and agrarian change in Chipinge district, Zimbabwe', *The Journal of Peasant Studies*, 38(5), pp. 1093-1122.

———— (2012) 'Agrarian change in Zimbabwe: politics, production and accumulation'. PhD thesis, University of Oxford.

Zimbabwe National Statistics Agency (Zimstat) (2019) 'Women and Men in Zimbabwe Report 2019'. Harare: Zimstat.'

———— (2020) 'Education levels and youths population in agriculture, 15-35 years'. Harare: Zimstat.

Interviews

Interview, Tawanda Feresu, ORA, Hwedza, 12 March 2016
Interview with Thomas Chikuze, Hwedza, 25 July 2020
Interview with Takudzwa Chitauro, Mvurwi, 27 February 2020.

12

Youth Sexuality, Gender Relations and Paid Sex: the discontents of developmental crises in Zimbabwe

Rekopantswe Mate

Introduction

Across sub-Saharan Africa, youth sexuality became a public policy concern in the 1990s as the HIV and AIDS scourge worsened and epidemiological studies pointed to youth as most at risk. HIV epidemiological studies revealed hitherto hidden youth sexual practices. Framed as illicit and immoral pre- and extramarital sex, youth sexuality fanned moral panics as risky and reckless through concepts such as 'intergenerational sex', 'cross-generational sex', 'the sugar daddy phenomenon', 'sex trade', 'survival sex', and 'transactional sex' (Stoebenau et al. 2016; Ojebode et al. 2011; Shefer et al. 2012 among others). Female youth's higher susceptibility to infection attracted more attention in research and policy debates as hapless victims of rapacious male sexualities or carelessness (Stoebenau et al. 2016). These blame games fanned distrust and tension in gender relations (Bandali 2011). What emerged was that young women's sexual practices were more nuanced and agentic than initially thought (Longfield 2004). Additionally, researchers argued that youth sexual practices indicated wider socio-cultural, economic and political change (Cole 2004; Groes-Green 2013). In Zimbabwe policy makers claimed cultural and religious sensitivities to sustain baseless claims that youth are asexual (Betts et al. 2003; Marindo et al. 2003; also Bhana 2017). This pre-empted robust policy and research debates. In the first two decades of independence there were few studies on the youth and their involvement in paid sex work.

This chapter uses Cole's (2004) notion of 'fresh contact', by which she refers to the novelty and creativity with which each cohort of young people encounter their own culture as they come of age in socio-economic and political contexts not encountered by previous cohorts. Such encounters force young people to selectively rethink and rework prevailing cultural practices. Zimbabwe gained independence when the world was undergoing tumultuous socio-economic change and as neoliberalism was taking root. Giddens (1992) describes this as the era of the ascendancy of individuality, volition and agency; with the deepening decoupling of sexual intimacy from reproduction and kinship, it became a recreational pursuit (see also Attwood 2006). In this vein, the chapter argues that youth participation in different forms of paid sex symbolises social change due to crises of reproduction because of contradictions of neoliberal globalisation. These contradictions are seen in conspicuous inequality, popular aspirations for social mobility, incitement to participate in the global consumer culture (Nyamnjoh 2005; Cole 2004), weakening social bonds increasingly driven by market logics, and growing individualism, hence unsupported or do-it-yourself (DIY) modes of existence (Kelly 2001). Bauman (2003) refers to such relationships as 'liquid love', to describe the logic of shopping, benefits, flexibility and commodification which percolates into social interactions leading to weak short-lived bonds. Giddens (1992) uses the notion of reflexivity where individuals engage in cost-benefit analyses while deflecting arguments against their choices. Episodic sexual relationships become convenient, whereas long-term commitments are seen as cumbersome. Changing communication technologies aid calculated interactions. Thus, while youth sexual practices symbolise change, their trailblazing practitioners risk accusations of deviance for embracing change or challenging social norms. The chapter proceeds by defining concepts of youth, sex work, and transactional sex, followed by a brief description of studies from which insights are drawn. The discussion is organised around four themes, as explained below.

Youth and social change

As a social category, youth is socially produced in specific socio-economic and political contexts. In Sub-Saharan Africa the phrase the 'crisis of youth', denoting young people growing up with limited access to or poor and deteriorating quality of services, is a common refrain (Peters and Richards 1998; Mains 2007; Masquelier 2013). This creates inertia or moratoria in transitions through the life course. Consequently, youth denotes extended liminality between childhood and adulthood because of a lack of resources. Thus, youth are caught between structures of inequality, such as patriarchy and gerontocracy, and contradictions of rapid social change under neoliberal globalisation. They are incited to participate in global consumer cultures through fashion, electronic gadgets, music, and new discourses of freedom, individuality, and choice albeit without the wherewithal to do so (Nyamnjoh 2005; Diouf 2003, Cole 2004; Groes-Green 2014). Without resources, or the support of families and governments, young people use their creativity to achieve these dreams (Zembe et al. 2013; Nyamnjoh 2005; Cole 2004). These DIY modes of existence typify neoliberal agentic selves (Kelly 2001), but also create anti-establishment youth cultures which include paid sex. These practices are risky and their outcomes unpredictable.

In Zimbabwe, tensions between the genders and generations emerged as relations became scrambled at household level. Respect for elders started to decline as their ability to provide became strained (Bandali 2011: 580), especially following the structural adjustment programmes from 1991 to 1995 and when the state and its agencies became conspicuously incapable to provide meaningful social services (Magaisa 2001). This is seen in the growth of child-headed households and the increase in the number of children living on the streets. Among the growing ranks of the poor, parental inability to provide dis-embedded young people from kinship relations into DIY transitions to adulthood forced them to provide for themselves, relying on their creativity and agency in defiance of ideals and norms of age and gender relations (Yingwana 2018: 285-60; Magaisa 2011: 107-109).

Paid sex practices, changing gender and age relations

Paid sex takes different forms and meanings in various contexts as practitioners grapple with respectability, or the lack thereof (Tavory and

Poulin 2012; Groes-Green 2014). Some researchers say transactional sex is different from the more stigmatised sex work (Barnett and Maticka-Tyndale 2011; Bandali 2011; Shefer et al. 2012, Hunter 2002, Zembe et al. 2013). Others say they are on the same continuum and equally stigmatised (Zembe et al. 2013; Tavory et al. 2012). Some women receive gifts and money to get by (so-called survival sex), while others seek to get ahead (sex for consumerist aspirations, for status) as noted by Zembe et al. (2013), Hunter (2002), Longfield (2004) and Groes-Green (2013, 2014). Across Sub-Saharan Africa, gifts for sex exchanges are rooted in complex moralities of respect, patronage, marriage, intimacy, and kinship norms, as well as notions of equity (Shefer et al. 2012; Groes-Green 2014: 238). However, as inequality between genders, social groups and regions widens, the moralities change (Hunter 2002; Nyamnjoh 2005; Cole 2004; Groes-Green 2013, 2104). Monetisation was grafted onto social exchanges of kinship and intimacy relations creating hybridised forms of exchange which continue to incorporate new commodities. Nonetheless, many Africans are affronted by sex-gift exchange for reasons including education, religion and westernisation. This too textures contestations in meanings of paid sex. In these contradictions, transactional sex serves many purposes, including cultivating gender connections/patronage, and providing the resources through which practitioners cope with adversities. It offers opportunities for upward social mobility (Groes-Green 2014) or not to look poor while in tertiary education (Ojebode et al. 2012; Masvaure 2010). It enables self-authoring and ideally confers respect from peers. Condemnation is commonplace, too (Nyamnjoh 2005).

Given economic crises and endemic unemployment young men's inability to save for bridewealth in conditions of deepening consumerism also precipitate paid sex both, for survival and consumerist reasons (Hunter 2002). The inability to perform marriage rituals undermines ideals of bridewealth as payment to elders for the sexuality of young women. In casual sexual relations, not only do young men dominate, they refute responsibility for pregnancies, arguing that women are manipulative and (can) use pregnancy to expedite marriage (Pattman 2005; also Groes-Green 2013). Thus, paid sex points to gender tensions and contestations over sexuality and propriety.

Zimbabwe's socio-economic changes, youth unemployment in the 1980s and 1990s

Zimbabwe's increasing school-leaver unemployment from the mid-1980s, and its implications for young people achieving social adulthoods, is widely publicised (Herbst 1989, Grant 2003). Less well known are gendered experiences of unemployment. Studies of youth unemployment largely focus on male youth's experiences and reactions through migration, informal sector work, patronage, and activism (Bennell and Ncube 1994; Gukurume 2017). The male biases are linked to fears of uprisings and crime (Munive 2010). It is as if female youth's social adulthoods are passive and dependent on action by male peers whose resources determine ability to marry thereby making young women wives and mothers. If, indeed, young women are waiting for men with resources to get married, what happens when men do not have the means to fund marriage rituals? If female youth have no formal work, and ,are not married what do they do? How do they survive?

Immediately after independence, there were moral panics about 'baby dumping' or the rejection (sometimes killing) of babies conceived out of wedlock. Adams (2009) shows that new ways of life in urban areas attracted young women who sought both money and fun. Magaisa (2001) shows that by the late 1990s, girls and women were resorting to sex work even in rural areas, the erstwhile citadels of morality, as a means to survive poverty and unemployment.

In 2002, when the Poverty Reduction Forum commissioned studies on the social aspects of HIV and AIDS, Zimbabwe was reeling from unprecedented socio-economic and political crises, as evidenced by political violence, deindustrialisation, unemployment, farm occupations, internal displacement, and mass migration. Donors had withdrawn funding en masse (Laakso 2002). There were deep political tensions and violence which forced people to leave their usual places of work and residence and go to nearby towns (Kriger 2008; Howard-Hassman 2010). Furthermore, Zimbabwe was in the middle of a drought (Sachikonye 2003). Inequality and vulnerability were palpable. Many citizens resorted to speculative economic activity such as hoarding basic commodities, smuggling, and cross-border trade. Life was commoditised as people tried to get by, to earn money to augment their incomes. These conditions worsened until 2009 when a Government of

National Unity was established.

In the early 2000s, around the same time that Marindo et al. (2003) and Betts et al. (2003) noted cultural and religious sensitivities vis-à-vis youth sexuality, discussion of paid sex was scandalous and unacademic. However, it was also a time of deepening crisis characterised by the emergence of and ambivalence towards illicit and quasi-criminal survival strategies as economic informalisation deepened (Jones 2010). Thus, debates about changing sexualities were sidelined, as other issues took precedence (see Nyamnjoh 2005; Cole 2004; Groes-Green 2013, 2014). Research on campus sexual cultures in tertiary institutions, however, did emerge (see Pattman 2001, Gukurume 2011, Masvaure 2010). Campus youth cultures came across as elitist, self-absorbed, hedonistic and hypersexual. It was easy to think of these studies as representing a minority rather than being a reflection of wider society. Studies of out-of-school youths remained few (Chikovore et al. 2002; Mate 2009).

This chapter argues that youth engagement in paid sex increased with economic crises. It argues that the pressure to survive borne by female youth who could not find partners who complied with the male breadwinner ideal was to blame. The chapter is based on insights from four studies done between 2002 and 2010.[1] The studies relied on qualitative research methods, individual and key informant interviews, focus group discussions (FGDs) and observations. The insights are presented chronologically and under four themes:

a) the deepening informalisation and commoditisation of social relations;

b) inadequate provision by parents versus invisible aspirational needs of girls;

c) male-biased turfing of relatively lucrative informal sector activities;

d) sex as currency and a commodity.

---

1 The four studies were funded by CODESRIA (Senegal) jointly with the Social Science Research Council in New York for the Gwanda study; NUFFIC for my PhD whose fieldwork was in Beitbridge; a small grant from the University of KwaZulu Natal (funded by the Andrew Mellon Foundation) for the Victoria Falls study and commissioned by the Poverty Reduction Forum (PRF), at the Institute of Development Studies (IDS) at the University of Zimbabwe for the social aspects of HIV and AIDS study.

These themes cut across all four studies but for purposes of clarity, I restricted each study to one theme.

Findings

Deepening informalisation and commoditisation of social relations in early 2000s

The smuggling of refined sugar to Mozambique was rife through Mutare in the 2000s. Male youths, locally called *matunge* (to describe head porterage), who carried the sugar by the carton through foot trails were sought after not just for their labour and knowledge of the illicit crossings, but also for the money they earned. Smugglers bought sugar from wholesalers and/or retailers and took it to Mutare by car, bus or by hitching lifts on haulage trucks.[2] Smuggling was a readily available form of work. It entailed 'easy' money which the young men spent freely and quickly on personal leisure (alcohol, paid sex, and night clubbing). Respondents noted that to catch the attention of women, most *matunge* produced a wad of Z$500 notes to buy a small item. These were overt displays of readily available disposable income.[3] On seeing the money, women asked for favours – drinks here, a meal there – and if so inclined, the *matunge* would have sex in exchange.

In Victoria Falls, young men in the curio trade talked about the joy of offloading money on women after a good sale. They said there was no time for courtship or dates because they wanted to attend to their stalls. Courtship was too time-consuming. They proceeded through bids. Without similar opportunities to earn money, girls knew to play along and ask about the 'offer'. The punters would haggle until they agreed and the exchange would take place in a forest, a shack or a room. Furthermore, young men spent their money on alcohol in the evening where more bids awaited.

In Beitbridge, food donations to a poor family would make the family turn a blind eye to their adolescent daughters' movements. In one confessional case, a businessman had a relationship with a 14-year-

---

2   From parts of Mutare one could see people walking up the mountain range that marks the border with Mozambique. Although security forces were stationed along the border, smugglers went about their business. Although sections of the border still had landmines from the 1970s war, local youths knew which foot trails were safe.

3   Note that people who used banks could not access their money because of a shortage of bank notes.

old girl using food and monetary 'assistance' to the family as a lure. Admittedly, one cannot generalise from one example, but on-going campaigns against child marriages point to the wider prevalence of this practice.

Border towns attracted female cross-border traders who needed transport for their onward journeys, as well as overnight accommodation and a means to avoid cumbersome import inspections checks. Any of these needs could be eased by exchanging sex with a facilitator or a knowledgeable truck driver. Truck drivers were especially handy as they offered accommodation, transport, and aided border crossings. Transactional sex was also used in exchange for transport to ferry bulky merchandise for sale outside the country or imported into it. Where smugglers were used, sometimes female cross-border traders did not have the money or chose to pay not in cash but through sex. With fast food chains introduced in Zimbabwe only a decade earlier, their expansion into smaller towns stoked a new craze. The new foods were exchanged for sex, especially with in- and out-of-school female youths.

Inadequate provisioning by parents versus invisible, aspirational needs of girls

In FGDs with female youth in rural Gwanda in 2004, female adolescent and youth needs were hidden or ignored by their families for cultural reasons or convenience. The needs included access to basic modern toiletries (scented bath soaps, deodorants, lotions), underwear, and pocket money for school lunches (Mate 2009). They desired products to mitigate or alleviate teenage skin care challenges such as acne and blemishes. Because of proximity to the border with South Africa and Botswana, store owners easily imported these modern goods. The girls wanted 'beautiful' lacy panties in synthetic fabrics, not the utilitarian fare their parents gave them. They wanted brassieres in attractive colours and fabrics, whereas parents provided T-shirts and vests. By contrast, parental views of basics included buying a bar of green soap (cut into pieces for laundry, bathing, and kitchen utensils). For skincare products, parents were content with simple, affordable, and ubiquitous petroleum jelly. When store-bought/factory-made varieties were out of reach, there were homemade alternatives.[4] Girls, however,

---

4   Made by melting candle wax and stirring cooking oil before the wax sets. The end product looks like petroleum jelly and is used as such.

said petroleum jelly (factory-made or otherwise) was bland and lacked sophistication. When used on the face, its greasiness precipitated skin breakouts and blemishes.

To alleviate parental inability to provide, some girls resorted to transactional sex to meet these private needs (Mate 2009). Money from male partners, peers, and older acquaintances filled the gap. With frugality, boyfriends' gifts were sufficient for low-priced items such as lotions, face creams, occasional biscuits, and snacks at school. Male peers did not have enough money for the relatively more expensive items such as brassieres. In this context transactional sex provided a route to discretionary spending. These needs were not recognised by parents as worth budgeting for.

Girls who fell pregnant out of wedlock were especially vulnerable because their personal needs and those of their babies were neglected as punishments for shaming the family through premarital sex, out-of-wedlock childbirth, and/or defying bridewealth norms. Respondents noted that parents said '*zibonele*', which means 'fend for yourself'. Where a young woman had no profession, or had dropped out of school, the despair that came with this stance landed many in transactional sex and eventually sex work. The cruelty of this needs to be unpacked. In many instances, families could not afford an extra mouth to feed. Many expected their daughters to marry well so they gained a son-in-law capable of paying bridewealth in order to get some relief from poverty. Consequently, some young women ended up migrating to South Africa or Botswana to undeclared occupations as long as they sent remittances. Later, in 2009-2010, my research in Beitbridge revealed the despair visited on young women with children out-of-wedlock, which often led to resorting to sex work to survive.

Male biased turfing of lucrative informal sector work

In Victoria Falls and its environs, lucrative informal sector work such as selling wood carvings was conspicuously male dominated. It was deliberately fenced and reserved for local male youths through bureaucracy, the gender division of labour, and local beliefs.[5] The carvings in local hardwoods included large and small sculptures of

---

5   Access to stalls was fenced because although there were female vendors of stone sculpture whom informants said came from Mashava in Masvingo, they were not allowed to have stalls. Because they could not engage in ambulant trade, they sold to local male youths who sold to tourists at a mark-up.

African animals, busts of elderly African men, ethnic masks, and stools imported from Malawi and Zambia. Save for imports, most carvings were produced by craftsmen in surrounding rural areas, purchased by members of cooperatives who finished them through sandpapering, polishing, engraving, and smoking. In 2004, the asking price for a one-metre high carved giraffe was between US$75 and $100 depending on the finish. Carved giraffes were most sought after.

Victoria Falls town, home to Zimbabwe's prime tourist resort, is surrounded by some of the poorest rural districts such as Hwange, Binga, Lupane, and Tsholotsho. These districts have limited infrastructure and services such as hospitals, tarred roads and secondary schools. Young people went to Victoria Falls to access schools and to look for work. As the national economy deteriorated, employment opportunities in surrounding towns such as coal mining in Hwange, tin mining in Kamativi, and the railways at Dete, declined. Tourism endured, albeit erratically. Youth came to Victoria Falls to seek work on the margins of the formal tourism sector as vendors of curios, entertainers and touts for adventure activities such as white-water rafting, elephant back safari and bungee jumping.

In 2004, there were eleven curio stalls within a ten kilometre radius of the resort along the Victoria Falls-Bulawayo road and several within the resort town itself. The stalls belonged to cooperatives of male vendors registered with the town council. Cooperative membership ranged between 55 and 180 members each. Busloads of tourists stopped at different stalls. Most cooperatives made a point of having good relations with drivers who worked for tour companies and hotels because the drivers determined tourist patronage.

During my fieldwork, the demand for stalls was high, with many applications pending at the town office.[6] Registered cooperatives had a circuitous process of admitting new members, citing 'congestion' and 'low sales' which indicated an interest to limit competition. Young men who could not join the cooperatives resorted to ambulant curio vending which entailed waylaying tourists on the sidewalks of busy roads. Their

---

6   Among other reasons, there were concerns that wood carvings fuelled the poaching of hardwoods in the province. However, tourists loved the carvings. Furthermore, environmental impact assessments flagged increasing human activity on the outskirts of the town and many stalls did not have running water and toilets because they were off the grid. This did not give a good image to tourists. Unregistered stalls also mushroomed along the road.

sales tactics were easy to observe. They carried backpacks to hide their merchandise but exposed it when tourists mobbed them. They specialised in sought-after carved pieces such as giraffes and masks.

In general, it was cheaper to buy from stalls, because ambulant traders' prices were inflated. Some ambulant traders also changed money from foreign currency to the Zimbabwe dollar. Because street trade in foreign currency was illegal and some tourists became victims of theft in the chaos, the town brought in tourism police who patrolled the roads and chased the curio traders. Those who were caught were fined, but often ended up giving the police 'something' to let them go. This practice was called *ukukhothisa* (Ndebele for 'letting someone lick'). By allowing the police to lick – giving then some money in hard currency – the traders survived on the street, much to the annoyance of the town authorities and members of registered cooperatives who were paying taxes to the council. Key informants from registered stalls complained that *imali ingaphansi kwejombo likangxoza* ('there is money under the boot of a police officer'), an indirect reference to corrupt activities of mutual benefit to the police and traders.[7]

Other unemployed male youths formed groups that sang traditional Ndebele songs, danced, told traditional stories and performed skits. They performed at hotels or at the busy campsite used by overland trucks, where I sometimes stayed. During my stays I counted over a dozen overland companies whose trucks and passengers stayed for a few days to two weeks while passengers toured the area.[8] Dancing and music performances were done at night, in anticipation of tips from guests. This was the only income for their efforts. Most of the groups were male, with females sometimes used as dancers.

Safari activities such as bungee jumping, white-water rafting, elephant back safaris, lion walks, and boat cruises were dominated by male youths. Respondents claimed that it was 'dangerous' as it entailed close encounters with wildlife and thus women could not cope with it. The only discernible reason is that most informal sector work (much like formal sector work) was turfed by ethnicity/hometown networks and gender norms. This kept many young women out of comparatively better paid informal sector work.

7   On seeing the police, the ambulant traders ran in different directions to lure the police off the street or to give them a bribe away from onlookers.

8   From Victoria Falls, backpackers could reach Zambia, Botswana's Chobe Game Park and/or the Caprivi strip in Namibia.

Why young women were excluded

Informants roundly said that carpentry was traditionally men's work thus young women had no business working with the carvings. In fact, curio stalls were seen as male spaces too. Young women were described derisively as *omaval'imali* ('people who block the flow of money'). This implied that female youths were a source of bad luck or that they were somehow polluted and polluting through their promiscuity or sexuality. Because young women were often suspected of engaging in sex with many men, they were perceived as having bad auras which disturbed the ambiance in male spaces. Male respondents said that they feared that the presence of young women would divert male tourists' interests away from buying their wares. Local young women endured running commentaries and verbal abuse when they came to stalls to visit husbands, boyfriends, friends, or brothers. Such visits were supposed to be short, and end as soon as a vehicle of tourists arrived. It seemed to me that the idea was also to prevent young women from learning about business in the curio trade. This also ensured that the young women would not know how much male traders spent on their personal leisure, including paid sex.

The refrain of *omaval'imali* was also mentioned by dance groups, who said female dancers drew more interest and attention from tourists, and sometimes more tips too. While this was good for any group, they resented being upstaged by women and having to pay them more for their charm or attractiveness. Thus, the female membership worsened inter-group tension. Female youths were better off joining groups with relatives such as brothers or spouses. Furthermore, dance groups rehearsed by day and performed at night, leaving little or no time for domestic work. Consequently, this was not practical for married young women or those who lived with their parents. Nor was it an option for young women who lived alone and had to pay rent and for their upkeep. These factors converged to create the belief that decent young women stayed in Chinotimba, the low-income residential area, and the informal settlements that surrounded it. Most tourists left Victoria Falls without seeing anything of its poverty-stricken backyard. It is here, hidden from view, unemployed and desperate young women lived. What did young women do to get by?

Working the 'night shift' or in Qethuka safaris: explaining young women's work

In an FGD with members of a social netball team of female youths, we discussed work and income-generating activities. Respondents were cautious at first until one said that many young women say 'they work at night' or 'always on night duty'. Asked to elaborate she said in Ndebele *'umsebenzi yisihule kuphela'* ('the only work is prostitution'). In a discussion punctuated with laughter, some referred to the same work as *'qethuka* safaris'. *Qethuka* means lying on the back. Others referred to it as *'siphundu* industries'. *Siphundu* is the back of the head, so work done while on one's back. They explained that they could neither get menial work such as washing dishes in hotels and lodges that dominated the town nor sell curios, citing turfing and verbal abuse by male vendors. Nor did they belong to any crafts networks or cooperatives. Many were not educated enough to qualify for formal work in tourism in the town or elsewhere. The married ones were stay-at-home mothers whose husbands were against them seeking paid work outside home because women who frequented the tourist part of town or interacted with tourists in the formal or informal sector were seen as loose. However, when married women lived next to women who engaged in sex work, they could not ask for cooking ingredients such as salt, tea leaves, sugar, or cooking oil when they ran short. Women in sex work would taunt them, saying *'uhlaleleni emendweni'* ('why are you still married [if your husbands cannot provide for basics]'). Thus, although marriage to a man in waged work meant that married women complied with gender ideals of depending on men, it is clear that the men were not always able to provide because of low wages or because they diverted their incomes to personal leisure such as extramarital sex, and alcohol. Consequently, many married men did not like to live with their wives in houses neighbouring sex workers. They feared that their wives would see through their challenged ability provide, and disrespect them. As noted by Yingwana (2018), the practice of sex work challenges patriarchal domination.

The work sites for *siphundu* industries, *qethuka* safaris or the night shift were ubiquitous. They included homes or shacks in Chinotimba, and informal settlements called 'DRC' and 'Kinshasa'[9] which mushroomed

---

9   These informal settlements were destroyed in May 2005 during Operation Restore Order.

outside Chinotimba due to the shortage of accommodation. Nightclubs in the tourist areas were also popular places of sex work.

I had occasion to observe several nightclubs in the tourist area where sex workers hung out. These establishments lured young women through free entry at 'ladies' nights'. One nightclub had popular themed evenings such as 'beach parties' at which female patrons wore skimpy clothing but men did not. Female patrons apparently understood that these dress codes and entry rules allowed them access to male patrons or for them to show off their bodies. Some clubs lured male clients through dancing competitions and beauty pageants with suggestive names like Ms Teen Delyte (sic). The contestants were adolescents in their mid to late teens lured by promises of modelling courses, fame and 'many more prizes'. The dances entailed sexually suggestive hip movements to applause and cheers by male patrons. The good dancers were tipped for their performances. Winners were given cash prizes, T-shirts, caps and in some cases three months probationary work (waitressing) at the nightclub. Key informants said few got permanent work after the probationary period. The work was a ruse for sexual favours to select patrons. The competitions meanwhile kept a revolving door of young women coming into the club. After three months these female employees often found themselves without work and no longer the centre of attention because there were 'new faces' on probation. The former employees had to move to another venue, leave town, or keep a low profile because of a tarnished reputation.[10]

Through paid sex young women were able to take care of themselves. Their rebuttal against warnings of risk was '*uzangithengela isepa yini?* ' ('will you buy me soap [if I stop doing what I am doing?]'). Soap was sometimes replaced with bread '*isinkwa*' or sugar '*itshukela*', indicating that many young women wanted to take care of themselves and clearly lacked adults to depend on or means to earn the money independently.

Sex: A currency and a commodity? Beitbridge 2009–2010

In February 2009, the government instituted a multi-currency policy which made the US dollar and regional currencies official tender as a response to the heavily weakened local currency. Although dollarisation led to price stability, many poor and unemployed people were excluded

---

10 Employers maintained low wage bills through of a stream of eager temporary waitresses and bartenders.

from the benefits of the multiple currencies.

A range of paid sex practices were in evidence as part of the coming of age in an economic crisis (Mate 2014). Female youths who at first worked as maids or bartenders decried the low wages of around US$50 per month. This was not enough for their own needs, let alone remittances. Paid sex was seen as a viable means of augmenting incomes.

Although male youths disparaged paid sex as degrading to both male and female partners, female youths had well cultivated arguments to counter such comments. Male youths said paid sex was convenient, albeit a less-than-ideal solution for single men. They were conflicted by it, arguing that it insulted older men by degrading their daughters by making them unmarriageable. It was perceived as immoral. Some young men saw spending money on fleeting pleasures as a waste, instead of saving, investing, or sending remittances to expectant kin. They also described paid sex as '*kuzvidyira pfuma yake*' which literally referred to female youth as 'receiving and spending [their own] bridewealth'. This is an aberration which usurped kinship norms, and made such women unmarriageable. Ideally, bridewealth is given to and shared among the bride's patrikin and rarely given to the bride herself. Unemployed young men were especially frustrated by the fact that even when they resorted to paid sex, they could not compete with men who enticed girls into paid sex through sought after fast foods such as fried chicken and chips from Kentucky Fried Chicken (KFC) from nearby Musina in South Africa.[11] During the study period, two pieces of chicken and chips from KFC cost ZAR27. This was relatively unaffordable for many young men and women.

Adult informants, however, argued that everyone was after money, hence girls expected men to pay for sex. Any man with ZAR5.00 could have sex with schoolgirls or young women who were waiting to cross into South Africa. ZAR5.00 bought a plate of food, a mini-bus ride within town, small units of airtime, toiletries, a packet of pads from China, or school snacks. For young people in transit, a ZAR5.00 plate food made the difference between going hungry and accessing sustenance. Thus, as little as it is, ZAR5.00 could not be scoffed at. The size of this payment

---

11 Many Beitbridge residents shopped in Musina while taxi drivers and owners of small trucks went there daily to ferry goods for cross-border traders. They had disposable income to afford fast foods more frequently than vendors.

pointed to the depths of poverty and despair young people were in. The ZAR5.00 price tag for sex was also derisively called 'bacossi sex', a reference to the controversial Reserve Bank of Zimbabwe intervention to control prices of basic commodities. The intervention was riddled with unsustainable contradictions and corruption.[12] Schoolgirls in need of school snacks, or products that were 'better' than those their parents provided, resorted to bacossi sex with peers and older partners.[13]

The idea that sex was a currency emanates from the fact that some young women got service providers to give them credit when they had neither the ability nor the intention to pay. Thus, enterprising young women would hire taxis (fixed fee of ZAR20/trip), get airtime, lunch, and drinks on credit. When service providers pursued their dues, they were offered sex. There were allegations that even within people smuggling, some women had sex instead of paying with money for services rendered.[14] For such young women, this was a survival strategy because they did not have the means to pay. A variation of this tactic was that young women would make a lot of demands on new partners. They wanted food, clothes, hairstyles, and toiletries. When the men were not forthcoming the young women would end the relationships.

Schoolgirls claimed that paid sex was compensation for the physiological degradation from sexual activity whose tell-tale signs were sagging breasts, and less than taut muscles around the thighs and buttocks. Apparently, these signs could be deciphered by elders, and men in general, leading to low bridewealth. This is corroborated by

---

12 The intervention was called the Basic Commodities Supply Side Intervention (BACOSSI). It entailed importing goods from South Africa, thus undermining local production. The imports were sold at prices that surprisingly undercut prices of local goods.

13 I observed the school lunches drama at the home of the now deceased elderly pensioner couple who hosted me. They lived with two grandchildren in primary school whose protests over packed lunch were energy-sapping for me because I also contributed groceries in exchange for accommodation. I used to buy wholewheat bread, peanut butter and eggs in Musina to cover school lunches. To my mind this was affordable and nutritious. On many occasions the children returned from school with the sandwiches untouched. They preferred polony sandwiches, potato crisps and similar factory-made snacks. When they got a KFC takeaway lunch, they would keep it for school the next day. No explanation about how unhealthy cold fast foods were would make them relent.

14 Given the abuses documented in people smuggling, it was not possible to discern when undocumented migrants actively decided to pay with sex or when they were sexually assaulted by smugglers. Furthermore, the idea of sex as a currency should not be construed as discounting or justifying violence.

a study of virginity testing in KwaZulu Natal in South Africa where along with physical examinations, elderly women claimed these signs indicated girls who had been deflowered (Scorgie 2002). Such beliefs are apparently commonplace in southern Africa. Consequently, respondents felt that paid sex compensated for some of these social costs. Additionally, young women argued that paid sex was also a test of ability to provide and pay bridewealth in case the relationship leads to marriage. Indeed, in many cases, relatives of female youths entrust them with the choice of a partner who can honour bridewealth payments. However, some key informants noted that girls who engaged in paid sex, *bacossi* or otherwise, were often abjectly poor heads of child-headed households.

Discussion and conclusion

This chapter has shown that sex work and transactional sex have a long history in Zimbabwe. It also provides a panoramic view of youths' engagement in paid sex between 2000 and 2010 during Zimbabwe's worst economic crisis. Paid sex was ubiquitous and seemed to increase in tandem with inequality and poverty. It has shown that labour markets continued to be gender biased and to exclude female youth from work, including relatively lucrative informal sector activities. Paid sex became a livelihood of the last resort among the desperate. Given cost recovery in many sectors, earning money meant the difference between destitution and survival (Bandali 2011). In many ways, resorting to paid sex led to a reworking of cultural ideals and practices. As noted by Magaisa (2001), even in conservative rural areas women engaged in sex work openly, some hiding their real names and some using vending as a front. Through sex work, women still paid homage to the ideal of the male provider, albeit in short-lived interactions. Women attached themselves, even for fleeting moments, to men with disposable income in order to earn something. These attachments presented multi-dimensional risks because of their fragility and short-term nature. They also point to wider social changes such as weak social bonds, and challenged the kin who could not fend for young women in need.

Male youths and older men took advantage of the breadwinner myth to pick and dump desperate young women using their resources as leverage. Although in most cases young women who engaged in these practices were seen as loose and unmarriageable, in others these practices were seen as transitory, ending with settled marriage (Adams 2009). As the crisis deepened, settling down through marriage became elusive.

The ubiquity of paid sex illustrates the unprecedented socio-economic and political change that confronted Zimbabweans in the last four decades. Furthermore, it shows the extent of exclusion and structural violence visited on young women. In Zimbabwean towns and rural areas, young women were without the means to make ends meet. They were actively or otherwise excluded from prevailing ways of earning money.

References

Adams, M. (2009) 'Playful places, serious times: young women migrants from a peri-urban settlement in Harare', *The Journal of The Royal Anthropological Institute*, 15(4), pp. 779-814.

Attwood, F. (2006) 'Sexed up: Theorising the sexualisation of culture', *Sexualities*, 9(1), pp. 77-94.

Bandali, S. (2011) 'Exchange of sex for resources: HIV risk and gender norms on Cabo Delgado, Mozambique', *Culture, Health and Sexuality*, 13(5), pp. 575-588.

Barnett, J.P. and E. Maticka-Tyndale (2011) 'The gift of agency: sexual exchange scripts among Nigerian Youth', *The Journal of Sex Research*, 48(4), pp. 349-359.

Bauman, Z. (2003) *Liquid love: On the Frailty of Human Bonds*. Cambridge: Polity Press.

Bennell, P. and M. Ncube (1994) '"Jobs for boys?": The employment experiences of secondary school leavers in Zimbabwe', *Journal of Southern African Studies*, 20(2), pp. 301-316.

Betts, S.C., D.J. Peterson and A.J. Huebner (2003) 'Zimbabwean adolescents' condom use: what makes a difference? Implications for intervention', *Journal of Adolescent Health*, 33(3), pp. 165-171.

Bhana, D. (2017) 'Love, sex and gender: missing in African child and youth studies' *Africa Development*, 42(2), pp. 243-256.

Chikovore, J., L. Nystrom, G. Lindmark and B.M. Ahlberg (2002) 'Denial and violence: Paradoxes in men's perspectives in premarital sex and pregnancy in rural Zimbabwe', in J. Chikovore, Gender and power dynamics in women's sexual and reproductive health: a study of male perspectives in women's sexual and reproductive health with a special emphasis on abortion, Umea University, Sweden

Cole, J. (2004) 'Fresh contact in Tamatave, Madagascar: Sex, Money and Intergenerational transformation', *American Ethnologist,* 31(4), pp. 573-588.

Giddens, A. (1992) *The transformation of intimacy: Sexuality, love and eroticism in modern societies.* California: Stanford University Press.

Groes-Green, C. (2013) '"To put men in a bottle": Eroticism, kinship, female power and transactional sex in Maputo, Mozambique', *American Ethnologist,* 40(1), pp. 102-117.

————— (2014) 'Journeys of patronage: moral economies of transactional sex, kinship and female migration from Mozambique to Europe', *Journal of the Royal Anthropology Institute,* 20(2), pp. 237-255.

Gukurume, S. (2011) 'Transactional sex and politics of the belly at tertiary education institutions in the era of HIV and AIDS: A case study of Great Zimbabwe University and Masvingo Polytechnical College', *Journal of Sustainable Development in Africa,* 13(3), pp. 178-193.

————— (2017) '#ThisFlag and #ThisGown Cyber Protests in Zimbabwe: Reclaiming Political Space', *African Journalism Studies,* 38(2), pp. 49-70.

Howard-Hassman, R.E. (2010) 'Mugabe's Zimbabwe, 2000-2009: Massive Human Rights Violations and the Failure to Protect', *Human Rights Quarterly,* 32(4), pp. 898-920.

Hunter, M. (2002) 'The materiality of Everyday Sex: Thinking beyond "prostitution"', *African Studies,* 61(1), pp. 99-120.

Jones, J.L. (2010) '"Nothing is straight in Zimbabwe": The Rise of the *Kukiya-kiya* Economy 2000-2008', *Journal of Southern African Studies,* 36(2), pp. 285-299.

Kelly, P. (2001) 'Youth at risk: Processes on individualisation and responsibilisation in the risk society', *Discourse,* 22(1), pp. 23-33.

Kriger, N. (2008) 'Zimbabwe's parliamentary election of 2005: The Myth of New Electoral Laws', *Journal of Southern African Studies,* 34(2), pp. 359-378.

Laakso, L. (2002) 'The politics of International Election Observation:

The Case of Zimbabwe in 2000', *The Journal of Modern African Studies* 40(3), pp. 437-464.

Longfield, K. (2004) 'Rich Fools, Spare Tyres, and Boyfriends: Partner Categories, Relationship Dynamics and Ivorian Women's Risks for STIs and HIV', *Culture Health & Sexuality*, 6(6), pp. 483-500.

Magaisa, I. (2001) '"We came to the Bridge for Money": Prostitution at a Rural Service Centre', in P. Hebinck and M. Bourdillon (eds), *Women, Men and Work: Rural Livelihoods in south-eastern Zimbabwe*. Harare: Weaver Press.

Mains, D. (2007) 'Neoliberal Times: Progress, Boredom and Shame among Young Men in Urban Ethiopia', *American Ethnologist*, 34(4), pp. 659-673.

Marindo, R., S. Pearson and J.B. Casterline (2003) 'Condom use and abstinence among unmarried young people in Zimbabwe: Which strategy, whose agenda?' Washington, DC: Population Council.

Masvaure, T (2010) '"I just need to be flashy on campus": female students and transactional sex at the a university in Zimbabwe', *Culture, Health & Sexuality*, 12(8), pp. 857-870.

Mate, R. (2009) 'Of perfumed lotions, biscuits and condoms: Youth, femininity, sexuality and HIV and AIDS prevention in rural Gwanda district, Zimbabwe', in D. Mwiturubani, A. Gebre, M. Paulo, R. Mate and A. Socpa (eds), *Youth, HIV/AIDS and Social Transformation in Africa*. Dakar: CODESRIA.

———— (2014) 'Grappling with emerging adulthoods: Youth narratives of coming of age in a frontier town, Zimbabwe'. PhD thesis, International Institute of Social Studies, the Hague.

Munive, J. (2010) 'The army of "unemployed" young people', *Young*, 18(3), pp. 321-338.

Nyamnjoh, F.B (2005) 'Fishing in Troubled Waters: "Disquettes" and "Thiofs" in Dakar', *Africa*, 75(3), pp. 295-325.

Ojebode, A., D. Togunde and A. Adelakun (2011) 'Secrecy, Security and Social Exchange: New Media and Cross-generational Dating in Nigeria', *International Journal of Sociology of the Family*, 37(2), pp. 307-327.

Pattman, R. (2001) '"The beer drinkers say I had a nice prostitute, but the church goers talk about things spiritual": Learning to be men at a teachers' college in Zimbabwe', in R. Morrell (ed.) *Changing men in Southern Africa*. London: Zed Books.

———— (2005) '"Boys and girls should not be too Close": Sexuality, the Identities of African Boys and Girls and HIV/AIDS Education' *Sexualities*, 8(4), pp. 497-516.

Peters, K. and P. Richards (1998) '"Why we fight": Voices of Youth Combatants in Sierra Leone', *Africa*, 68(2), pp. 183-210.

Sachikonye, L. (2003) 'From "Growth with equity" to "Fast Track" Reform: Zimbabwe's Land Question', *Review of African Political Economy*, 30(96), pp. 227-240.

Scorgie, F. (2002) 'Virginity Testing and the Politics of Sexual Responsibility: Implications for AIDS Interventions', *African Studies*, 61(1), pp. 55-75.

Shefer, T., L. Clowes and T. Vergnani (2012) 'Narratives of transactional sex on a university campus', *Culture, Health & Sexuality*, 14(4), pp. 435-447.

Stoebenau, K., L .Heise, J. Wamoyi and N. Barbrova (2016) 'Revisiting the understanding of "transactional sex" in sub-Saharan Africa: A review and a synthesis of the literature', *Social Science & Medicine*, 168, pp. 186-197.

Tavory, I. and M. Poulin (2012) 'Sex work and the construction of intimacies: meanings and work pragmatics in rural Malawi', *Theory and Society*, 41(3), pp. 211-231.

Yingwana, N. (2018) '"We fit in the Society by Force": Sex Work and Feminism in Africa', *Meridians: feminism, race, transnationalism*, 17(2), pp. 279-295.

Zembe, Y., L. Townsend, A. Thorson and A.M. Ekstrom (2013) '"Money talks, bullshit walks": interrogating notions of consumption and survival sex among young women engaging in transactional sex in post-Apartheid South Africa: A qualitative enquiry', *Globalization and Health*, 9(28).

13

Youth and informality in Zimbabwe[1]

Simbarashe Gukurume and Marjoke Oosterom

Introduction

At independence in 1980, Zimbabwe's informal sector was largely invisible and insignificant. However, due to protracted economic and political crises it has moved from the periphery to the centre of the country's economic landscape. According to Mlambo (2017), by 2015 an estimated 90% of people were unemployed and forced to eke out a living in the informal sector. In fact, the informal economy has now become the country's largest employer and accommodates millions of Zimbabweans, the majority of them being young people (Gukurume 2018).

This chapter traces the historical reconfiguration of the informal economy in Zimbabwe since independence. We focus on the contribution that the sector has made to the lives and livelihoods of the 'born free' generation and, equally, how the youth have been at the centre of politics of the informal economy. We view the informal economy as a space through which to understand the temporalities of youth agency and resilience in Zimbabwe. We demonstrate that 'informality' in the case of urban Zimbabwean youth refers not only to the many informal economic activities they do to sustain themselves, but also to the 'informal politics' of ZANU-PF in urban spaces that have been a central feature of youth living from informal work.

We deploy the conceptual frame of the 'hustle' to understand young people's everyday struggles and ways of making do and getting by in Zimbabwe's informal economy. Drawing on longitudinal ethnographic work among young, urban informal workers, we assert that in spite of its precariousness, the informal economy has provided young people with the space to navigate uncertainty.

The chapter is divided into six sections, covering the two periods from 1980 to 1999 and from 2000 to date. We first conceptualise the youth hustle and situate it within the informal economy. We then discuss the development that led to the growth of the informal economy: how the government sought to mimic colonial strategies of managing informality between 1980 and 1990, through what Kamete (2017) referred to as 'warehousing'. In the next section we explain how the adoption of neoliberal economic reforms accelerated the growth of not only the informal economy itself, but also the number of youth generating livelihoods in the sector from the early 1990s to 2000. In the subsequent sections, we focus on several interrelated themes in relation to state action, youth and the informal economy. We argue that the ways in which the government dealt with urban informal workers was the result of how it perceived urban youth as a threat. The second theme is the resultant politicisation of the informal sector and how the ZANU-PF government sought to control and use the informal sector for political mobilisation, especially during elections. The final section explains how the 2017 coup and subsequent political transition reconfigured parts of the informal economy, displacing informal workers from the city centre to designated markets, and shows how this affected youth vendors.

The informal economy and youth hustling

With deepening economic crises and skyrocketing unemployment, the streets have become an important economic resource supporting the livelihoods of many youth. We deploy the concept of 'hustle' as a window through which to unpack and understand the configuration of youth livelihoods in the informal economy. In this section we discuss the concept of youth 'hustle'. Hustle is a productive theoretical concept which enables us to understand young people's everyday struggles, how they deploy their agency and how they navigate existential anxieties and the complex politics in the informal economy (Gukurume

2018; Oosterom 2019). Thieme (2013) conceptualised 'hustle' as a culturally nuanced navigational capacity used by youths to get by in conditions of uncertainty, precarity and survivalism mainly in the informal employment sector. Thieme also asserted that hustle relates to the everyday dealings associated with uncertainty and accepted informalities that pervade realms of life amongst youth in precarious urban geographies. These often illegal, survivalist and opportunistic activities are akin to what Jones (2010) referred to as '*kukiya kiya*' or '*kujingirisa*' (see Gukurume 2018). For some scholars, hustling constructs urban youth as uncertain, and vulnerable, albeit not without logic and agency that can simultaneously circumvent and accentuate conditions of uncertainty and adversity (Saitta et al. 2013; Mwaura, 2017; Thieme 2013). For Thieme (2013) youth hustle is an implicit critique of the state's failings and a blatant rejection of the previous generations' conception and experience of 'licit work'.

In our conversations and interviews with young people, the majority of them referred to their activities in the informal economy as 'hustling'. For instance, Andrew, who was a foreign currency dealer in the streets of Harare, remarked, 'There are no jobs and there have been no jobs for a long time, so we have to hustle, many young people like myself are 'hustlers'.

This was not unique to Andrew, but resonated with the narratives of many other young people we interviewed and interacted with in the urban markets in Harare. Andrew told us that he has a diploma in accounting but has never worked formally after his graduation in 2017. Graduating into the streets has become a common feature and reality for many young people in post-colonial Zimbabwe. Many unemployed youth venture into trading second-hand clothing, electronics and automobiles, phones and airtime credit, or car washing, in the streets of Harare. In designated markets, registered vendors pay the city council but may encounter political brokers who levy fees, as we shall discuss. Where activities are enacted in the streets, however, 'illegal' youth vendors pay no council fees and constantly engage in running battles with law enforcement agents.

Within Zimbabwe's urban political context, with intense rivalries between ZANU-PF and the opposition, the informal economy is rife with partisan politics (Kamete 2017; Kriger 2012; Oosterom 2019). We therefore also deploy the concept of 'political informality' (Goodfellow

2020) to discuss the practices of ZANU-PF and its local agents to control urban informal workers. Political informality refers to a 'realm of diverse political processes and practices' (ibid.: 279), some of which complement formal rules and regulations, while other practices may unintentionally or deliberately undermine formal institutions. Clientelism is one of these informal practices, and we shall demonstrate that ruling party patronage is an informal political practice that targets young informal workers.

Warehousing the informal sector

At independence, Zimbabwe inherited an industrialised and largely formalised and diversified economy (Carmody 1998; Gibbon 1995; Mlambo 2017). Carmody (1998) asserted that Zimbabwe had the most industrially developed economy in sub-Saharan Africa outside of South Africa. Mlambo (2017) echoes this, highlighting how Mugabe inherited a thriving and diversified economy anchored by three pillars: agriculture, mining and manufacturing. As such, the informal sector remained small and economic growth was higher than many other African countries, averaging about 4% per annum (Carmody 1998). In the early 1980s, the real Gross Domestic Product (GDP) annual growth rates averaged 4.5%. This was made possible by inherited colonial policies that promoted large-scale investment in both agriculture and manufacturing, and the large influx of foreign capital after the lifting of economic sanctions imposed on the colonial regime (Mlambo 2017). According to the African Development Bank, Zimbabwe recorded its strongest post-independence economic growth during 1980-1990, with GDP growing by an average of about 5.5% which was higher than the average for sub-Saharan African countries (AfDB 2011). However, although Zimbabwe inherited a highly developed and sophisticated manufacturing sector, it was the sector that benefited mostly the minority white population (Mlambo 2017). The post-independence government inherited not only a highly sophisticated and thriving economy, but also a highly unequal one. Although the history of the informal sector dates back to the colonial period, when poor and unemployed black urban dwellers resorted to street vending, it was small and insignificant. The Rhodesian government deployed repressive laws to curb the growth of the so-called 'African economy'. For instance, the Town and Country Planning Act (1946), the Vagrancy Act (1960), the Urban Councils Act and the Vendors and Hawkers by-laws (1973) were enacted to frustrate the growth of informal sector activities (see Dhemba 1999). Strict legislation and city by-laws restricted the informal economy to specific spaces and discouraged its growth (Brand et al. 1993). Consequently, during this era the informal economy emerged, largely as an underground one. During this period, the informal sector was an unattractive option for many young people who preferred, and easily secured, white-collar jobs in the formal sector. Kamete (2017) asserted that 'warehousing' – the confining of informals to very specific spaces – dates back to the colonial period and continues to be a common strategy, albeit with modifications through which the informal economy is governed in the global south. Warehousing was not always successful, and often faced resistance from the people. Indeed, moments of change tended to have limits to the ways in which the colonial and post-colonial state policed and regulated informality.

At the dawn of independence, the majority of colonial city by-laws and strategies of managing the informal sector were largely adopted by the newly independent government and sustained for a number of years. Just like the colonial regime, the post-colonial state viewed the warehousing of informality as an important strategy for regulating and modernising the sector as well as maintaining some form of order in urban spaces (Tokman 2007; Hansen 2004). This strategy of controlling informality was based on specific forms of urban city planning and modernity which closely mirrored the British planning systems. Indeed, supporters of this strategy regard this as the evidence of inclusive city planning, where the poor's livelihoods are accommodated (see Kamete 2017; Gumbo 2013). Gumbo (2013) asserted that the informal sector grew by 17% under the socialist policies of the 1980s. For Gumbo, this increase was in part due to over-urbanisation because the urban labour force increased at an average of 3% per annum compared to the formal economic sector that generated employment at an average of only 2.2% per annum throughout the 1980s. This therefore meant that job creation in the formal sector was no longer keeping pace with the growing demand for formal sector jobs. Similarly, state-owned enterprises were underperforming and inefficient because of the lack of a profit motive (Carmody 1998).

Economic Structural Adjustment Programmes (ESAP) and the growth of the informal sector

From the late 1980s, Zimbabwe shifted from socialist to a neoliberal market policy orientation. Bretton Woods institutions imposed economic reforms as preconditions for accessing loans and grants, and the Economic Structural Adjustment Programme (ESAP) was adopted in the early 1990s. ESAP led to massive job losses due to retrenchments and shrinking of the formal sector, hence it triggered a rapid growth and expansion of the informal economy (Gibbon 1995; Mupedziswa and Gumbo 2001; Musoni 2010). For instance, by 1991 the informal economy accounted for about 27% of total employment (McPherson 1991) and employed more than 450,000 people. Dhemba (1999) argued that structural adjustment saw urban poverty rising from 12% in 1991 to 39% in 1995. It also sparked an influx of people into the urban informal sector (Kamete 2006). Migration out of the cities became commonplace as people could no longer afford the expensive city life. Consequently, as large-scale formal organisations adjusted their operations in the wake of ESAP and growing global competition, employment generation declined to an average of 1% per annum throughout the 1990s (Gumbo 2013). As a result, the informal economy grew rapidly and employed 61% of the labour force by 2001 (Gukurume 2010; Gumbo 2013). Following this, Moyo (2018) asserted that the growth of urban informality should be explained and understood through the complex shifts in the Zimbabwean economy. Apart from urban-rural migration, there was also massive migration into neighbouring countries and to Britain and USA (Crush and Tevera 2010), and remittances from the diaspora have sustained many families and shielded the country's economy from a total collapse. In our interviews with youth vendors, it emerged that remittances also played a key role in the establishment of small and micro enterprises. Remittances flowed into the country through both formal and informal networks. Due to the 'illegal' status of some Zimbabwean migrants and the high transfer charges, remittances were often sent through informal networks. This led to the emergence of networks like the 'Malayitshas' in South Africa and other ways of transferring money on and beyond the margins of 'formality', 'legality' and the purview of the state.

The economic crisis that deepened in the 1990s had clear implications for youth. Many young graduates could no longer be guaranteed jobs in the formal sector. Worse still, those who made it into the formal sector were paid low wages that offered limited prospects for upward mobility. Consequently, many of these young people were compelled to 'hustle' in the informal sector to complement their earnings, establishing micro, small and medium enterprises (Gukurume 2018). As such, the privatisation of the economy and the attendant retrenchment of employees, which affected the largely inexperienced youth in both the private and public sector, pushed thousands of people into the informal economy, like many other countries that adopted the neoliberal economic reforms (Hansen 2010). Following this, the informal sector rapidly expanded with the economic and political crisis that ensued after 2000, as we turn to next. It made the informal economy reconfigure into what some scholars started calling *the* economy, supporting the livelihoods of the majority of Zimbabweans (Kanyenze and Sibanda 2005). Interestingly, while acknowledging the important role that can be played by the informal sector in creating employment for the youth and spearheading socio-economic development, the Zimbabwean government and authorities' perception of the informal sector has remained ambivalent and ambiguous (Kamete 2008; Gukurume 2018).

Controlling the informal sector and urban youth

The formation in 1999 of Zimbabwe's main opposition party, the Movement for Democratic Change (MDC), and its subsequent successes in urban areas formed the onset of major political and economic crisis from 2000 to 2009. ZANU-PF lost its electoral grip in most urban spaces after 2000: in the 2002 elections, the MDC almost won all the parliamentary seats in Harare. Frustrated with the deepening economic crisis and skyrocketing unemployment and poverty levels, many urbanites saw the MDC as a better alternative to ZANU-PF. Economic mismanagement, corruption and the controversial fast track land reform programme produced a crisis that culminated in 2008 with hyperinflation and cash shortages, and produced a further influx of thousands of people into the cities (Chikulo et al. 2020; Gukurume 2015; Potts 2011). According to the African Development Bank (2011), the years 2000 to 2008 saw a protracted economic crisis and a broad-based decline of the economy leading to a cumulative drop of about 50% in real GDP growth. Matamanda et al. (2019) argued that apart from the protracted economic crisis, politics has had a huge impact on the proliferation of the informal sector in the country. The streets have become an important economic resource supporting the livelihoods of many youth. Additionally, in spite of its criminalisation and marginalisation, the informal sector contributes significantly to the national economy and has become the country's largest employer (Gukurume 2018).

After successive electoral defeats to the MDC in urban areas, the ZANU-PF government sought to reassert its dominance in the cities through several strategies, one of which was to influence city councils by directly interfering with their operations, replacing professional civil servants with partisan officials, sacking mayors and councillors, and appointing ZANU-PF aligned 'special councillors' (McGregor 2013; Muchadenyika 2015). It was also involved in land deals in informal settlements to tie residents into party patronage (McGregor and Chatiza 2019). Another strategy was to control the informal economy (Kamete 2006). This saw the rapid politicisation of the informal sector as well as the unleashing of the state security apparatus in an attempt to clamp down on informal sector players, especially those in the streets or operating outside designated spaces. ZANU-PF and its political henchman saw the informal economy as an important economic resource to through which to accumulate wealth and space for political mobilisation (Maringira and Gukurume 2020). For instance, agents used designated markets like Mupedzanhamo, Magaba/Siyaso and the Mbare Musika markets not only to collect money through informal levies and other market fees, but also to reward their loyal supporters with stalls (Kamete 2017; Kriger 2012), a practice that continues to exist as our interviews conducted between 2018 and 2020 demonstrated. Indeed, markets are viewed by ZANU-PF as strategic spaces for party recruitment, instilling their party ideologies, and collecting fees that undermine the revenue of the city authorities.

The government has periodically engaged in 'clean-up campaigns': the evictions of informal vendors from the city centres and demolition of illegal market structures. The most destructive and controversial operation occurred in 2005, Operation Murambatsvina ('clean the filth'). Murambatsvina was viewed by critics as a political operation and punishment of the urban population for its support to the opposition in the March elections (Bratton and Masunungure 2006). Under this operation, 'illegal' and 'informal' market structures and houses were razed and vendors violently pushed off the streets. An estimated 700,00 people were displaced or lost their livelihoods (Tibaijuka 2005). While this affected everyone in the informal economy, young people were particularly hit hard (Bratton and Masunungure 2006), many of them losing their informal jobs. Civil society groups and the international community castigated the government for this operation and regarded it as a violation of human rights (Tibaijuka 2005). In response, the government initiated another operation, 'Garikai' ('Live Well'), constructing a few alternative markets for jettisoned vendors to use and relocating evicted dwellers to new informal settlements.

The literature demonstrates how young vendors bounced back. While the operation cleared the vendors off the streets for a number of months, it did not take long for youth vendors to desert the so-called designated spaces and return to the streets from which they had been removed (Kamete 2008; Musoni 2010). Many complained that they could not access space at designated markets, nor afford the exorbitant rentals and levies for stalls at the markets. Others noted that the newly constructed markets were far from the city centre and hence lacked customers. The return to contested spaces and the streets, is one of the many ways through which youth vendors resisted and subverted state authority (Kamete 2010). It also demonstrates the resilience of young vendors to political and economic shocks, and to recurrent police brutality.

This violence and harassment was particularly pronounced against vendors selling in the streets outside the designated markets. The informal economy is home to a wide range of economic activities or hustles,ranging from trade in mobile phone accessories, airtime, fresh fruits and vegetable, public transport touting, foreign currency dealings, and second-hand clothing. These activities have been produced and reproduced over time and space by the reconfiguration of the country's economy. For instance, the introduction and adoption of mobile money services in 2011 by companies like Econet and NetOne saw the emergence of mobile money agents, and speculative dealers (Gukurume and Mahiya 2020). In the 1990s, the informal sector was largely dominated by food and newspaper vendors and a few dealers in second-hand clothing. However, over the past few years a diversity of informal activities emerged in the streets of Harare. For instance, street foreign currency dealers emerged and expanded at the height of the country's economic and political crisis (Mawowa and Matongo 2010; Gukurume 2015). However, after the dollarisation of the economy in 2009, the economic stabilisation pushed foreign currency dealers off the market. Indeed, the economic stability that punctuated the GNU period saw a steady decline of the number of people surviving through the informal sector, while those who were there reported thriving business. At markets like Mupedzanhamo, the MDC negotiated access into the previously dominated ZANU-PF structures and accessed a few tables through the MDC dominated city council. Political violence subsided. However, after the end of the GNU, ZANU-PF and Mugabe regained total control in the 2013 elections. The economy began to decline and violence at the markets re-emerged with the expulsion of MDC aligned vendors from Mupedzanhamo.

Informality, youth political mobilisation and violence

Realising the mammoth task of creating jobs for the thousands of unemployed young people, former President Robert Mugabe often condoned the growth of informality (Mupedziswa and Gumbo 2001). For instance, in the early 1990s, the government promoted and condoned informality and provided various forms of support (ibid.). In response to the outcry about Operation Murambatsvina, the government declared that it would promote the role of the informal sector in the economy, but that registered 'small and medium enterprises' (SMEs) were favoured (GoZ 2005: 8). The government created a Ministry of Small and Medium Enterprises in 2002 at the peak of the country's protracted economic crisis to spearhead the growth of SMEs. Similarly, the Ministry of Youth Development and Employment Creation (MYDEC) asserts that its role is 'to lobby for the recognition of ... micro enterprises, the informal sector and cooperatives in .... government policy' (MYDEC cited in Kamete 2020: 932). Mugabe has sometimes offered ZANU-PF youth land and open spaces in the city for housing and vending activities,[2] yet these practices can be understood as part of its party patronage strategies. During the 'meet the people' rallies in 2014 Mugabe and his wife ordered the council and police to allow vendors to work in the city

---

2 'Grace Mugabe drawn into vendors' saga', *NewsDay*, 4 June 2015; 'Servicing of land for youths begins', *The Herald*, 22 August 2016.

centre and were criticised for inspiring lawlessness.[3] Mugabe and his government saw the informal sector as the panacea to the skyrocketing levels of unemployment for the youth and as mitigating the growing urban poverty. This was an attempt to win back the urban youth vote and a way of strengthening and widening his patronage networks in the informal sector (Maringira and Gukurume 2020; Chirisa et al 2019).

For Mugabe and his allies, unemployed urban youth were a potential resource to be used during political campaigns, national events and often to do violence and mobilise on behalf of him and his ZANU-PF party (Chitukutuku 2017; Oosterom and Gukurume 2019; Maringira and Gukurume 2020). From the mid-2000s, a number of politically connected youth groups emerged that violently controlled certain informal economic activities and spaces. One of these, a powerful militia group Chipangano, controlled large sections of urban informal markets and bus termini in central Harare (Kriger 2012; Mutingwizo 2014). The group was at the centre of ZANU-PF patronage networks and violent accumulation. Supported and protected by some powerful ZANU-PF politicians, the group collected rents, terrorised MDC-aligned vendors and mobilised political support for Mugabe and his political henchman (Maringira and Gukurume 2020; Oosterom and Gukurume 2019). Newspaper reports show how ZANU-PF members have taken advantage of this politicisation to establish powerful networks of 'land barons' (brokers) who use informal markets and other spaces to create and cement partisan patron-client relations.[4] This was echoed by Chiweshe (2020) who asserted that land barons were exploiting political power for primitive accumulation, with politicians and politically connected individuals using land and urban markets as an economic and political asset. These networks are largely gerontocratic and tend to not only exclude young people, but also to fleece them of their hard-earned money through rentals and levies.

Some ZANU-PF-aligned youth deployed Mugabe's rhetoric of 'youth empowerment' to lay claim to urban spaces where they set up makeshift stalls. Interestingly, President Mugabe and the then Minister of Local Government and National Housing Ignatius Chombo often ordered the city council to allow vendors to operate in the city centre,

---

3   Grace Mugabe inspires vendor lawlessness;, Zimbabwe Situation, 12 December 2014.

4   'Zanu PF land barons exposed, what next?' *NewsDay*, 12 December 2019.

especially towards elections.[5] In return, vendors were required to attend party and national events such as Heroes' Day and Independence Day celebrations presided over by President Mugabe and ZANU-PF. Indeed, our research participants at Mupedzanhamo market recalled how ZANU-PF youth and market committees always ordered the closure of markets for these events. ZANU-PF has put in place its own district coordinating committees, party branches or cell structures to control strategic urban and peri-urban markets. ZANU-PF politicians and agents then use these structures to mobilise support and entrench their influence in the informal economy (Kamete, 2017). Indeed, membership to ZANU-PF is often regarded as a prerequisite for one to access a table or stall in these markets or claim space in public areas often used for street vending. Following this, scholars have argued that land has emerged as a political resource used and instrumentalised to control and amass political mileage and votes for ZANU-PF political elites (McGregor and Chatiza 2019; Chiweshe 2020). At the same time many young vendors complain that it is impossible for them to have their own stalls at the markets; they can only rent them. Many pay exorbitant rentals to relatively older vendors who accessed stalls in the 1990s (Kamete 2017). In addition, young people in the informal economy encounter precarious working conditions. Their work is characterised by meagre salaries, long working hours and the risk of unfair dismissal, police brutality, and political violence. Consequently, many of these young people continue to long for a formal and 'decent' job.

The practice of politicising urban, informal economic networks became central to ZANU-PF strategies to consolidate its powers, and this continued under the Government of National Unity and thereafter (Kriger 2012; McGregor 2013; Oosterom 2019). Revolving funds were also incorporated into these partisan patronage networks to stimulate youth businesses (Oosterom and Gukurume 2019). When the struggle intensified over the succession to President Mugabe and its accompanying factionalism within ZANU-PF, this filtered down to the local level where factions were contesting the local spaces and informal economic networks (Oosterom, 2019). Some ended up on the losing end, like the former ZANU-PF provincial youth chairperson and Chipangano leader, Jimmy Kanuka, who had joined the Mujuru

---

5   '"Chipangano" leader bashed', *Zimbabwe Situation*, 13 November 2014.

faction and lost his political credentials soon after 2013.[6] Factionalism, which had caused divisions across state and party institutions, including the ZANU-PF youth league and Zimbabwe Youth Council (Oosterom and Gukurume, 2019), thus affected who became the locally powerful henchmen on behalf of ZANU-PF.

After the 2017-coup: the reconfiguration of the informal sector

The ouster of President Robert Mugabe in November 2017 through a military assisted transition/coup configured a new regime of state control and spatial regulation of the informal economy. The Mnangagwa regime quickly pushed vendors from the city centre to designated spaces. The politically connected vendors who had inundated every corner of Harare were forced to relocate to the margins of the city centre by the law enforcement agents, including city council officers. This particularly affected second-hand clothing vendors, of which youth constituted the majority. For Mnangagwa, the young informal workers posed a potential threat to his power, given the role that some vendors' associations had played in mobilising protests against Mugabe (Matamanda et al. 2020). Indeed, vendors' associations and prominent leaders like Stan Zvorwadza and Promise Mkwananzi, leader of the #Tajamuka movement, had played a huge role in mobilising protests and other forms of resistance to the Mugabe regime. Therefore, for Mnangagwa, young informal workers constituted a potentially threatening constituency that needed to be contained and dispersed to undermine their potential for organising and revolting against his government. This was understandable given that many young people had become frustrated with the Mnangagwa government's failure to create the jobs he promised on his inauguration.[7] Realising this frustration and growing restlessness among the youth, Mnangagwa's allies began to claim that the government had created over two million jobs, albeit in the informal sector.

The removal of vendors from the city to designated markers resonates strongly with the city council's vision of transforming Harare into a first-class city by 2023 and reclaiming its 'sunshine city' status.

---

6   Ibid.

7   'Zimbabwe's Mnangagwa promises jobs in "new democracy"', BBC News, 22 November 2017; 'Zimbabwe's Emmerson Mnangagwa promises "jobs, jobs, jobs" in "new democracy"', *Evening Standard*, 22 November 2017.

This vision resonates powerfully with President Mnangagwa's vision of the country becoming a middle-income economy by 2030. Mnangagwa believes that this vision can be driven by large multinationals[8] and formalised SMEs. Kamete (2020) argued that the vision of a modern city has no space for ambulant youths using space in contravention of planning controls. Ironically, the Co-operative Societies Act, which governs the country's informal sector, has no provision for informality (Kamete 2020). Consequently, clashes between youth and the urban planning and law enforcement officials are commonplace. In the same vein, the Mnangagwa regime seems to be openly encouraging the formalisation of the informal sector so that it can play a part in his vision 2030.[9]

At the onset of the COVID-19 lockdown, all informal sector activities were ordered to stop and the government demanded that informal traders sector be registered and formalise their businesses in order for them receive relief funds and to resume operations.[10] This quest for formalisation is not new. In fact, Kamete (2008) argues that the post-independence state has always been obsessed with formalising informality. Registration and/or formalisation is a prerequisite for state support. For instance, in interviews with Zimbabwe Youth Council (ZYC) and Empower Bank officials, funding for youth empowerment is only extended to those with formally registered SMEs; youth in the informal sector have hardly benefited from such funds. Formalisation is also supported by the city council because it enables them to collect levies from vendors. Following this, and support from the government, the city council has adopted a heavy-handed approach to dealing with informality, particularly street trading.

All the while, since Mnangagwa took over in 2017, restrictive urban policies that consider informal activities to be illegal have been forcefully implemented to promote order and cleanliness in the city. This has seen the government and city council pursue a stringent, modernist approach to urban development, confronting informal workers with severe security crackdowns. The violence used to quell protests after the 2018 elections and again in response to protests in January 2019 gave a clear signal that the new dispensation would not

---

8   'New mines to drive middle class vision', *The Herald*, 17 July 2020.

9   'President rallies SMEs for economic growth', *The Herald*, 12 December 2020.

10   'Informal sector demands social, financial support', *Daily News*, 22 June 2020.

tolerate such actions. The lockdown in response to Covid-19 saw an upsurge in human right abuses and brutality by police and security forces, in particular regarding the protests announced for 31 July 2020 (CZC 2020). However, with Zimbabwe's economy again contracting in 2019 due to poor performance in mining, tourism, and agriculture, and the deepening economic crisis due to the pandemic in 2020, the informal economy will remain vital for the country's population for a long time to come.

Conclusion

This chapter has shown how the informal economy has expanded as the result of consecutive crisis in Zimbabwe and how this has had implications for youth working in urban settings. It has shown how 'informality' relates both to the economic activities that help urban youth to sustain themselves and to ZANU-PF's tactics of controlling partisan networks in the informal economy to absorb resources and for political mobilisation. While urban councils have consistently tried to enforce a modernist form of planning, party actors subvert formalisation by inserting themselves informally into networks and markets. Young informal workers have experienced the brunt of evictions, and political mobilisation in urban spaces. They have also demonstrated great resilience, bouncing back after evictions, and subverting and resisting partisan influences. The Mnangagwa government appears to be less tolerant of informal workers than the previous regime, as suggested by the upsurge in political violence since 2018.

Acknowledgements

This chapter has used some of the interview data collected through the research project 'Learning on the Streets', which is funded by the Economic and Social Research Council (ESRC) in the United Kingdom (grant number ES/S000127/1, Principal Investigator Dr. Marjoke Oosterom, Institute of Development Studies, Brighton.

References

AfDB (2011) 'From Stagnation to Economic Recovery', in *Infrastructure and growth: An action plan for sustained strong economic growth.* Tunisia: AfDB.

Brand, V., R. Mupedziswa and P. Gumbo (1993) 'Women Informal Sector

Workers and Structural Adjustment in Zimbabwe', in P. Gibbon (ed.), *Social Change and Economic Reform in Africa.* Uppsala: Nordiska Afrikainstitutet.

Bratton, M. and E. Masunungure (2007) 'Popular Reactions to State Repression: Operation Murambatsvina in Zimbabwe', *African Affairs,* 106(422), pp. 21-45.

Carmody, P. (1998) 'Neoclassical Practice and the Collapse of Industry in Zimbabwe: The Cases of Textiles, Clothing and Footwear', *Economic Geography*, 74(4), pp. 319-343.

Crush, J. and D. Tevera (2010) 'Exiting Zimbabwe', in J. Crush and D. Tevera (eds), *Zimbabwe's Exodus: Crisis, Migration, Survival.* Cape Town: Southern Africa Migration Programme.

Chikulo, S., P. Hebinck and B. Kinsey (2020) '"Mbare Musika is ours": An analysis of a fresh

produce market in Zimbabwe', *African Affairs*, 119(476), pp. 311-33.

Chitukutuku, E. (2017) 'Rebuilding the liberation war base: materiality and landscapes of violence in Northern Zimbabwe', *Journal of Eastern African Studies*, 11(1), pp. 133-150.

Chiweshe, M.K. (2020) 'Money, power and the complexities of urban land corruption in Zimbabwe', *African Journal of Land Policy and Geospatial Sciences*, 3(3), pp. 130-141.

Crisis in Zimbabwe Coalition (CZC) (2020) 'Wither democracy and human rights in SADC: Covid-19 Lockdowns and Basic Rights'. Harare: Crisis in Zimbabwe Coalition.

Dhemba, J. (1999) 'Informal Sector Development: A Strategy for Alleviating Urban Poverty in Zimbabwe', *Journal of Social Development in Africa*, 14(2), pp. 5-19.

Gibbon, P. (ed.) (1995) *Structural Adjustment and the Working Poor in Zimbabwe: Studies on Labour, Women Informal Sector Workers and Health.* Uppsala: Nordiska Afrikainstitutet.

Goodfellow, T. (2020) 'Political Informality: Deals, Trust Networks, and the Negotiation of Value in the Urban Realm', *The Journal of Development Studies*, 56(2), pp. 278-294

Government of Zimbabwe (GoZ) (2005) 'Response by Government of Zimbabwe to the Report by the UN Special Envoy on Operation Murambatsvina/ Restore Order'. Harare: Government of Zimbabwe.

Gukurume, S. (2010) 'The Politics of Money Burning and Foreign Currency Exchange in Zimbabwe: A Case Study of Mucheke Residents in Masvingo', *Journal of Sustainable Development in Africa*, 12(6), pp. 62-73.

——— (2015) 'Livelihood resilience in a hyperinflationary environment: Experiences of people engaging in money-burning (*kubhena mari*) transactions in Harare, Zimbabwe', *Social Dynamics*, 41(2), pp. 219-234.

——— (2018) 'Navigating Precarious Livelihoods: Youth in the SME Sector in Zimbabwe', *IDS Bulletin*, 49(5), pp. 89-104.

Gumbo, T. (2013) 'On deology change and spatial and structural linkages between formal and informal economic sectors in Zimbabwean cities (1981-2010)'. PhD thesis, Stellenbosch University.

Hansen, K.T. (2004) 'Who rules the streets? The politics of vending space in Lusaka.', in K.T. Hansen and M. Vaa (eds), *Reconsidering informality: perspectives from urban Africa*. Uppsala: Nordiska Afrikainstitutet.

——— (2010) 'Changing youth dynamics in Lusaka's informal economy in the context of economic liberalization', *African Studies Quarterly* 11(2/3), pp. 14-27.

Kamete, A.Y. (2006) 'The return of the jettisoned: ZANU PF's crack at re-urbanising in Harare', *Journal of Southern African Studies,* 32(2), pp. 256–271.

——— (2010) 'Defending Illicit Livelihoods: Youth Resistance in Harare's Contested Spaces', *International Journal of Urban and Regional Research*, 34(1), pp. 55-75.

———. (2017) Governing Enclaves of Informality: Unscrambling the Logic of the Camp in Urban Zimbabwe. *Geoforum,* 81C (2017), pp. 76-86.

———. (2020) 'Neither friend nor cnemy: Planning, ambivalence and the invalidation of urban informality in Zimbabwe', *Urban Studies*, 57(5), pp. 927–943.

Kriger, N. (2012) 'ZANU PF politics under Zimbabwe's "Power-Sharing" Government', *Journal of Contemporary African Studies*, 30(1), pp11-26.

McPherson, M. (1991) 'Micro and Small Scale Enterprises in Zimbabwe:

Resultsof a Country-wide Survey'. Gemini Technical Report, No 25.

Magure, B. (2015) 'Interpreting Urban Informality in Chegutu, Zimbabwe', *Journal of Asian African Studies*, 50(6), pp. 650–666.

Maringira, G., and S. Gukurume (2020) 'Youth patronage: Violence, intimidation and political mobilization in Zimbabwe'. *African Peacebuilding Network APN Working Papers* 28.

Matamanda, A.R., I. Chirisa, M.A. Dzvimbo and Q.L. Chinozvina (2020) 'The political economy of Zimbabwean Urban informality since 2000 – A contemporary governance dilemma', *Development Southern Africa*, 37(4), pp. 694-707.

Mawowa, S. and A. Matongo (2010) 'Inside Zimbabwe's roadside currency trade: The "World Bank" of Bulawayo', *Journal of Southern African Studies*, 36(2), pp. 319-337.

McGregor, J. (2013) 'Surveillance and the City: Patronage, Power-Sharing and the Politics of Urban Control in Zimbabwe', *Journal of Southern African Studies*, 39(4), pp. 783-805.

———— and K. Chatiza (2019) 'Frontiers of Urban Control: Lawlessness on the City Edge and Forms of Clientalist Statecraft in Zimbabwe', *Antipode*, 51(5), pp. 1554–1580.

Mlambo, A.S. (2017) 'From an Industrial Powerhouse to a Nation of Vendors: Over Two Decades of Economic Decline and Deindustrialization in Zimbabwe 1990–2015', *Journal of Developing Societies,* 33(1), pp. 99–125.

Moyo, I. (2018) 'Resistance and Resilience by Informal Traders in Bulawayo, Zimbabwe: Beyond Weapons of the Weak', *Urban Forum* 29, pp. 299–313.

Muchadenyika, D. (2015) 'Land for Housing: A Political Resource – Reflections from Zimbabwe's Urban Areas, *Journal of Southern African Studies*, 41(6), pp. 1219-1238

Mutingwizo, T. (2014) 'Chipangano Governance: Enablers and Effects of Violent Extraction in Zimbabwe', *Africa Peace and Conflict Journal*, 7(1), pp. 29–40.

Musoni, F. (2010) 'Operation Murambatsvina and the Politics of Street Vendors in Zimbabwe', *Journal of Southern African Studies*, 36(2), pp. 301-317.

Mupedziswa, R. and Gumbo, P. (2001). *Women informal traders in*

Harare and the struggle for survival in an environment of economic reforms (Nordiska Africainstitutet. Research Report No 117, Upsala, 2001).

Ndawana, E. (2018) 'Sacrificing urban governance at the altar of political expediency: Illegal street vending in Harare', *African Security Review*, 27(3-4), pp. 253-277.

Oosterom, M.A. (2019) 'Youth and social navigation in Zimbabwe's informal economy: "Don't end up on the wrong side"', *African Affairs*, 118(472), pp. 485-508.

———— and Gukurume, S. (2019). '*Managing the Born-free Generation: Zimbabwe's Strategies for Dealing with the Youth'*, CMI Working Paper No. 2, October, Michelson Institute.

Potts, D. (2011) 'Making a livelihood in and beyond the African city: The experience of

Zimbabwe', *Africa* 81(4), pp. 588–605.

Saitta, P., J. Shapland and A. Verhage (2013) *Getting by or getting rich? The formal, informal and criminal economy in a globalized world.* The Hague: Eleven International Publishing.

Thieme, T.A. (2013) 'The "hustle" amongst youth entrepreneurs in Mathare's informal waste economy', *Journal of Eastern African Studies*, 7(3), pp. 389-412.

Tibaijuka, A.K. (2005) 'Report of the Fact-Finding Mission to Zimbabwe to assess the Scope and Impact of Operation Murambatsvina by the UN Special Envoy on Human Settlements Issues in Zimbabwe'. New York: UNHCS Habitat.

Tokman, V.E. (2007) 'Modernizing the informal sector'. DESA Working Paper No. 42. New York: United Nations Department of Economic and Social Affairs.

14

Conclusion

Rory Pilossof

Zimbabwe in 2020 was a very different entity from what it was in 1980. In 1980, the coming of independence and majority rule created a wave of positive and hopeful visions for the future for much of Zimbabwe's population. Many people looked forward to a settled and secure livelihood, with well paid jobs in a newly independent state. Being part of the civil service was seen as a solid career choice for nurses, doctors, teachers, and administrators. Many believed in long-term employment with the hope of a pension. Young adults looked forward to an expanding education provision, for themselves and their children, and to becoming members of the middle class and professional services.

But, by 2020, many of these visions of the future had long faded from popular memory. As the chapters in this book outline, the economic and social realities in Zimbabwe since 1980 have undermined education and social provisions. The informal economy has moved from the periphery to the centre of most people's lives, and the hopes of stable, waged employment with long-term prospects and even a pension had disappeared. Even work in the civil service is no longer seen as a way to make a living, with continued rumours of strike action and dissent within the cohorts of state employed doctors, nurses, and teachers.

As a result, the youth of today have a far different outlook on what the state can and should do for them. They have had to find new forms of livelihoods and ways of being in both urban and rural areas. As Gukurume and Marjoke observed in Chapter 13, the informal economy moved from the periphery to centre of economy over the last 40 years, with over 90% of people eking out a living in this space. The dramatic rise of informality, it must be noted, is not only limited to the employment sector or the workplace. Across Zimbabwe, young people have been forced into informal living arrangements, informal schools and places of learning, informal travel activities and border jumping. As the state has abdicated responsibility, modes of informality have risen.

This collection has provided insights into a wide range of youth experiences in Zimbabwe from 1980-2020. By focusing on education, social and political interaction, and work and livelihoods, the book covers much important ground and illustrates the complexities of life in Zimbabwe for successive generations of youth. Across the collection, several key themes consistently re-emerge. As outlined above, informality is clearly one and this is addressed directly by many of the authors. Other themes include hardship and trauma, politicisation of the youth, and migration.

Hardships and trauma: The collapse of the state and the severe political and economic crises that have plagued Zimbabwe since the 1990s have negatively impacted on social provisions such as health care and education and have radically undermined waged employment opportunities. These processes have resulted in many adults struggling to provide for their families. Poverty has had a severe impact on the quality of life of many youths. In addition to the traumas of poverty and loss of livelihoods, the state itself has consistently used violence and coercion to control and manipulate many populations in Zimbabwe. Elections consistently raise the spectre of targeted violence, and the reinstatement of the National Youth Service Programme in 2021 seems likely to continue this trend.

Politicisation: As Mikhe and Reeler have shown in their chapters, the youth have been constantly politicised. Reeler observed that the youth have been a continuous site for political contestation, and 'feared for different reasons depending on the viewer's political affiliation. For ZANU-PF they were the threat at the polls due to the size of the youth demographic, and, for the MDC, they were the "green bombers", a violent youth militia intent on disruption of any election campaigning.' Although many youths have actively avoided these political spaces, the threat of violence and coercion, and the role of youth in these spaces, continue to define local politics in Zimbabwe. This violence has left lasting impact on generations of youth and is an area of study that deserves more critical attention.

Migration: As noted in the introduction, migration is another theme that cuts across this collection and is important in understanding the youth experience in Zimbabwe. The Youth Empowerment and Transformation Trust's 2019 report ranked Zimbabwe as one of the countries with the highest proportion of youth who had migrated, or wanted to migrate (YETT 2019: 99). Of those in their study 22% said they had given 'a lot' of thought to leaving the country and only 23% had no intention of moving. This shows the levels of instability and insecurity faced by many youths, who see migration as a means of ensuring safety and finding work. These were the two most common reasons for migrating, according to the YETT report. Internal migration was also a key issue, as shown in the chapters on informal work, mining, and agriculture.

Policy implications

The findings and observations in this book have several policy implications going forward. As the YETT report makes clear, youth constitute most of the country's population and the challenges they face often exclude them from political and economic spheres (YETT 2019: 106). Because the youth are such a large part of the population, and Zimbabwe is clearly a young country, there is a critical need to ensure that they are given opportunities to develop and grow in Zimbabwe; the country needs to address the concerns and requirements of the youth, to ensure that the challenges they face can be adequately and meaningfully addressed. There are solutions to the problems that pervade Zimbabwe, but they require political will to follow through with reforms. As with so many issues affecting Zimbabwe, this political will is in disappointingly short supply.

If that will does emerge, there are key areas where policy could assist the youth. For example, as many of the chapters note, the marginalisation of the formal economy means school leavers have few employment opportunities. The stabilisation of the economy could ensure that waged work could become a key provider of livelihoods again. In addition, key informal sectors such as mining need to be better managed and regulated to make the working lives of those in and around mines safer and better protected. The youth are key contributors and actors in this sector and thought needs to given into how they can be recognised and represented as such. In addition, as Shonhe and Muchetu show in their chapter, agriculture is an important sector for growth and development, and yet the new youth continue to struggle to gain access to land and plots. Legal mechanisms to protect and offer land or mining claims is a key area for state intervention (YETT 2019: 109)

Politically, many youths are engaged and have a deep interest in the political fortunes of the country. Democracy and representation are important, as Reeler's chapter makes clear. The youth seek avenues for political activity, even if these are not official channels, as Marjoke and Gukurume show in Chapter 8, and make obvious that they do indeed want more democratic processes and are keen to see the better functioning of the state. With elections planned for 2023, there is a drive to get youth involved. Once again, they are seen as a key catalyst for change and an important constituency for reshaping the political landscape. At the same time, however, there is widespread fear that many of the youth will be utilised as the violent enforcers in the state's campaigns of intimidation.

Many of the chapters here also highlight the gendered dynamics of informal work and social interaction. The chapters from Mate, Muwonwa, and Chandaengerwa and Bourdillon are illustrative here. Women and young girls are often excluded from formal and informal livelihoods and thus are often forced into more risky and dangerous activities in order to generate income. Policies need to be enacted to ensure equal access to resources and key markets to protect women and the work they can do to provide for themselves and their families. The key here is to develop mechanisms to ensure that the involvement of women in informal and formal economies is beneficial and offers long-term opportunities.

The youth are not a homogenous group. There are clear divisions and faultlines in this cohort. For example, there are significant differences between rural and urban youth, that are important in any policy considerations. In addition, the youth are also divided along gender, class, and ethnic background, which are key differences that impact their experiences. These differences speak to the political polarisation in the country, but also to the vulnerability of many groups who have fallen outside of the state's view. The collection also makes the point that successive generations of youth have had different experiences in Zimbabwe, and this is important to recognise. The book highlights this and show the ways in which the youth navigated and managed the social, economic, and political crises that have enveloped the country since 1980. Many youths have been able to face these obstacles with remarkable ingenuity and resourcefulness. As the future looks increasingly bleak for many young Zimbabweans, this resourcefulness and ingenuity looks likely to be tested. The visions of Zimbabwe's future in the 2020s are very different from those of 1980 and represent a sad indictment of the first 40 years of independence.

References

Youth Empowerment and Transformation Trust (YETT) (2019) *Decades of Struggle and Hope: A Zimbabwean Youth Compendium*. Harare: YETT.